GETTING THE *BEST* OUT OF COLLEGE

GETTING THE
BEST
OUT OF COLLEGE

〓〓〓〓〓〓〓| REVISED AND UPDATED |〓〓〓〓〓〓〓

Peter Feaver, Sue Wasiolek, and Anne Crossman
FOREWORD BY Coach Mike Krzyzewski, Duke University

TEN SPEED PRESS
Berkeley

Library of Congress Cataloging-in-Publication Data
Feaver, Peter.
  Getting the best out of college, revised and updated : insider advice for
success from a professor, a dean, and a recent grad / Peter Feaver,
Sue Wasiolek, Anne Crossman. — 2nd ed.
    p. cm.
  Summary: "A guide to optimizing all aspects of the undergraduate college
experience, written for students by a professor, a dean, and a recent
college graduate"— Provided by publisher.
  1. College student orientation—United States. I. Wasiolek, Sue. II.
Crossman, Anne. III. Title.
  LB2343.32.F434 2012
  378.1'98—dc23
                        2011051246
ISBN 978-1-60774-144-2
eISBN 978-0-307-78880-1

Printed in the United States of America

Cover design by Alan Hebel, The Book Designers
Design by Colleen Cain

10 9 8 7 6 5 4 3 2 1

Second Edition

To the faculty mentors who helped me get the best out of my college and graduate experience, and to the mentees who help me get the best out of being a professor.

PETER

To my mom, who continues to inspire me to become a well-educated person. Thanks for studying with me, taking me to the library every Sunday, and buying me every book I ever wanted. (Just think, you won't have to buy this one!)

SUE

With gratitude to my parents and grandparents for their tireless love and sacrifice in propelling me toward my dreams; to my husband, Josh, for helping make those dreams a reality.

ANNE

CONTENTS

ACKNOWLEDGMENTS

Writing this book has been an adventure all its own. Peter and Sue toyed with the idea of writing a book for nearly a decade, advancing it by baby steps because most conversations took place at the gym or loud college functions. It was not until indefatigable Anne joined the merry band as a recent grad that we got this book steadily under way.

That being said, we could not have written the book without the countless students, faculty, and administrators who, over the years, have shared with us their lessons learned the hard way. Some will easily find themselves in the anecdotes we have included; others will have to look a bit harder, but we assure you that you're here—in the stories, in the counsel, and in our most sincere gratitude.

We eagerly thank all those who read the draft manuscript, in whole or in part, and gave us the kind of trenchant feedback we needed. We especially thank Dorothy Lou Bailey, Andrea Beschel, Lauren Betz, Autumn Bonner, Nick Bonner, Tanvi Buch, Hans Buder, Barbara Carlson, Josh Crossman, Lisa Disbrow, Rebecca Duckworth, Brian Fawcett, John Feaver, Ruth Feaver, Carol Fidler, Joshua Foromera, Helen Giles, Arunabha Guha, Onome Ofoman, David Selinger, Philip Whisenhunt, Beth Whitehead, Billy Zarzour, and John Zink.

Thank you to Sheila Curran, who led us to the good people of Ten Speed Press, and to the Crown Publishing Group for encouraging us to pursue a second edition. We are also immensely grateful to Emily Timberlake, our editor, for taking our book to a new level of excellence, and for Jean Blomquist and Molly Woodward, who scrubbed the manuscript shiny bright.

Above all, we would like to thank our families, who were supportive, patient, and long-suffering through this process. A special thanks to Karen, who too many nights caught Peter sending furtive emails of chapter drafts after he'd already spent a long, hard day at the White House, and to Josh for giving up countless weekends of kayaking to stay home with the kids so Anne could warm a seat at the public library.

Getting the Best Out of College

FOREWORD

Coaches don't win games, players do. But good coaching can help players win. The right coaching can help a player go to the next level. And bad coaching can lead a good player far away from success.

That, at least, is how I approach my job, and that is how this book approaches college. This book aims to coach students toward academic and personal success at the collegiate level. The authors are my Duke colleagues, and among them they have many decades of experience helping students make the most of the natural talents and the opportunities which life has presented them.

This book does not guarantee success any more than I could draw up an X's-and-O's play that guarantees a game-winning basket. Players still have to execute that play when the whistle blows, and students still have to apply the advice to their own personal situations. But if you read this book and take the counsel it offers seriously, you will be better prepared for success.

In my world, there are lots of ways a team can get off track, especially in a long season of competition. An important part of my job is to help my athletes avoid those pitfalls and to identify the best ways to navigate to a successful conclusion.

That is what this book does for any student who reads and applies it. The premise of this book is that anyone reading it has already mastered one part of the collegiate experience: picking a college and getting in. That, however, is the easy part.

Based on their extensive experience working with students, the authors argue that the choice of college is less important than all the choices you make once you are in college. You can go to an elite school and get a lousy education if you make a lot of bad choices. You can go to a less well-known school and come out with a superior education, if you take full advantage of what that school has to offer. (Come to think of it, there may be a basketball analogy here, too: everyone knows that a Cinderella team can make a run if they face a major program that doesn't take each game seriously.)

Things were a bit simpler for me when I went to college. I was fortunate to go to a great school, the US Military Academy at West Point, and one of its many strengths was that it provided students with an exceptionally regimented system of do's and don'ts, especially back then.

College today could hardly be more different. Students face a bewildering array of choices—choices of where to live, what classes to take (and whether to go to class—this, by the way, is *not* a choice for members of the Duke men's basketball team!), what to major in, what to do after class, and so on. Some of the choices involve timeless concerns; we knew what fermentation did to barley and malt back in my day. But some of the choices involve developments as recent as yesterday's news and tomorrow's technology. And students can find themselves on their own confronting each and every one of those choices.

Students who just coast along will find that the choices are being made, but by default and without much thought to how one thing affects another. Such students may graduate (or they may not—it happens all too often), but they won't have made the most of the extraordinary opportunity that college represents.

I hope you won't be that kind of student. I hope you will read this book and get the most out of it—and let it help you get the best out of college.

Mike "Coach K" Krzyzewski
Head Coach, Duke Men's Basketball Team
Head Coach, USA National Team

INTRODUCTION

There are lots of books telling students how to get into the college they want and how to pay for it once they do. This is not one of those books. This book begins where they end.

As hard as it is to select and pay for college, many people find a way. The unexpectedly hard part—the part that in our opinion most people get wrong—is getting their money's worth. Paying tuition is a significant stretch. But making the most of that tuition is harder still.

As a prof, a dean, and a recent grad, we have advised thousands of students on how to get *into* the college they want and how to get *out* of college what they need. We have learned that few students (and even fewer parents) appreciate a fundamental secret: it matters less where students choose to go than what they choose to do once they get there.

Bright, eager students work unbelievably hard to get into college and are willing to shoulder an enormous financial burden for years to come. Despite that huge investment of time and money, those same students settle for a mediocre college experience. Too many graduate without the skills or glowing recommendations they need to succeed at the next level. Every spring we hear the same graduate groan, "I wish I had known *that* as a freshman."

But not you. This book is, in a way, an antidote to the uneven advising that afflicts most colleges—even the most prestigious ones.

Designed to help you start well and finish strong, this book will be of greatest benefit to the incoming student, whether a freshman or a transfer student, beginning with the most common concerns about dorm life, leaving home, and deciding the fall schedule. But that doesn't mean this book is limited to newcomers on campus. These pages contain a wealth of wisdom based on almost sixty cumulative years of experience and is written for students at all stages of their undergrad career, with topics such as how to decide between the summer internship or paying job, how to balance the desire for an attractive GPA with a respectable course load, when and how to ask professors for that glowing recommendation (and how to actually earn one), and how to make memories as an undergrad that you'll enjoy remembering. After decades of advising students, we have learned—and watched others learn—these lessons the hard way so that you don't have to.

Parents tend to believe the purpose of college is to gain an education, while students often see it as a rite of passage into adulthood with a few classes thrown in. As such, we encourage both parents and students to read this book, and have structured it somewhat chronologically to foster discussion around curricular and extracurricular expectations.

What qualifies us to help you get the best out of college is a distinctive blend of perspectives and a shared passion for making higher education worth the price tag. Peter Feaver has won two teaching awards as a professor of political science at Duke University. He is prominent in research and public policy–making circles largely in the area of American foreign policy, but he has written this book because some of his most rewarding experiences have been student interactions, both in and out of the classroom. Sue Wasiolek, assistant vice president for student affairs and dean of students at Duke University, is known as "Dean Sue"—a seasoned administrator who has been mentoring students and troubleshooting student life for over thirty years. She has regularly taught classes during that time but is best known on campus for her commitment to and support of students in the extracurricular parts of their college experience. Anne Crossman, a recent Duke alumna, founded a student group at Stanford as a freshman to mentor first-year students as they slalomed through the college scene; she transferred to Duke halfway through her undergraduate career. Anne taught both public high school and college students before becoming a full-time mom and author. She recently published *Study Smart, Study Less* in order to further help students reach their potential.

Simply put, we are people who have spent a long time helping students get the best educational experience possible, and we are honored to join you in your journey.

CHAPTER 1

"You Expect Me to Live with a Stranger?"

Managing Life in the Dorm

It's been played countless times across the theater of your imagination. Perhaps desperately—inspired by those days when your little sister plucked your last nerve. Perhaps wistfully—when she wrote you that sentimental birthday card and you got misty-eyed thinking that you wouldn't get to watch her try out for the school play next fall. Heck, maybe you tried a dry run when you were six, filling your SpongeBob suitcase with Pop-Tarts and getting as far as the mailbox. And now you are leaving home for real. Your parents' car is packed to the hilt, your welcome packet is at the ready, and any minute now you will be pulling up to what will become home for the next four years.

You are not alone. Tens of thousands of peers are heading in the same metaphorical direction. And one (or more) is heading quite literally to the exact same place: your room.

Life with a roommate will be full of surprises—from a scenario so awful it's worthy of a novel, to best friends who found a multibillion-dollar company and whose children later intermarry to form a dynasty, and everything in between. What to expect is anyone's guess.

Here is our confident prediction: your roommate will be another flawed human being with complementary strengths as well as aggravating weaknesses. Learning to manage this is probably the first hurdle a freshman faces (which is why we begin a book about college in your bedroom). It is a big part of the rite of passage that college has become. But you should not let it determine the success or failure of your college career.

Sharing personal details, inadequate space, and possessions can be tense at times—and that's assuming both parties get along. Yet, after a brief period of adjustment, most students describe their residence experiences on campus as being a highlight of their college careers, enabling them to find timely support that often led to friendship.

A positive experience can make your college career gleam, while a negative one can be devastating; our goal is to help you avoid the latter. The former is kismet, meaning there is only so much you can do to make it happen. The latter is also partly a matter of luck—bad luck—but that doesn't mean you need to build a shrine with magic trolls to keep evil at bay.

The wise student learns how to manage this relationship *before* any crises occur so it never becomes so tense that it leads to a full-blown crisis. There are lots of areas in this book where we will encourage you to push yourself to get the best out of college; however, in this chapter we will advocate the opposite philosophy. As influential as your roommate experience might be on your day-to-day happy meter, of all the areas of college life needing your attention we recommend this area be low on your list of priorities. In other words, rather than maximize the upside, minimize the downside.

It's not that the roommate relationship doesn't consume your life; it's that it shouldn't. We wouldn't dare suggest that your roommate isn't worth your time; a metatheme of this book is that relationships matter. But the natural inclination of most students is to invest too much time in this piece of the college experience and not enough in the others, which is why we tilt against it and advise heaps of thoughtful communication early on so the relationship will continue smoothly and require little course correction from there.

Night Owl or Early Bird?

Filling Out the Questionnaire

Shortly after mailing in your acceptance card saying "I choose YOU," you'll receive a rather plump packet in the mail, most likely full of brochures on classes, student rights on campus, and, somewhere within the ream, a roommate questionnaire. *Don't blow this one off.*

This is one of those applications that parents love to fill out and oftentimes—with the best intentions, of course—parents will answer the questions with a fanciful interpretation of who their child could be in the hopes that the new roommate will fit this description and rub off on Junior. Or students will fill out this form afraid of what their parents will read and so they don't really tell the truth, particularly when it comes to habits and traits they might be ashamed of, like smoking. This is not the time for subtlety. If there is something you feel adamant about concerning your roommate or your own personality, be as clear as possible.

Sometimes the questions are elaborate, like "If you were a toaster pastry, what flavor would you be?" while others are fairly bland but straightforward, such as "Do you study late at night or early in the morning?" Unless you know someone in the residential life office, you probably won't know which questions are the most heavily weighted and decide your fate, so put equal effort into each of them. One of the most critical questions is whether or not the roommate smokes, and it's typically a key decider in the matching process.

The most basic rule of filling out this form is honesty. Don't answer questions as if you were the person your parents think you are, the person your parents want you to be, or the person you wish you were—stick with who you are.

Granted, you will change in college. We all did. But start out by telling your interests. If you like leaving your room messy, say so. If you think having a non-color-coded sock filing system is a near cardinal sin, say that too. Some forms ask about sleep schedules and others ask about musical preferences. (Please: just tell the truth, even if it is a horrible truth, like you can't get to sleep without listening to *Love Songs from the '80s.*) It leads to a much better chance of matching you with an appropriate roommate, and, should conflicts arise later, your resident advisor (RA) may refer to what you wrote on this form as a starting point in reaching a compromise. The key is not to agree to something on the form that you aren't willing to actually do, because you will most likely be held to your word if a problem arises later.

One last point: be considerate. We know of an RA who was called in to referee a particularly thorny dispute. Apparently some young woman had strongly requested a nonsmoker on her roommate questionnaire and was granted one, but she didn't bother to mention that she was a smoker herself. Confused? She later told the housing staff that she requested a nonsmoker because she thought two people smoking in one room would have been too much.

> One of my friends from back home didn't turn in her housing request form on time. As a result, she didn't get into the dorms and ended up renting an apartment about a mile and a half off campus. She disliked the commute, especially when it was raining and she had to bike. Nearly every time we hung out, she would tell me I had it good since I lived right on the campus in the middle of all the action. It is a whole lot easier to make friends simply by being in the dorms or the food courts the first two weeks of school when nobody really knows anyone and people are happy to hang out with strangers and make new friends.
>
> **Brian—freshman, U of Oregon**

Back Away from the LoveSac
Packing for College

Ridiculous as it may sound, a couple of years ago a student arrived on campus with a U-Haul on freshman move-in day. As he backed it up to the entrance and rolled up the door, everyone was in suspense—what could he possibly be bringing that required a moving truck? Out came his dolly with a full-sized fridge. It got as far as the dorm's front stoop and was wisely sent back by an insistent RA.

What many freshmen may not realize as they pack is they can't duplicate what they have at home, and all that stuff won't be necessary in order to feel at home anyway. Assemble what you feel like you can't live without, then pack only 60 percent of that. Try to imagine how you will store your stuff in the off-season once your parents' minivan isn't around and you have to pay for every cubic foot you fill. Take an honest look at each memento and be sure you absolutely need it, and that you are willing to pay (over and over again) to store it for the next four years.

Besides hauling it, a key factor in deciding what to pack is whether or not your school is located near a Big Mart. If yes, then it's probably worth erring on the side of taking too little. Other than a toothbrush, a change of clothes, and towel, it is very unlikely that you'll need absolutely everything from day one.

Okay, maybe you need a little more than a toothbrush, but you certainly need less than you may initially want to pack. Even if there isn't a Big Mart, most on-campus stores will have the basics.

To combat your desire to pack your LoveSac, some colleges mail a brief list of what you will need to bring to campus: typically a set of sheets, a bath towel, a warm coat, toiletries, and a pillow. It's pretty stark. You won't immediately need Halloween decorations. Or scrapbooks. Or your library. And you most certainly won't need your antique guitar or your grandmother's diamond earrings. Belongings can get damaged or "lost," so it's best to leave the valuables at home with the folks. Clay *did* bring his brand-new acoustic guitar and discovered his roommate etching his frustration into it one day with a cafeteria knife. If you play a musical instrument and want to bring it along, super, as long as it's not a family heirloom. Even the most practical valuables get dinged, such as Michele's laptop, which ingested half a can of beer when an inebriated hall mate stopped by to say hello. $*-@!

> In packing for college, assemble what you feel like you can't live without, then pack only 60 percent of that.

Here's a left-field suggestion: don't pack a full year's wardrobe. To start, the closets are super tiny (as most things in your room will be), and yours won't hold all you're used to storing at home. Moreover, there tends to be an abrupt style shift that happens in the second half of the year as people return from studying abroad and from holiday shopping. Whereas high school sort of melded together one academic year at a time, spring and fall have a very split feel to them, almost as if they were separate years of study. If staying au courant with fashion is important to you, hedge your bets and save your money and some closet space for January; there will most likely be a new look and you'll want to be ready for it. (These deep wardrobe insights were brought to your attention by none other than the coiffed and fashionably astute Peter Feaver—as they say, those who can't do, teach.)

> I couldn't agree more with the advice here on packing light. That said, there are some things you can easily overlook. A minifridge is a must—when it's 1:30 a.m. and you can't think because your body is cannibalizing itself and the dining hall closed at 6:30 p.m., you need a solution. Second, bring more than two pillows—your bed will frequently double as your couch!
>
> **Hans—recent grad, Duke U**

If you are the type who really must have every T crossed before you arrive (and don't worry, we are more empathetic with that sort than we sound—if pressured, one of us could be forced to admit she even packed *crates* of soy milk when she moved into her freshman dorm), a lot of schools now provide the dimensions of the rooms and even CAD drawings online so you will have fewer surprises about what fits where. Be forewarned that your roommate might have her own ideas about how to arrange the furniture and may not want to sleep in a bunk bed just so you can fit the recliner in your room. In fact, your school may not even permit lofts for liability reasons. One thing you'll definitely want to know is whether or not the residence hall is air-conditioned. If not, and you are heading toward humidity, a fan or two (or three!) is a must, even starting the first night.

One final note, and we'll leave you to your suitcase. It's worth mentioning that some students feel pressured to buy everything up front while they can still saddle Mom and Dad with the bill—a wise economic strategy from the student's point of view. However, it creates perverse incentives to buy stuff you don't need and may tax your folks' budget. The compounding purchases may cause them to balk at some spending where they might have been generous otherwise. Consider making a deal. Ask what they have set aside for your dorm purchases and whether or not they intend for you to pay for everything else once your feet hit your dorm stoop. Depending on their expectations, you may be able to split the amount and spend 60 percent now and 40 percent later. Or perhaps they would be willing to set up a bank account where they automatically deposit some fraction of that amount each month, minimizing discussions about your spending habits. We realize that an enterprising student might say that he would like 100 percent now and then another 50 percent in January. Of course, we can't recommend that. This book is about getting all that you can out of college, not your parents.

> It can be hard battling the desire to bring it all when packing for college. What helped me was to map out the nearest grocery store, shopping mall, and Target relative to campus *before I left home* so I knew how easy it would be to find the extras once I was at school.
>
> **Andrea—freshman, Carnegie Mellon U**

How Sweet Is a Suite (or a Single)?

Of all your years, freshman year is the best time to have a roommate. Deciding on how many roommates to have . . . now that's a good question. Some colleges give you a choice, and some surprise you with a threesome in a double-sized room just because they are short on space. (Another GREAT reason to pack less.) Regardless, unless you have some sleeping disorder that causes you to wake screaming each night at 2 a.m. and you are worried about your reputation in the dorm, consider opting for one or more roommates and save the single for grad school or your senior year.

Steve opted for a single by accident when he filled out his roommate questionnaire. For some reason, he thought he was checking the box requesting a single roommate as opposed to two or three roommates. It turned out to be a very lonely experience the first few weeks, and it was harder to win friends in the dorm because his hall mates assumed he was antisocial.

You'll find that it's easier to move from a double or suite into a single than the other way around. Another incentive is that having a roommate will bring social traffic into your room, which will in turn broaden your network on campus. The bottom line is you'll be missing out on one of the fundamental elements of the college experience if you decide to room alone. And, anyway, it's only for a year.

On the other hand, opting for a four-person suite may be more than you bargained for. The number of roommates you request is a highly personal decision that depends entirely on your capacity for delightful entropy. A lot of it depends on how many siblings you have or wish you had, whether you consider yourself an introvert or extrovert, and what sort of setting will make you feel most at home.

Two housing alternatives offered by some colleges are campus apartments or student cooperatives. Since the value and challenges of each vary from campus to campus, it's difficult to make broad-sweeping recommendations. No matter how wonderful these alternatives might be at your school, we would advise living in a dorm your first year on campus because it's nearly always the busiest hive of activity. Beyond that, if you are interested in campus apartments or co-ops for the future, spend the year querying upperclassmen. Ask questions about parking (will you need a car, or is there adequate bus service for buying groceries and getting to class?), safety (what kind of police or security surveillance is provided?), how people interact (is it just a large group of cliques that never intermingle?), and trends of being involved on campus (do students seem to disappear from campus life once they leave mainstream housing?). It could be a winning combination of independence and community or a social bomb, and your sleuthing will be able to determine the best fit for you.

> I didn't have any roommates either my freshman or sophomore years of college, and it is one of the bigger regrets of my college experience. I had never shared a room before (except for begrudging cohabitation with my sister on vacations), so I figured I would be way better off in a single room. I didn't realize that I was missing out on great friendship opportunities, participation in the college freshman's default small talk subjects, and the standard shenanigans of roommate-dom, which, even if they were wild at the time, make for great stories afterward.
>
> **Rebecca—recent grad, Point Loma Nazarene U**

Steel-Toe Boots or Flip-Flops
First Impressions and Putting Your Best Foot Forward

Some colleges give students the option to contact their roommates before the school year starts, while others prefer the sink-or-swim approach and save the introduction for the dorm doorstep. If you're given the choice, our advice is to opt for a conversation beforehand but to limit it to very superficial sorts of topics to get to know each other. Don't dive right into the nuts and bolts of life just yet, and certainly don't put too much stock in your roommate's Facebook page. Though we recognize we're in the age of email and online chats, we recommend you handle the first couple of conversations by phone. Here's why.

THE PHONE IS YOUR FRIEND

Jessica was so excited to meet her new roommate that, the day campus housing forwarded her Emily's email address, she poured her life story into an email and eagerly awaited Emily's response. A day went by and no response. Jessica started to wonder what was up, so she reread her email and thought perhaps that she had left the section about class schedules a little unclear, so she sent off a quick follow-up email. And waited. Another day went by and Jessica became worried that maybe she had said too much or offended her new roomie, so she sent off a quick apology. Days went by and no response. After a week, Jessica started to get frustrated with Emily: Was she unwilling to forgive Jessica's mistake? Was she just being rude? Did she not care about developing a roommate friendship? Ten days after her original email, with no response from Emily, Jessica was about to send off a scalding email when she got a note from Emily apologizing for her slow response—she had been camping with her family in Montana for the past two weeks and had been without Internet access the entire trip.

Email is such a delicate medium. We all know how difficult it can be to decipher (or express) emotion accurately, whether there are emoticons or not. Since you don't have any goodwill to spare in this relationship just yet, we suggest you prevent any potential miscommunication and stick to the phone. See this phone conversation as a great opportunity to hone the standard spiel you will give a couple hundred times over the next few weeks about who you are, where you're from, why you came, and what you want to do with the next seventy years of your life.

But what about that uncomfortable, eternal pause when no one knows what to say? Consider scheduling the conversation via email so that you can have your head in the game when you sit down to talk. And—this may seem a bit overkill but you will thank us later when silence erupts—consider writing a list of five to ten questions you want to ask during the call and then perhaps a nice line·or two to signal that you're ready to end the call. It will also help you remember which details you want to cover, such as if he's bringing a coffee pot and does he mind sharing it.

Your first conversation should be about interests at home and what you hope to do while you're in school (such as auditioning for a play or finding a crazy work-study job). Dorm gadgets are also a safe topic as well as a great money saver, since you won't need more than one minifridge. If your roommate seems willing to share (and you are able to give as well as take), then synchronize. Printers, refrigerators, microwaves, coffee pots, a sound system, and NASA-quality video gaming equipment are cumbersome, and there is little reason to have two of each. You may want to discuss potential room configurations or the notion of borrowing. Some students enter with the mind-set that there are certain items they are willing to share from a practical standpoint and others they are not. Even if you don't resolve this question entirely during the first conversation, it's okay to at least get the topic on the table. Of course, if you don't have the benefit of synchronizing inventory before the first day, you can still purchase that microwave (assuming it's allowed in the dorm). Once you've met your roommate in person and worked out the details about shared space, your folks can return it if necessary.

Feel free to share some generic background about yourself, such as if you like to train for marathons or will be gone every weekend playing golf. If your faith is important to you, you are welcome to mention it briefly, but now is definitely not the time to persuade him to adopt your worldview. Keep the info minimal, and as you listen to your roommate's story be careful of forming too strong an opinion. It's difficult to know how the freedoms of college will affect and change a person. Also, figure his parents—who want to know all about you too—are standing nearby as you talk, so he may not feel as relaxed during the conversation as he'd like.

Other conversations, such as how to handle overnight guests or whether or not you should institute a lights-out curfew, are probably better discussed in person. Your dorm will give you information and regulations on these topics, among others, when you arrive, so there is no need to go into them beforehand.

It's best to treat this person as a prospective friend, not an automatic one. Don't set expectations (either with yourself or promises to each other) of how close this friendship will become. What often happens when those sorts of expectations are made and folks don't click is that someone gets miffed, and then the situation gets awkward. Instead, let the friendship develop naturally, as will all your other relationships on campus.

Move-In Day

It's your first and probably only "freshman move-in day." However new it may feel, since you are not the first freshman ever, don't feel like you're encountering this new phase alone. Your college has done this many, many times before and most likely will have some sort of plan to help you overcome the initial hurdles. Read their instructions. Follow their instructions. Show up where they say and when they say. There's no need to arrive ridiculously early, but don't be late either.

While we're handing out "don'ts," here's another one: don't cling to your first impressions of your roommate or her family, especially if they are negative. Chances are she has endured an awkward car ride with parents and great physical strain trying to defy gravity in hefting things upstairs in the heat, is a slight bit queasy about what the year will hold, and is trying to help her parents deal with their own empty-nest upheaval—it's an emotional powder keg. Promise yourself you'll hold those initial impressions lightly. Also, try not to focus too much on what your parents think of your new roommate. They don't have to live with her—you do!

While you're at it, you may want to hold your furniture hopes lightly as well. If you haven't had a chance to coordinate with your roommate in advance—or even if you have; people have been known to change their minds—you will most likely have two of some items when you really only need one. The first day as roommates offers up an unnecessary test of who will give up their whatever-it-is first. Be the first one to compromise if you find that your coordinated plans with your new roommate fall short of the mark. Avoiding small battles early could make a big difference in preventing larger skirmishes later in the year. It's not that you need to roll over for every minor complication, but it doesn't hurt to be the generous one up front so you have a greater say on the big-ticket decisions that may come later.

SHOULD YOU ROOM WITH A FRIEND?

If you are attending a college in-state along with other graduates from your high school, you may be given the option as a freshman to room with someone you know. We've had a number of students query us on this point, and our answer is that we've seen mixed results. We know of some students who were great friends before becoming roommates but then were terribly disappointed by the experience and it dinged their friendship. And then we know of others where rooming together galvanized their friendship all the more. Since this person is already your friend, consider stepping out of your comfort zone and rooming with someone new in the hopes of making even more friends.

> When I realized one of my close friends had decided to go to the same school as me, we considered rooming together. Instead, we decided to leave it up to fate and get randomly assigned. This was one of my best decisions of my freshman year because it gave me the opportunity to expand my circle of friends. My roommate and I knew different people, which gave us the ability to act as an outlet for each other when our other friends caused us stress.
>
> **Lauren—sophomore, Northeastern U**

Compromise Isn't a Four-Letter Word
Writing Your Roommate Agreement

Yes, we know you can count as well as spell, but some people don't recognize compromise for the art form—as opposed to expletive—it truly is. Offering to go the extra mile is a good introductory move. It is also a useful frame of mind to have for the first couple of weeks. It's a mistake to approach roommate discussions like you are the United States and he is North Korea. At least with roommates, compromise can be a show of strength that will not inevitably lead to international nuclear blackmail. If things get rough, you can always appeal to the RA, who is a lot more capable of effective action than the UN.

One of the most important things you will do your first week of school is fill in some sort of roommate agreement, typically given out by your RAs, to help guide you over the next year. Some schools may not provide a formal agreement but will encourage you to establish some ground rules and then talk with your roommate whenever there is any sort of misunderstanding. (If that's the case, feel free to use the headings in this chapter to lead your conversation.) Putting your roommate agreement down on paper can certainly help identify any potential misunderstandings before they occur, but whether it is written or not, it is CRITICAL that you discuss expectations ahead of time in order to avoid conflict. Kick off the conversation by discussing the lighter stuff: whether or not you have a food or animal allergy, if you want to have an agreed time for lights out and quiet, whether or not it's okay to have family members sleep on the floor when they visit from out of town, and, if the setup of the room is less fair to one of you, what changes can be made to balance the score for second semester. Feel free to ask your RA for help in either identifying potential concerns or in mediating your discussion should conflict arise.

CULTURAL DIFFERENCES

Should you be assigned roommates from a different cultural background or a different country, recognize that they may have unique forms for expressing dislike and working out compromises.

Allie grew up in a small town and was excited to discover on move-in day that her roommate, who had a name she wasn't sure how to pronounce, was from Thailand. What Allie didn't realize was that, as an international student, Prasert had arrived days earlier and had been enjoying her solitude until an entourage of parents and boxes arrived and overwhelmed her with clutter. As the year wore on, Allie learned that "okay" didn't always mean okay, and that Prasert valued saving face and a type of humility that meant not standing up for herself whenever there was tension. She also learned that when Prasert gave her a gift, it was important to display it in a place of honor for a time to show gratitude. This might seem an unfair expectation of Allie, but given that Prasert was adjusting to life in a new country, it was a small challenge, if that. Having Prasert for a roommate also gave Allie the privilege of introducing her to college football and the pregame bonfire, not to mention the opportunity to escape campus with Prasert to explore Thai restaurants in the city nearby when her double major in engineering and computer science got to be too much. It was an unforgettable year for both with a lot of great memories.

Whether or not she is an international student, your roommate will most likely arrive with needs or communication styles that won't be like yours, so it's best to assume that up front. Should you find yourself living with a Prasert of sorts, recognize that she may find it odd and more than a little alarming that students paint themselves in school colors and prance half-nude in front of thousands of strangers, not to mention news crews. Collegiate athletics is an American thing. Try to see it through an international student's eyes. And consider yourself fortunate, since having an internationally astute roommate could become a valuable part of your college education.

OVERNIGHT GUESTS

There are bigger questions as well, such as whether romantic guests should be allowed and, if so, how to notify each other to prevent an embarrassing situation. Students usually try to be very understanding of their roommates' requests but often don't know how to respond when those requests get out of hand, which they can do in a short time. It's best to be clear about your expectations up front and to hear your roommate's side of things as well, and then to go with the highest standard—meaning, if one of you says, "There's a 'no vacancy' policy," then consider the rule concrete, even if you disagree, and move on. Your room is a shared space where both of you should feel safe and welcome to return at any time.

ALCOHOL

Alcohol can become an issue when a drinker and a nondrinker room together. The drinker wants to make the room party central and uses the nondrinker's smoothie maker for margaritas or, worse, the drinker returns to the room at some obscene hour looking green and gray. There are people on staff to help with that, particularly the latter scenario. Grab the closest RA and ask for help and even a quiet place to sleep while your roommate recovers.

The best way to avoid these uncomfortable situations is to be clear about your expectations from the onset.

In a situation where you are uncertain how much alcohol your roommate consumed, it is absolutely important that you let someone on staff in your hall know that your roommate is not doing well. RAs are less concerned about underage drinking than they are about the potential for alcohol poisoning, and unless you have been trained to make that sort of diagnosis, it's best to bring in some outside help. (In fact, to encourage students to protect each other's health and to prevent alcohol-related deaths, many colleges provide a sort of backdoor policy so you can take a friend to the ER without anyone being penalized.)

Diagnosing whether or not your roommate has had "too much" to drink will be complicated by your not knowing his health history, such as if he's taking meds that react negatively to alcohol. Your safest bet is to assume your roommate needs help if he is unable to tell you coherently why he does not.

We know of one freshman named Pat who returned to his dorm room clearly ill after a party one night, but whose roommates assumed he was simply drunk. What they didn't realize was that, along with having had too much to drink, Pat also had a very fast-developing form of meningitis. Tragically, once they did get help, it was too late and he died a few hours after being taken to the ER. Given the possibility that your roommate may be at risk—and this may sound harsh, but it's the fact—it's better to risk looking like a tattler than to prioritize your social sticky stars over your friend's well-being.

DRUGS

Most colleges reflect the prevailing view in society: drug infractions are taken far more seriously than alcohol infractions. You and your roommate will come to some understanding about drugs and whether you will or won't allow them in your room. Whatever your agreement, remember that the responsibility (and culpability) for what happens in the room rests with *both* of you. So your decisions about drugs could have consequences for you both, even if you don't plan to partake. Some schools hold students accountable for the deeds of their roommates. There are ways to toe the line without feeling like a rat, and your RA is a great resource on this question. Not to worry, your RA doesn't have to report everything, especially when you're just looking for info and asking hypothetical questions.

> Remember that your relationship with your roommate is a dynamic one; it will be constantly changing. It will look like one thing when you first meet, another thing a couple of weeks later, and still something else halfway or even all the way through the year.
>
> **Helen—sophomore, U of Chicago**

VALUES

One issue that typically isn't an issue, though some might assume it, is religious or political values. It's easier to share a room with a flaming politician from the "wrong" side than it is for the über-organized to live with the organizationally challenged. While you may converse in polite terms on these sorts of subjects, there may be a point when you don't want to discuss them further. Your roommate—like you—will most likely have an opinion about everything in your life, and since you are living together will know more about you than you may want to reveal to most people. Figure out an appropriate boundary for sharing opinions. Agree on some sort of code or response that wraps up the conversation when one of you has had enough so you never have to resort to punching the red button. Sometimes it's best to agree to disagree, and call it a night.

Most Common Roommate Complaints

We began our discussion of roommates by talking about the value of compromise, but at times compromise is not possible or is not enough. In digging for anecdotes on this topic, we've ended up with some fairly anemic examples—not for lack of drama, of course, but because they lose something in translation. Most scuffles between roommates tend to be so petty that it's ridiculous to put them into print. Something happens early on in the relationship that sets the melee in motion, and the straw that turns the proverbial camel into a paraplegic is that one roommate used the other's dishwashing detergent without asking. Of course, more lurks beneath the issue than stolen soap, but that's all that exists on file and so what results is a set of bitter roommates whose complaint can't be truly resolved because it can't be isolated at its source.

COMPLAINT #1: DIFFERENT DEFINITIONS OF "CLEAN"

Hygiene may not appear on the roommate agreement, but, hands down, it wins the dubious honor of being roommate complaint #1. The slob and the neatnik usually butt heads. If you find yourself in this situation, you may feel tempted to draw a line down the center of the room, demarcating "your" territory and "hers," but that kind of compromise rarely works since odors don't respect boundaries. The problem can be further exacerbated if the neat roomie decides to straighten up for the cluttered roomie and ends up losing or misplacing something important. Aim for a preventative agreement on this one—like who vacuums which weeks or where the dirty dishes will be stored to keep the room from reeking. And, by all means, come to an agreement about this early in the game while your room is still relatively clean!

Getting the Best Out of College

COMPLAINT #2: DIFFERENT STUDY HABITS

There are two key components to this complaint: when to study and how to study. Are you an early riser? Do you plan on setting your alarm for 5 a.m. so you can head to the library? This might cause your roommate some angst, considering he was up studying until 3 a.m. and just entered his sleep rhythm as you started bustling about the room. Do you require absolute silence, or do you need to hear something with a beat when you hit the books? Do you take frequent breaks, or do you need a marathon of uninterrupted intensity? Differential workloads may also be a cause of contention, since the lit major appears to be lounging around reading on his bed while the bio chem major is hunched over his desk crunching numbers. The easiest solution is that neither of you use your room as a primary place of study.

> On my roommate questionnaire, I filled in flexible hours since I'm a pretty flexible person, thinking going to bed "late" meant 11:30 p.m., but oh was I wrong. It turned out that I got a roommate who was a true night owl, staying out until, sometimes, 3 a.m. My classes started at 8 a.m., so even though I thought I was staying up late by going to bed just before midnight, in comparison to my roommate I was an early bird. Adjusting to his schedule the first few weeks was tough because I am a very light sleeper and I woke up every time he came back. As time went on, I started noticing him less, and now I am a much heavier sleeper and rarely notice his returning.
>
> **Brian—freshman, U of Oregon**

COMPLAINT #3: DIFFERENT BEDTIME RITUALS

One roommate may want to sleep with the window open in the dead of winter while the other is from Arizona and thinks anything under 70°F is frigid. Or one may need to fall asleep to white noise while the other prefers zero noise.

The good news is that, should you someday marry, these sorts of roommate discussions will come up again (and then it will be permanent!), so consider it great practice. It may be that you need to help buy your roomie a down comforter or suggest she listen to soundscapes on her headset instead of the stereo. We could fill the remainder of the section with suggestions, but you're smart enough to come up with them on your own. The point is that the two of you should reach some sort of compromise that is equally *unsatisfactory* to you both, which is how you know it's a true compromise.

COMPLAINT #4: PROBLEM-SOLVING VIA THE INTERNET

Few people like conflict—and even fewer people want to be roommates with those who do! Most people try to avoid conflict by ignoring the problem, hoping it will resolve itself. This is actually a pretty good way of dealing with petty problems, and we recommend this if the alternative demands intervention by the United Nations Security Council every time your roommate leaves a wet towel on the floor. When the problem really does need to be addressed, however, ignoring it won't work and neither will something much worse: a crisply worded email. It is much easier to vent and press Send than to sit down and talk it out. However, email is a *terrible* medium for resolving disputes, and the brusque email usually triggers an even more arch response that requires an exasperated rebuttal and soon PEOPLE ARE SHOUTING AND COMPARING EACH OTHER TO NAZIS. This, of course, introduces a further risk that in a moment of weakness one of you might forward the email thread to others and leave both of you looking infantile. A good rule of thumb is if the problem is too small to talk about in person, ignore it; if it is too big to ignore, it is too big for email and requires a face-to-face conversation. If necessary, bring the RA in, but leave the Internet out.

ADDRESSING ROOMMATE COMPLAINTS

In general, the most successful strategy for dealing with a disagreement is to speak up long before the issue becomes so painful that it cannot be resolved.

Feel free to propose your RA as a mediator early on in a conflict. It doesn't need to sound like a threat, such as "If you don't stop, I'm going to tell the RA," but more of "Hey, let's talk with the RA and see if he has any advice." If your roommate is unwilling to see the RA, then go to him on your own. Though it may seem like you're talking about your roommate behind his back, even that is preferable to suppressed rage, which can end catastrophically. On the little stuff, early sacrifices pay off in bigger dividends than you might think.

At the end of the day, talk is just talk and actions are actions. If the talk doesn't lead to actions, try to restrain yourself from making a beeline to the housing office to request a new roommate. It's very unlikely you'll be granted a change in the first quarter for the simple reason that the dorms are packed and there may not be other options available. Sure, it doesn't hurt to ask, but prepare yourself for a no. Even if there are rooms available, the housing office is often unwilling to participate in room-mate exchanges because they consider the art of compromise part of the college experience. In some senses, they're right. There is something very meaningful about learning to live with people different than you.

However, if the situation hinders your ability to perform in your classes or you start sleeping elsewhere just so you don't have to return to your room, it's time to take the matter to the authorities. Amy had to resort to applying for a change in roommates the second week of her freshman year when her roomie's reverse sleep habits and consistent pot use within their room made a compromise impossible. For a case such as this, the university was happy to move Amy into a healthier situation and did so within the week.

Real Life Lessons, Compliments of Your Dorm

View college life as a round-the-clock learning experience. (Under-standably that's what happens when you live at school.) Even your dorm will offer up nuggets of insight. Let's take, for example, the often-overlooked service the university performs in cleaning up after you. If you live in a residence hall, it is likely that the university provides housekeeping services for public areas such as hallways, bathrooms, and lounges. (Don't get too excited; you're still responsible for cleaning your own room.)

It happens without request, just like magic. Only it isn't magic. It can be nasty work, often because—dare we suggest it—college students can sometimes appear to be ungrateful slobs. (In reality, they're probably just oblivious, but puddles of vomit after Friday night's party are rarely left with an apology note for the guy who has to clean it up.)

Even if they were accustomed to doing chores at home, most students quickly acclimate themselves to the luxury of a housekeeping service, and since it's "part of tuition," never give a thought to cleaning up after themselves. The resulting filth can make for a demeaning experience for the housekeeping staff.

We are here to make a bold suggestion: over these next four years, notice the people who are enabling you to focus on your studies and show your gratitude. The parking attendants, the security guards, the sanitation service, the groundskeeper, the dining hall staff: they all make our lives a little easier, and many have not had the opportunities you have before you now to further yourself. The mature student will recognize this and find ways to respect their dignity.

In my freshman year of college, I decided to live in an all-boys dorm. I found out after one week what hundreds of boys all living in close proximity (without their parents) are capable of. To call the dorm disgusting would be an understatement. After the first weekend, the hall was completely trashed. I woke up to a loud BANG BANG BANG on my door Sunday morning. I jumped quickly out of bed to find it was the maid vacuuming up against my door. Through the next few weeks I got to know her and tried to keep my area of the hall a little cleaner; in turn, she never woke me with vacuuming again.

Billy—sophomore, High Point U

"This Is Not What I Had in Mind When I Left Home"
Unusual Roommate Scenarios, Thoughtfulness Required

Much as we hate to suggest it, we would be remiss if we didn't hit upon a few roommate situations that might diverge from your expectations. The chances of you actually encountering any of these are almost the same as those of you being elected student body president. However, chances are more likely that you may know of someone who is in this situation. So for his sake and for the enhancement of your own wisdom, read on. Here are five situations that could make for a complicated residential experience.

POSSIBILITY #1: SHE FORGETS THE "DO NOT DISTURB" SIGN

You walk in on your roommate and the love of her life in what lawyers call "in flagrante delicto" (or, an embarrassingly passionate entanglement). This is not a teachable moment. This is not a moment for a lengthy explanation of your changed schedule or lengthy apologies. This is a moment for a quick "sorry" and a hasty retreat. Give the situation about an hour to cool off and then consider it safe to go home. Knocking might not be such a bad idea. Be sure to spend the hour thinking about what sorts of activities you feel comfortable taking place in your room. If you'd rather this one not be repeated, be up front about it. Couples have been making whoopee in campus hideaways for years, so it's not like they'll be deprived. This room is your home too and you need to have the freedom to come and go as you like.

POSSIBILITY #2: HE TRIES TO END HIS LIFE

Your roommate attempts or threatens suicide. It goes without saying that this can be devastating for all who know this person. First off, get professional help for you and for your roommate, assuming he is, we pray, unsuccessful. These are deep waters and you should not try to navigate them for any length of time without a professional guide.

A few things to consider while you are seeking help: First, your roommate's decision to end (or attempt to end) his life is not your fault. Figure that a lot has gone into the making of this person and you are not responsible. Once you've taken yourself off the dartboard, look for opportunities to reach out to your roommate and his family. It's probably obvious, but this is not the time to be Mr. Popularity by regaling the dorm with tales of roommate woes. It's best to be discreet; your discretion will prove you are mature and trustworthy.

Most likely, your roommate will take time off from school and you will be assigned a new roommate. Give that person a clean slate, assumption-free. Of course, your roommate could also choose not to leave campus but to stay and seek out help. If that's the case, you will gently want to discuss with him expectations for the rest of the year. Since this is a difficult time, it might be best to ask, "Hey, do you mind if I bring our RA in on this conversation? I don't want to say anything stupid, and I really don't even know what to expect about your recovery. I'd like to hear his advice." Undoubtedly your roommate will feel like everyone is talking behind his back, so being up front will hopefully be a relief for him and will start you both back on the right foot.

This advice also applies to other health issues, such as noticing your roommate is struggling with depression, alcohol and drugs, or an eating disorder. Be a friend and ask for help. Ignoring the situation will only allow it to escalate and make recovery that much more difficult.

POSSIBILITY #3: SHE COMES OUT OF THE CLOSET

Your roommate tells you she's a lesbian. In such a situation, communicate openly with her: if your roommate has told you she's a lesbian, it's because she wants you to know and she probably anticipates some sort of response. Feel free to revisit the topic with her after you've had a few days to think about it and say just that: "I've had a few days to think about it and I was wondering if we could talk more about how you see this influencing our roommate situation." Consider it a mature way to proceed forward. If you are uncomfortable or feel you may become distracted by the potential for sexual undertones in your rooming situation, speak with your housing office about the possibility of finding a new room. Wanting to remove the sexual dimension doesn't make you homophobic any more than choosing not to room with someone of the opposite sex makes you heterophobic. It's not a bad idea to loop in an RA or an administrator to these discussions, but check with your roommate first—just because she's come out to you doesn't mean she's ready to come out to the rest of the world.

If *you* are the gay or lesbian roommate, our advice is likewise to encourage honest conversation. You may feel absolutely certain that there is no reason for your roommate to feel awkward, but she may feel otherwise. It might be worth checking with the RA or an administrator about what room-swapping options are available before you tell her, and asking an RA or administrator to join your conversation—assuming your roommate is okay with it—certainly couldn't hurt.

POSSIBILITY #4: HE *CAN'T* QUIT WHENEVER HE WANTS

Your roommate is a frequent drunk, and not a happy one at that. If you find your roommate is overly prone to this sort of behavior, you would be wise to lean in the other direction and avoid drinking with him entirely. Be assuaged that you won't need to clean up his vomit for the rest of the year, but a sacrificial gesture early on is wise on a number of accounts. After you've seen what's in store for the year, begin to discuss ways for him to either manage his drinking or have some of his drinking buddies care for him in his stupor so you don't become his designated doormat. Especially take note if he blacks out—a reaction that is far more serious than passing out, or losing consciousness, after too many drinks. *Blacking out* is distinct in that it affects the brain's ability to recall the past or manage long-term memory, somewhat similar to amnesia. Essentially his drinking has become so intense it is damaging his brain. Repeated abusive drinking is not a sign of a fun-loving party animal: it is a sign of alcoholism that requires professional help.

POSSIBILITY #5: SHE'S ON THE COVER OF *PEOPLE*

Your roommate is someone famous. She could be "Someone's" daughter, a teen TV star, or a rising athlete. Should you end up rooming with a notable, first consider how *you* would like to be treated were you that remarkable person. (When all else fails, the golden rule makes for a nice fallback plan.) Everyone needs downtime. Everyone needs space where they can relax and be themselves.

As you put yourself in her stilettos, you'll come up with some likely scenarios of what to do and not to do. (We're sure you won't line her desk with carbon paper so you can get handwriting samples to sell on eBay.) No matter what this person has done or whom she's related to, chances are she'd just want you to treat her like she's normal.

"My Roommate's a Neanderthal . . . Am I a Loner for the Rest of the Year?"

Take heart, a bad rooming situation doesn't destroy your chances of a decent collegiate social life. In fact, it doesn't even need to ruin your year. On the other hand, if you expect to be best friends forever it could cause problems. A substantial number of roommates swap after their freshman year. This is not a life sentence or even a marriage. It's more like dating. Even in the rare instances that roommates become the best of buds, it's exceedingly rare (not to mention a tad bit unhealthy) that they become each other's entire social life.

For the vast majority, the roommate relationship is a good experience. For all the horror stories we've heard, there are many more of roommates being bridesmaids and godparents and lifelong friends. Forging these friendships is itself a learning experience. We all have to learn to work with people, share office space, and perhaps share a home with a spouse. The roommate situation is a wonderful laboratory for refining these skills. Remind yourself (often) that you are learning life skills that will be useful for a number of work, home, or military settings, where you will be forced to live in close proximity. Experts call these skills "emotional intelligence," and they are critical to your future success.

CHAPTER 2

Leaving Home, Phoning Home, and the First Trip Back to the Mother Ship

Maintaining Relationships Back Home

Home is one of the toughest parts of college. Many students discover that maintaining healthy relationships and connections with the old home while getting established in the new home stretches—and sometimes stresses—them in surprising ways. Some miss home too much and stagger around campus like a weepy Hallmark commercial. Others don't miss home enough, or at least feel guilty that they don't, and strain against the proverbial cord as if it were a noose. Still others find that home is changing almost as fast as they are and don't know what to make of it. The truth of the matter is, whether you're enrolled in state or studying three thousand miles away, relationships back home will affect how well you transition into this new phase of independence.

Things have changed. Your room has possibly been turned into a craft center for Mom. Your high-school friends may seem immature. Your kid sister no longer believes you are All That. And though you have only been gone a short time, upon returning you find your parents remarkably smarter than when you left them.

Leaving the nest can be a bit rattling for everyone involved, and well-meaning parents can have as hard a time as any (mistakenly keeping the cord a bit too tight or cutting it a bit too completely). Even the most self-sufficient of students can find themselves daydreaming of home when they should be studying. If any of this is starting to sound familiar, don't worry—you're not an alien, and you're not alone.

"How Do You Explain School to a Higher Intelligence?"
Relating to Your Folks as an Adult

Most likely you grew up hearing stories about the good ol' days when Mom and Dad were in college livin' the high life. Their tales of meeting each other in the cafeteria line or skipping class on a Monday just because it was a nice day at the beach or visiting Chinatown with a Chinese roommate and experimenting with herbs at the apothecary have probably been romanticized a tad. Okay, bump that up to *a lot*.

Just because they are nostalgic and oh so old doesn't necessarily mean their suggestions will be irrelevant. Human nature has not changed dramatically since they were in college; though your major may not have existed back then, a lot of their wisdom may be sound.

That said, the college campus *has* changed dramatically in the last twenty years, so some of their advice may no longer fit the situation. For instance, they might not be aware of the depth of support staff available to students, but they are probably more aware than their own parents were that you will need such support.

What we are trying to say (delicately, if possible—who knows who may be reading over your shoulder) is this: the natural undergrad reaction that Parents Don't Know a Thing is only a *smidgen* true.

Here's the kicker: you are changing in ways that neither you nor your parents fully appreciate—possibly in all senses of that term. Before you file your folks under "antiquated," keep in mind that of all the people in your life, your parents have thought about your future longer than anyone else. Picture them standing over your crib two days after your birth, musing over who you will become. Then, out of love for you and wanting you to become your very best, they sacrificed the upgrade on the car, a vacation here or there, and even the wardrobe they would have liked just to make sure you had braces, tutors, soccer uniforms, and a whole host of other gifts. That long-range perspective is what drives their interests and actions. And, while that may at times feel like they are trying to control your decisions or prevent you from steering your own future, being aware of this dynamic will help put your conversations in perspective. Most likely, they have your best interests at heart.

We doubt you will be surprised to hear that there may be moments of conflict as you differ with your parents about how to make a success of your future. On the whole, parents don't typically care what their child does at college, but they *do* care that what he does might have lingering negative effects on his future. As one wag put it: they don't worry that you will make mistakes, they worry that you will make the wrong mistakes.

"You Could Be Happy Here— I Could Take Care of You"
The Growing Pains of Leaving Home

"The day I drove off to college was the most emotionally charged moment of my life—even more than my wedding day a few years later," said Kyla. "It was almost like attending my own funeral the way my mother kept avoiding eye contact so I wouldn't see her puffy eyes, or how my brother was angry because he'd just realized that I was going to miss every one of his band performances. I was excited and then felt guilty that I was excited. I was frightened and then giddy with the possibilities ahead of me. It was exhausting. And I almost wish I could do it again."

Kyla's experience of leaving home may have been more of an emotional roller coaster than yours will be, since she was the first child to leave the nest and the only girl. This heightened response tends to be true if you are the first, last, or only child leaving home. Parents are usually very proud of their children for taking on new challenges and bettering themselves (as in going to college), and as a result they may experience some mixed emotions—panic, resentment, pride, and maybe even envy—all at the same time. Parents who did not go to college may experience even more heightened emotions and their pride may be tinged with embarrassment that they did not have the same academic achievement. The best advice we can offer up front is:

- Be aware that this will be an emotional time for everyone involved.

- Try not to take your family's reactions personally.

- Don't feel like you must make them understand everything you are going through.

There will be time for decompressing and debriefing after the emotional flurry has settled. For the time being, focus on the journey that is ahead of you and know that, in the end, your family wants the best for you.

What all graduating high-school seniors need to realize is that their grand entrance into college life is (typically) much more bitter than sweet for their parents. Certainly both students and parents will miss each other to some extent. But if the relationship was a healthy one to begin with, parents will experience the "empty nest" as a major loss of closeness and a dreaded change—things will never be the same again.

During freshman orientation, my mom was going through some pretty serious premature empty-nesting, since she was seeing her youngest child off to college. The result was a kind of hyperactive, nervous doting that left my eighteen-year-old self feeling smothered and annoyed. Looking back, I feel terrible that I wasn't able to rise above my own momentary concerns and recognize what she was going through emotionally. By preparing yourself for this mentally ahead of time, you'll acquit yourself better than I did.

Hans—recent grad, Duke U

Your parents will be doing their best to negotiate their own transition into this new condition of life. In some respects, they are losing a child (although gaining a friend). It will take time for your relationship with your folks to adjust to all this . . . maybe even years.

None of this is to make you feel guilty. By all means, go to college. It is not only a privilege, it's also a rite of passage into adulthood that is good and necessary for jump-starting your life. We only mention all this about your parents' emotions so that you can manage the transition well by being that friend they hope you will become.

Your parents' view of your college experience will be a combination of what they hear from you, what they read in the media, and any newsletters your college sends home—all filtered through their own experiences from years ago. It's a bit of a jambalaya. In almost every case, they will be wiser than you, but increasingly you will find yourself more knowledgeable than they are—and not just in areas of pop culture.

In college, the knowledge gap (note, we emphasize "knowledge gap" not "wisdom gap") starts to approximate where you thought it was when you first crossed into puberty: you actually *do* start to know important stuff that your parents don't know or can't remember. Though they might surprise you by how well they can hold their own in a conversation on transcendentalism, most likely you will be sharper on the subject since you just completed two hundred pages of reading on it last week.

So far we've mentioned the emotional isolation and physical distance your parents are braving. Let's tack onto that the financial pressure of footing the bill for this adventure. Ah, so here you may chime in that you will be helping chip away at the debt by pursuing a work-study job. That may be true, but in most cases parents are shouldering a big part of the load. Even if your parents can somewhat afford writing the tuition checks, each signature still represents luxuries they are sacrificing to send their baby far, far away so she can be happy. The joy of seeing her happy is tinged by that loss—losses some parents may never communicate but you can bet your minifridge they are feeling. This, combined with that long-term perspective we mentioned earlier, will set the stage for a lot of their conversations with you.

> What all graduating high-school seniors need to realize is that their grand entrance into college life is (typically) much more bitter than sweet for their parents.

For most parents, their child's college opportunity represents the largest investment they have ever made besides the family home. For you, the investment may seem secondary to the rite of passage that college represents (and perhaps you feel you deserve). When the two perspectives collide, expect your parents to weigh in heavily on getting the biggest return on their investment.

To sum all this up, anticipate one of two reactions from your parents as you prepare to leave: neediness or dismissal. You may feel smothered by their fear of the empty nest and worries about your capability to get the best out of college, or you may feel disconnected if they emotionally distance themselves from you to help buffer their feelings. (This may have even been going on since you started your senior year and "the end" was in sight.) Sometimes it is a combination of the two. And sometimes parents are able to disguise these emotions and put on their best face so that you will head off to school none the wiser about how much duct tape they are using to keep themselves together. A good thing of which to remind yourself in all of this is that they have been extraordinarily patient (or at least tried to be, anyway) with your insane pubescent emotional roller coaster for the last eight years, so cut them a little slack. Be loving, be gracious, but go.

What to Do When the Mother Ship Gets a Makeover
Adjusting to Change Back Home

The three pieces of news from home that tend to be the most difficult are parents separating, a newly diagnosed illness of a family member, and some tragedy befalling the family pet. Students often assume—either consciously or not—that while they are in college, life will remain the same at home. It seems a reasonable expectation after all, since life at home hasn't changed that much over the years. Home will always be home. Mom will have the same haircut. The house will be the same color and the furniture will be in the same place. The expectation provides a sense of stability.

Sadly, however, this expectation is unrealistic since your family dynamic changed from the moment you left. If the change influences you directly (such as redecorating your room), it will hopefully have been communicated in advance. But there is no guarantee. In some ways, the safest bet is to expect that your family will have changed as much as you have since you've been away at college; that way you won't be surprised by any makeovers and may be comforted to find that a few things stayed the same.

> During my sophomore year, my parents decided to move without telling me. I felt a mixture of hurt, anger, and nostalgia because of the fact that I would never really be able to go "home." However, when I asked my parents about it, they seemed really excited about the prospect of moving and I felt ashamed that I had put my needs over theirs, considering that I was in college and at home for only one month a year. When I went to visit them over Christmas break, I loved the new house. Granted, I will miss my childhood home, but all that matters is that we are happy and together.
>
> **Onome—junior, Stanford U**

PARENTS SEPARATING

A new car is easy, but some bombshells are not. The most heartbreaking change is death or divorce. We aren't suggesting that your parents are about to die or file—in fact we hope they don't. But both do happen and, sadly, it's likely that someone you know on campus will be going through this misfortune. In fact, divorce is often more likely *because* the kids have gone to college. Many parents in troubled marriages hold on until their child has left high school. Other folks don't even realize they are in a troubled marriage until the one thing they still have in common—their child—is gone. The sad truth is that the psychological consequences of divorce on a child are not lessened just because that child is living away from home.

To improve your chances of a positive weekend should your parents decide to visit, here are a few do's and don'ts we've gleaned from years of observation and experience:

- Introduce your parents to your friends and their parents—other than coming to see you, it's why they're attending the functions.

- Prep a tour so they can see just how far your chem lab is from your writing course, or where you grab your morning bagel. These will make for a nice mental gallery as they picture you in your new life after they have returned home.

- Clean your room. Even if your parents aren't coming, your roommate's parents might be and they will want the full tour; it is always a good idea to put your best foot forward.

- If you have formed a close working relationship with a couple faculty members, arrange *well in advance* to introduce your folks to them.

- Even if you don't have a lot of work, let your folks know in advance that you won't be able to spend the full weekend with them. It's okay to meet up after breakfast.

- Most campuses offer special shows or programs during parents' weekend, but the tickets can only be purchased by students. If this is something you think they'd enjoy, you'll want to buy tickets a few weeks in advance.

- Make the good-bye easier on Mom and Dad by sending *them* a care package or putting a nice note in their car. It will remind them how much you love them and will help them see you as an adult.

- Take a few photos of your time together and forward them to your folks as a thoughtful souvenir.

Hopefully, if the parents are adamant that a divorce is necessary, they will wait to tell their student until they can do so face-to-face. This word is for parents—if bad news of any kind must be given, please engage the help of the residence life staff or the dean's staff before delivering the news. If you are willing, the staff can be there when the news is shared. If a student is going to encounter any sort of family tragedy, it's best to work with the counseling services on campus, where they can be ready and available at a moment's notice.

To the student, we recommend you use the counseling services on campus to help you evaluate how this news is affecting your course work. From there, talk with your academic advisor and your profs as soon as possible. Profs may not make good counselors, but they *do* need to know why your performance is impaired so they can be more supportive. Oftentimes there are extensions available when the situation warrants, so it's worth asking.

RECENT DIAGNOSIS IN THE FAMILY

Family illness is another big blow. Again, we hope that all of your loved ones remain healthy and that this will never apply to you. Our biggest suggestion on this front is to take some time off from school if it is a family member you are particularly close to. Since your head won't be in the game anyway, it's the healthiest thing you can do to give yourself a break and go home to support your family, saving your tuition for when you are better able to focus. Most schools recognize the benefit of taking a leave and will work with you to make certain that your scholarship or other financial aid will not be adversely affected.

Why not get a job stocking shelves to pass the time and earn some extra money for books or espressos while you are home? Most schools are very accommodating and willing to work with students so they don't lose academic ground in these situations. There may even be a way to finish one or two classes from home and withdraw from the rest. This is where it is important for the student to communicate with the appropriate people on campus *immediately*, if only so you know where to find the eject button. (The best way to figure out who those "appropriate people" are is to start with your RA and academic advisor so they can steer you in the right direction.)

Your parents shouldn't feel that they need to arrange all this for you—it should be something you take care of so that every decision is *your* most comfortable decision. That doesn't mean you shouldn't consult your parents, but that ultimately the decision is up to you.

Often in the case of divorce, some students want to stay as far from the tension as possible and remain on campus. That's totally understandable; do what works best for you. Ultimately we suggest that you not go the distance alone and that you seek help early.

Sadly, most deans and professors find out about a troubled family situation or illness too late in the process, when the student has already dug himself a hole so deep that no one can help. Most faculty and staff take the stance your future employers will: it is up to you to make sure your home life does not undermine your work. The responsible thing to do if home is consistently affecting work is to tell the folks in charge. They don't need to know all of the details, but if it affects your work, it's your responsibility to let them know so everyone can adjust their expectations accordingly.

THE FAMILY PET

As for the last heartbreak of losing a beloved family pet, there is probably little comfort we can give. While the situation does not typically warrant taking time off from school, the initial news may make it feel that way. During his junior year, one student of ours—Philip—lost Max, "the most wonderful dog in the world," the dog that had stayed with him through twelve moves before Philip graduated from high school. He admits that the news hit him hard for a couple weeks but that he recovered eventually. He didn't feel like going home, but he did visit some friends who had a dog that appreciated a good belly scratch. For some, the loss of a pet is no big thing, while for others it is a symbol of the home life disintegrating. Whatever your pet means to you, reach out to friends (whether furry or not) so they can help.

Paving the Way

This is one of those sorts of sections we recommend both you and your parents read and talk about one night over pizza. There are three significant seasons as a parent where said parent may have unspoken expectations about said child: leaving for college, getting married, and bearing the first grandchild. These seasons of change tend to flow much easier when all of you are on the same page and talking about it ahead of time.

Is There a Vaccine for Homesickness?
Missing What You'll Miss

Oh, how we wish there were. In prepping for this section, we realized we would be talking out of both sides of our mouths. On the one hand, homesickness is normal and definitely nothing to be ashamed of. On the other hand, it's not something to indulge.

Even if you want to, and even if home is only a short drive away, our biggest push on this point is that you shouldn't go home every weekend—certainly have some planned trips home but also plan some diversions for those other weekends. Try not to be pulled home by that overwhelming urge to be in the familiar again, because it actually makes it harder for both you and your parents to adjust to the notion of you being a self-sufficient adult.

Another bonus to staying on campus is that you will be able to focus your attentions not only on your studies but also on your second family that you will develop by getting to know hall mates and peers. Even hanging around on a weekend with no plans creates an opportunity to engage in campus life and make unexpected connections, and that will never happen if you keep going home. Sorry, Mom.

If you're looking for ideas of what to do (especially on the cheap), check out your campus visitor center. Many college websites also list cultural and sporting events in the area so students can get involved in life where they live. Don't feel like you have to discover every cool book nook, market, theater, and museum on your own—at the very least, the visitor center will help you weed out places that would be a waste of time.

But what about going home to see your friends? That's a tricky one, and it varies from student to student. Some neglect their high school classmates entirely and dive into new friendships on campus. Some stay connected with former classmates and do it in a healthy way that still enables them to make new friends on campus. Some try desperately to maintain their high school friendships in exactly the same form and priority that they were before graduation, which rarely turns out well. While there is nothing wrong with the first two scenarios, the last one clearly hinders personal growth. Friendships should enable you to become the best person you can possibly be. What you will likely find over your undergrad years is that you will naturally prune your high school friendships. Some will fall away to be revived in unexpected ways at future reunions, while others will have you desperately trying to remember the names of people who were the sun and moon and stars for you in high school. Some old friendships may deepen in ways you did not expect and could not have planned.

Speaking of planning, "Don't plan on the hometown honey lasting all the way through college." That is what one prof we know tells her advisees at the beginning of each year, and most of the time she's right. But there are exceptions. One student in particular—we'll call him Tom—was a smart football player with a bit of a sarcastic wit. Upon hearing his advisor's pronouncement, he challenged her and said not only would he graduate a math major (she had just finished the spiel about changing your interest in majors a couple times prior to graduation day), he would also keep his high school girlfriend. The complication in this budding romance was that his girlfriend attended school forty miles away, which is an unmanageable distance when you don't have a car. The happy ending is that four years later, Tom graduated a computer science major and a math minor (close enough!) and his advisor flew to Texas to attend their wedding and eat crow. A few years back, she was invited to the baptism of their infant daughter and she is thrilled to admit they are happily married.

It's a sweet story (and not an altogether impossible hope, for those of you with high school sweethearts out there), but we would be remiss if we didn't tell you that it is exceptional. The futures market on high school romances is bearish. (Take an econ class if that analogy makes no sense to you.) Over the next four years, the two of you will grow and change a ton—even if you attend the same institution. In some cases, being on the same campus puts the success of the relationship at even greater risk since your interactions can become smothering and not allow for the independent growth you need.

Of course, don't feel like you need to break up with your boyfriend upon finishing this chapter. (And if you do, please do not tell him that it was because of what we wrote.) We are not trying to be Dr. Kevorkian–meets–Dr. Phil. These relationships tend to follow a natural life cycle of drifting apart, and as a result they don't require drastic steps toward euthanasia. If it dies, let it die naturally.

It isn't healthy to cut off all home ties and immediately expect college to be your entire life. This is true across all fronts—family, friends, interests, and significant others. A healthy perspective is to blend your former and current lives, beautifully marbling the best relationships in each so they can survive and become a foundational part of who you are.

I attend a university that is in a different state than my hometown, but my roommate's family lives just a short car ride away from our dorm. At first I was a bit envious of her proximity to home, but after a month or two, the fact that she was spending every weekend with her family meant that she was missing out on some great parts of college life. Most of the Nerf gun ambushes, wax-paper-in-the-oven experiments, and living room interpretive dance parties are spontaneous, and since she wasn't around, she was often left out of the fun that we spent the next week talking about.

Rebecca—recent grad, Point Loma Nazarene U

Your Cell Phone—Life Preserver or Anvil?
Communication Strategies That Build
Healthy Adult Relationships Back Home

What may be one of the hardest adjustments of all is that while your parents will be deeply involved in your college experience (in most cases, emotionally if not financially), they can no longer be intimately involved in your day-to-day life as they were in high school. At least, they shouldn't be.

Thanks to modern technology, it's far easier to stay in contact with your parents than it was for previous generations of freshmen, and the nature of contemporary middle-class society sees a lot more instant communication than we dare describe without dating ourselves. The technological arm seems to stretch farther and faster every day.

As a result, this is one area where you must be exceptionally wise and sensitive to your family. If you find that your parents need more contact with you than you need with them, it shows your maturity to compromise in your parents' direction. Part of being an adult is respecting someone else's needs rather than merely assuring that your own are met. You may think that being an adult means being independent—and it does, to a certain extent—but all the more, it means transitioning from "taker" to "giver." It doesn't mean you are letting your parents control your life, it just means you are checking in to see that they are doing well for their sake. At the same time, your parents need to understand that there are some limits on how often they should expect to hear from you. For instance, multiple times a day is probably unrealistic and unhealthy.

On the other side of the equation, if you are the needier one, our advice is to resist the temptation to check in as often as you would like—especially if you find you are speed-dialing home multiple times a day. This area cries out for moderation, so lean against your natural inclinations and you will likely get the balance right.

Students who phone home too much will find they have restricted their own growth by involving their parents in the minutiae more than they should. If you are calling home with hourly updates, you're asking for it! By stringing your parents along on your yo-yo days of ups and downs, don't be surprised when they call your advisor or dean or room-mate's parents to iron out snafus and be supportive.

Unlike most students, I was *not* ready to go off to college, not because I didn't feel ready to be on my own or because I didn't think I could handle college life, but simply because I liked living at home. I quickly adjusted to college life and found that I liked it much more than I had thought I would. There was, of course, one problem: communication with the folks back home. I found that I would go weeks at a time where I wouldn't even talk to them. Aside from visiting my siblings' Facebook pages, communication was lacking. After going back home from college for the first time, I realized that it was okay to call them more often because I had officially adjusted to my new life. I was not calling them because I was homesick but because I liked talking to them and missed them.

Billy—sophomore, High Point U

There are multiple ways to interact with folks back home, and it's best to think through the advantages and disadvantages of each before communicating absentmindedly. The cell phone is convenient and it's oh so easy to dial your mom after class to let her know how your test went—but are you missing an opportunity to talk to your professor or teaching assistant (TA) as you both meander the same direction to lunch? Okay, so you opt for the text message. That is certainly expedient, but then neither of you gets the warm fuzzies of hearing a live voice. Maybe there is a better time you can catch up so that your inter-actions are more meaningful. Or maybe by scheduling only a few conversations a week you will have more to tell her than what you just ate for lunch. As you set a communication pattern for calling home, try to make it flexible to accommodate the various schedule changes you will encounter in your college life, as well as sustainable for the long haul.

To close off this topic, here's a little FYI that might save your neck someday. In our techno-centered age, it is not uncommon to see people multitasking with email while on their cell phone and ordering lunch at a diner simultaneously. In fact, it's almost encouraged. Be forewarned, however, that there are varying receptions to this sort of behavior depending on the generation you are communicating with at that moment.

The student generation probably expects this to be the case and may not think it's rude to hear you typing in the background during a phone conversation (though, some would disagree and say they are still offended). However, step back one generation (such as your parent's age group): while they may suspect you are multitasking, there is still the hope that you will attempt to mask it so that it doesn't look like you find the conversation dull. Step back two generations (between your parents' and grandparents'—think CEO and future boss): multitasking is seen as the height of rudeness.

This can create intergenerational tensions not only at home but in the workplace, so keep your social radar tuned to make sure you aren't sending the wrong signal. After all, you don't want your sixty-year-old hostess to spit in your burger because you were curt with her while emailing your parents about your urgent change in flight plans while on hold with the airline.

Homesickness is not something to be ashamed of. Even though you may feel the pull to go home or spend hours on Skype, try to avoid it. If anything, remember you are not alone in what you are feeling; I was able to become much closer to people in my dorm as a result of our mutual homesickness. It also helped because we were able to reminisce and share stories about our homes and the people we missed, which brought us closer.

Helen—sophomore, U of Chicago

"Me human. Boy. Elliot. Ell-i-ot."
For the Male Reader

Indulge us as we take a brief detour into the quicksand of gender stereotypes. Taken from personal experience over the last thirty years, it is the parents of males who tend to complain the most about their child's lack of communication. It doesn't seem to matter which parent is speaking. Both seem to find their son less talkative than they'd like. Parents are generally more surprised by news from sons than they are daughters, since their daughters are more likely to have kept them informed of little progresses along the way. For good or ill, the parents of males say they are the last to know when their sons have a new girlfriend, but they seem to know immediately if their daughters have a new boyfriend on the scene.

Certainly the old adage of "boys will be boys" is clanging somewhere in the background and, if you are the aforementioned male, you may not want to change. If nothing else, be advised that you may be erring on the side of nontalkative and your folks may need a little more tele-time. If you aren't willing to communicate for their sakes, do it for your own; emotional intelligence (that is, reading and responding appropriately to the needs of others) is just as important as mental intelligence, and it's a critical skill to master as early as possible.

Avoiding the Worst-Parent-Ever (WPE) Award

(Word to the wise: We think parents should read this section. However, if you plan on sharing it with them, it would be best if you restrained your enthusiastic highlighter. You might also want to preview the WOE Award on page 48 before they pointedly hand it back to you.)

Loving your child is not and should never be a crime. However, the ways parents go about expressing that love can be complicated at times. The Worst-Parent-Ever Award could easily go to parents who respond to their children's departure by becoming Too Distant, but in our experience most finalists are in the Too-Involved camp.

THE TOO-INVOLVED PARENT

The typical worst parent is the one who feels that the only thing his son or daughter should be doing is studying. Period. Therefore, this parent does everything the student needs up to the point of taking her tests and writing her papers for her. This parent calls to handle his son's bounced check or his daughter's speeding ticket, or calls his daughter's professor to find out how she can improve in class. Though parents' motives are admirable, as a result of Mom becoming her sophomore's Girl Friday, that sophomore doesn't learn how to manage the day-to-day distractions of life while accomplishing a greater goal.

There was one parent of a recent freshman who was practically awarded a WPE *plaque* as a result of her behavior the summer before her student ever stepped foot on campus. Between two administrators, they tallied fifty emails they had received from this mother covering every worry she could imagine about her child leaving home. Her son was away from home for the summer and the whole time he was gone, she fretted about his course deadlines, whether or not he had registered for the right classes, if she could get the syllabi in advance, and so on. While administrators are typically prepared to receive one or two emails of this sort from parents (especially parents sending their first or only child off to college), they were overwhelmed by the quantity of emails from this one woman. Generally her son's courses looked fine and they tried to reassure her that he would have a two-week window like all the other students to make sure they were a good fit. Sadly their reassurances did little to assuage her. The message most colleges send home to the folks is that, while they are available should parents ever have a concern, the parents should consciously try to develop new outlets for their time now that their children have left home.

In keeping with the idea of helping their student focus on studies, parents will often come running when their child calls home sick. Too many parents have a propensity to come to campus and shepherd their child through the medical system at the first sign of minor illness. (For major illness or surgery, this sort of help may be warranted and sometimes the university will ask a parent to come to campus—but not for bugs that can be knocked out with a quick prescription or a weekend in bed.) This is another example of an opportunity to develop a new life skill—one that is sadly lost when Mom or Dad show up with the best intentions. In order to help your parents keep illnesses in perspective, the onus is on you to communicate it in a way that doesn't send them into a tailspin of panic.

At this point, it may be helpful to note that, historically, colleges have had an implicit understanding termed *in loco parentis* (L., "in the place of a parent"). The idea is that undergrads are not children but are also not yet adults and so still require some sort of parental guidance; since the parents are not there to provide it, the responsibility falls to the school. In ancient days, the faculty acted in loco parentis on behalf of their students by chaperoning parties, monitoring curfews, and the like.

Students and professors both happily celebrate that this is no longer the case now that campuses have developed a huge complex of student life administrators who are able to provide advice, support, and a measure of accountability. Sure, the bureaucracy may require a few extra steps beyond the quick call home, but it's a fairly apt halfway point between on-call parents and flying solo as an adult—like a climbing harness as opposed to a safety net. The staff will not mother students but are certainly available to provide more hands-on care than students would receive if left on their own.

Like any new venture, there is a possibility of little failures along the way—both you *and* your parents should expect them. We know of one phone call that exemplified the need to reset this expectation all too well. Julie asked her professor if she could call over break to discuss her final grade with him, and he agreed. The conversation went something like this:

Julie: Now that semester grades are out, can you tell me what grade I got on the final?

Prof: You got an 85.

Julie: [Whispering in the background.] Well, what was the grade for class participation?

Prof: An 87. It works out to an overall final grade of 85 when combined with your other papers and tests.

Julie: [More whispering.] What is the weight given to quizzes?

Prof: 10 percent.

Julie: [More whispering.]

Prof: Would you like me to talk with your mom directly?

Julie: Yes! [Hands the phone over.]

Mom: Now, I was a sociology major in college—why did my daughter get this grade in your class? You don't understand, my daughter is not like the other students. She is studying in the library on Saturday nights, she reads all the material, she . . .

We didn't make that conversation up—Scout's honor. It really happened just like that. While the mother may have a greater understanding of her daughter's performance as a result of that call, she undermined her daughter's sense of independence and confidence by returning her to the days of high school. The mom did less damage to the professor's perception of the student than one might think—in fact, the professor had some sympathy for her and her relationship with her overly involved mom as a result. Which reminds us to remind you once more: as strange as your professor may seem, we can state with utter certainty that your professor has been a student before and has dealt with parents before (and may even be a parent himself), so whatever you are going through, chances are the professor can relate at least a smidge.

On the other hand, in situations where parental control is too great on subjects of future importance—like choosing a major, career, or grad school—it may be beneficial to have your professor talk to your parents. We can't promise that your professor will be willing, but don't be so embarrassed that you forsake asking altogether. Have your parents call him during office hours (on their tab). Because the prof is an adult (and may even be a parent—certainly he had parents of his own), he will most likely be aware of the challenges you face, and sometimes a conversation like this can go a long way in helping you and your parents reach an amicable compromise.

Be forewarned in all this that there are various federal laws that restrict communication between the school and the parent. A student's educational record can generally not be shared with anyone—including, at times, the parent—without the student's authorization, so parents should not be surprised if college officials or faculty will not share details about the student's performance. On the other hand, the law *does* allow info to be shared regarding alcohol and drug violations, so it is in the student's best interest to call home before the dean does if such violations have . . . ahem . . . occurred. Most profs don't keep abreast of privacy law and so they may be willing to talk with your parents without your knowledge, but that may be the exception to the general privacy rule. Understandably parents are frustrated when they are barred from the conversation—one father told us, "It's like I just bought a new car that I will never be allowed to drive."

THE TOO-DISTANT PARENT

So far, these bits of wisdom have been aimed toward the most prevalent scenario: the too-involved parent. But what about the other possibility—the one where Mom and Dad seem to have lost all interest or concern for their child now that he has left home?

Liam was a student raised by well-educated parents who were supportive of him as a youngster in his many academic endeavors. But once his treads hit the quad and they had unloaded their minivan, they went home to clean out his room (without telling him) and to return to life as it was before he was born. In their desire to send him off into adulthood, they didn't write letters, didn't call, and didn't send care packages. They waited for all communication to be initiated by him. And, while this fostered a spirit of independence in the lad, it also left an unsettling feeling of abandonment. Partway through his education they made it known to him that, though they had the means to continue to financially support his basic needs, they were pulling all funds and tuition checks so he could learn to make it on his own. Liam had very little time or warning to transition into life as an adult and as a result it placed an undue amount of emotional and financial stress on him. The stress was so great that he dropped out of college.

So parents can fall off the horse on either side. Just when they think the constant fretting about whether or not they are raising Junior properly is over, they find themselves maneuvering the most delicate tightrope of all. We tip our hats to any and all attempting this feat and we wish them the best.

Avoiding the Worst-Offspring-Ever (WOE) Award

It wouldn't be fair to hand out such a dubious award to parents without making one available to their children as well, now would it?

Just as your parents want the best for you (even if you think they have an odd way of showing it at times), we suspect you are grateful that they birthed, clothed, fed, housed, and raised you. Chances are, however, that you may have odd ways of showing your gratitude at times.

The best place to start is to look for opportunities to be extra sensitive to your parents' feelings. The WOE Award goes to the student whose self-centeredness is so inflated that it chokes off all sympathy or empathy. No matter how hard you try, it will be obvious to all when you come home for the first holiday (often Thanksgiving) that your first priority is seeing old high-school friends and your second priority is expressing how much you miss being with your new college friends.

We ask you to consider a third priority: reconnecting with Mom and Dad. When your mom apologizes that her wardrobe is outdated, or if your dad tries to ask your advice on a topic that may or may not be of interest to you, try to hear their underlying message: they miss you, they are proud of you, and now that you are on your way to adulthood they want *you* to be proud of *them* too. Prove how much of an adult you are by being mutually encouraging.

Ultimately, be teachable. Just because you've reached college doesn't mean you should no longer ask for (or take!) advice. Folks will be dishing it out for the rest of your life (heck, we do it for a living), so whether it comes from parents or faculty or the custodian or a book, hear what they have to say and then sift. Just because you may think you know it all doesn't mean you should act like it.

But what if you *do* have a better idea of how to spend your future than your parents? Delana came to us complaining that her parents wanted her to take a high-paying job, whereas she wanted to travel and study abroad. They argued that they paid her bills and she insisted that it was her life—and both were right. Whose argument wins? First off, this should be a conversation and not a fight (slamming the door or ending the call midsentence are clear winners for the WOE Award). But it is a conversation that will at some point require a compromise and a conclusion. At the end of the day, certainly, it *is* your life and *you* have to take ownership of it—that's appropriate. But part of taking ownership and being an adult is living with the consequences of your decision. If Delana chooses to give up an opportunity to take a well-paying job so she can teach English in Asia, she can't very well expect her parents to wire her a couple grand if she gets stranded in Vietnam.

Be sure to talk with your folks about what they expect their financial role will be as you work through school. Some stop doling out the dough in high school, some go through grad school, some pay for up to a year after college. It's much better to have that conversation early on in your career. That way you can adjust your expectations and set your course from there.

We've talked a lot about talking in this chapter. It's something you will live and die by. We've also made a lot of generalizations about parents in this chapter, some stemming from the types of parents we've had and others from the types of parents we've seen. We tried to hit the extremes. Yours likely fall somewhere in the middle, and that's great. Maybe none of this chapter applied to you because you have already struck the perfect balance. In that case, just remember that a college education involves learning lots of stuff that, so far as you can tell, has no direct application to you right now. That might also apply to sections of certain books about college.

CHAPTER 3

"I Have the Perfect Schedule—All My Classes Are on Wednesday!"

Writing the Personal Narrative Called Your Transcript

Unlike the other college study guides out there, we are going to suggest that you *not* pick your courses.

That's right. From our perspective, and that of your future employers, you are not picking courses, you are creating a narrative of your educational journey (your school calls it a "transcript"). The narrative doesn't need to be ploddingly linear, but you should be able to make some sense out of it in retrospect. If there are mistakes, they should be balanced by subsequent successes. If there are successes, they should culminate in conquests.

The key to much of this is choosing professors rather than choosing courses, since the professor you pick will make or break any course.

Let's say you enter college thinking you will be a business major. Logically you'd start off with some econ and accounting courses. But halfway through the term you can barely stomach your weekly readings and you wake up every morning dreading the day's classes. Shock of all shocks, the biology course you are taking called "Mechanisms of Cellular Organization" to complete your science requirement has turned out to be fairly fascinating. You like the professor so much that you take another class from him and get his recommendations on other profs in the department you should consider.

By your junior year, you're a biomed major. Remember those business classes that turned out to be a dud? Well, you've started noticing some parallels, in that it seems the survival of businesses reflects a lot of evolutionary dynamics. Add to that the anthropology and sociology courses you took—"Tribal Stories of Origin" and "Culturomics" —as well as perhaps fulfilling your PE requirement with "Aboriginal Dance"—and you are looking pretty learned and well-rounded.

While that may not be your personal narrative of choice, the point is that the resulting transcript is one of breadth and depth; there is a broad range of courses but also a deep engagement in one or two areas. To turbocharge this sample transcript, you might take a couple of grad-level courses to show real mastery beyond merely fulfilling graduation requirements.

What if venturing out into unknown fields of knowledge leads to a couple of landmines (also known as bad grades)? Good question. The fear of bad grades often prevents students from getting the best out of college, and it shouldn't. Bad grades in your freshman year are more easily explained than they are in your senior year—so in the scenario above, that graduate could easily explain how losing interest and failing in his business major led to a newfound passion in the economics of survival. However, had this student waited until his junior year to admit defeat in his business courses and experiment elsewhere, it would have been much harder to explain.

Should you fall short of the ideal GPA, try at least to build an interesting narrative. The example we gave showed a rather obvious pattern. Obvious is nice; however, it isn't necessary.

We have seen transcripts that at first blush suggest total random whimsy. However, it turns out the students took as many courses from "star professors" as possible, resulting in a hopscotch across the pantheon of the university. What they lost in systematic progression, their narratives more than made up in quality of individual chapters.

A diverse transcript with a spectrum of profs across your major department and across departments in the university will speak well of you even if your GPA is a bit lower than another student who took a safer route, since it shows you are not afraid to take calculated risks. If you perform well in at least one or two of those classes, you will hopefully earn a strong letter of recommendation that emphasizes your intellectual courage and puts the rest of your GPA in context.

Pick your courses according to the following priorities:

1. Reputation of the professor as a teacher/scholar

2. Reputation of this particular course as a course

3. Your intrinsic interest in the topic

4. Level of difficulty so you can balance out your schedule

5. Any graduation/distribution requirements

6. The convenience of the time slot for the course

Most students select their courses using the exact opposite priority scale. Most students, as a result, are not getting the best out of college.

Beyond your own satisfaction at having gotten the most bang for your buck in your college experience, the overall goal in building a narrative via your course selection is to present a thoughtful, well-educated, well-rounded individual to future employers. While they do tend to look at an applicant's GPA, the transcript coupled with your resume are in some ways a teaser that will hopefully make you an intriguing prospect for an interview. Then, should you make it as far as the interview process, the opportunity to discuss the themes behind your educational narrative will make your application all the more interesting. And, as we all know, the more interesting the candidate, the more interested the employer. The same holds true of applying to grad schools.

If you aren't a top-down thinker (meaning that you find it difficult to plan beyond next semester), don't panic. We've got some bottom-up strategies spelled out later in the chapter to help you secure your footing as you make your way through the course guide.

When I got to college, I couldn't wait to pick my schedule. I have never been a morning person, but I soon realized that taking only afternoon classes made my day significantly less productive, so the next semester I switched it up. By taking classes in the morning (maybe not all at 8 a.m., but certainly a large percentage of early classes), I was able to finish my studies well before I would have even been awake the previous semester. This gave me more time to get things done and made it easier to manage my time.

Lauren—sophomore, Northeastern U

"I Refuse to Take a Class That Starts Before Noon"
The Best Way to Pick a Course

Granted, you may have pushed yourself through endless mornings of 5 a.m. alarms in high school with the promise that once you got to college you wouldn't roll out of bed until noon, but we're about to serve up some disappointment: choosing your schedule based on how late the courses allow you to sleep in is not the breakfast of champions.

Your best bet in selecting classes is to start off by asking your peers which professors to take. Be sure to set aside a fair chunk of time to do this (meaning, not the night before registration begins), since you will need to ask advice from a wide range of students to hedge against the possibility that one or two had a trivial pet peeve. You'll want to ask questions that are specific about the students' likes or dislikes in terms of course load, timing, teaching style, grading scale, fairness, availability, and so on—and weigh their teacher preferences accordingly. Look for firsthand advice from upperclassmen as opposed to hearsay from newly minted freshmen.

Specific questions to ask:

- What were highlights/lowlights of the course?
- What seems to excite this prof?
- How manageable is the workload, and do you have any advice on making it work?
- What was the quality of feedback for grading (and did your final actually have grades/comments on it, and did you pick it up)?
- Did you feel prepared for this course?
- Did you find that the information taught in this course was worth your investment of time and tuition?

Other sources of information on professors include, not surprisingly, professors! However, while profs may know a great deal about the backgrounds of other professors, they won't necessarily know much about how that professor teaches. In fact, for professional reasons, they may be reluctant to tell you what they know about the professor's reputation—like, "avoid that prof—but they may be willing to suggest colleagues you might enjoy, so listen just as carefully to what they don't suggest as to what they do.

There are also online evaluations to consider, but be wary here. These sorts of tools tend to be very skewed; they cater to the extremes, drawing students who more often feel the need to vent than to praise, and at times even allowing profs to leave their own reviews.

Finally, once you have narrowed your search to a few potential professors, consider attending one of their lectures a semester beforehand to observe their style and how the students respond in class (panicked, attentive, snoozing, on the edges of their seats, and so on. When we said start your seach early, we meant it!). You might even be able to walk out with a couple of students after class and ask a few specific questions about their experience with this prof and whether or not today's lecture was typical. Should you decide to follow our advice, take two things into account: First, please choose a large lecture where your presence will not be noted (and thus disruptive). Second, give very little value to the fact that you will feel completely lost by the content, since that is to be expected.

If the professor you are interested in observing doesn't offer lectures but is primarily a seminar instructor, keep reading.

> Be wary of people who give you advice on course numbers instead of specific professors. While a class's content on its own might seem good or bad, a good professor can make a bad class worth it and a bad professor can turn a good class into a nightmare.
>
> **Helen—sophomore, U of Chicago**

"I Learn Best When Profs . . ."

No matter what advice you hear, remember that it's only advice, not divine command (or popular vote). In fact, we have some advice about the advice you will be getting: filter it through a sieve called "know thyself." Two anecdotes make our point.

Without realizing what she'd done, Pearl requested "Literature and the Arts" to fulfill her freshman writing requirement first semester, primarily because the description of the course sounded fascinating. However, once she arrived on campus, other students started to warn her that she had picked the hardest freshman lit class at the university and that it would be a ton of work and she should try to switch immediately—actually multiple sources agreed. She panicked. But the textbook looked so amazing, and the one day of class she had attended made her want to memorize everything the professor said. In the end, she found one former student who admitted that the course was a lot of work but also argued that it was well worth it. He gave her a few tips on how to balance the load and how to discern the must-read from the nice-to-read on the syllabus, and with that she kept the class. Years later, if you ask Pearl what was her favorite course of her college career, she will cite "Literature and the Arts" as an easy winner.

By the way, she *did* make good use of her peers' advice. Rather than being caught unaware and later being overwhelmed by the impossible workload, she was ready for it and knew a few moves to keep herself afloat. In the end, her research paid off.

Want another course-hunting anecdote?

Sure you do. Jerry was looking for a good course in the history department, so he began asking around about a professor whose course description sounded interesting. Of the two or three people he asked, all adamantly disliked the professor. They said her teaching style was mind-numbing because she used PowerPoint slides with bullets for every single point she made, her syllabus was color-coded (which they found insulting), and she assigned a ton of reading to compensate for only having two lectures a week. Jerry signed on immediately. Why? After asking very specific questions about this professor, what he heard was that her teaching style didn't match his friends' learning styles, but it *did* match his.

He had been having difficulty following some previous professors' lectures, so the idea of a PowerPoint outline was a relief. And, not willing to admit it to his friends, he color-coded his lab notes because it helped him stay organized and ahead of his deadlines. Sure, no one likes a ton of reading, but since he'd already taken a look at the subject matter, it didn't seem as daunting as they made it out to be. It turned out to be a great match for him.

The key is discovering early on how you learn best. Part of that discovery will be learning which teaching styles definitely *don't* work for you. But rather than learning the hard way—stuck in a course you dislike for a whole semester—you could swing by the counseling center in the first few weeks of the semester to have them help you pinpoint your learning style. Or check out the book *Study Smart, Study Less* to help identify and work toward your learning strengths.

This is some of the best advice you could get: choose your courses by professor and make other considerations secondary. During my sophomore year, I was nervous about taking a constitutional law course with a famous law professor because the final exam counted for 100 percent of the final grade. Lucky for me, I didn't let that scare me off. The course turned out to be one of the best I ever took. My classmates thought so too—at the end of the last lecture all 120 people in the lecture hall gave the prof a standing ovation. It literally gave me chills.

Hans—recent grad, Duke U

"Since I Took Eight Courses in High School, I'll Take Seven in College"
Blunders Best Avoided in Weighing Your Course Load

Every university has a different way of counting credits and course hours. Whatever that method may be, do your best to stick with the average recommended by your advisor for your freshman year: too few courses and you'll probably waste time and run the risk of working inefficiently; too many courses and you'll run the risk of burnout, not to mention have little possibility of building friendships.

Professors understand the way courses are weighted at their university and for the most part will stick to that definition in assigning workloads in their courses. Unless you've got a particularly devious prof, he won't grant his course a low number of credits and then assign work as though it were worth the greatest number of credits possible. Of course, the real challenge is that not all equivalently weighted courses are, in fact, equivalent in workload. Across departments and within departments, some courses are harder than others.

It takes great skill to balance the number of time-intensive courses each term (such as labs or lit courses with a ton of reading and extra assignments) with "easy" courses. (Be aware that even though these "easy" courses are meant to lighten your load, they still require diligence, and a poor grade here will carry the same weight as a poor grade in a harder course.) Also, taking five "easy" courses worth three units is not the same as three "hard" courses worth five units, even though both scenarios total fifteen units. The more courses you sign up for, the more professor relationships you will need to manage, the more syllabi you will need to track, the more classes you will need to attend, and the more finals you will need to ace. Your advisor is there to help you strategize your semester lineup, so why make the process unnecessarily difficult by trying to figure it out on your own?

Knowing yourself as you do, if you really think you can handle an extra course above the average for a semester, then give it a go. Register for the class and use your one- to two-week window to practice balancing all those courses at once.

Be sure to communicate your intentions with the prof of this extra course in advance, and explain that you are trying to choose courses cautiously. This will build a professional rapport with your prof. Should you have to back out at the end of week two and take the course next term, you will have begun a mature relationship with the professor and possibly have earned her respect as well. Of course, this means that if you decide to back out, you do so at the university's appointed time. Waiting until a few weeks from the end of the semester to beg forgiveness for your frailties and ask that you be deleted without record from the course won't go over so well. At most schools, it can't be granted regardless of how smoothly you make the request.

If location is an issue with close scheduling (meaning that taking two courses back to back will make you either miss out on the end of one or be consistently late to the other), work it out with your profs *in the first week of class* to be sure you have their blessing.

It almost goes without saying that this trial period only works if you are in fact doing all of the assignments and attending every class. Since most profs don't take attendance or require weekly homework, it is easy to shirk some of the workload and give yourself a false sense of security that you can handle the load. The amount of work in the first two weeks may be less than what is ahead for the rest of the term (only the course syllabus can tell you that); be diligent and make the trial as close to realistic as possible. If there is a paper due in a month, start it now just so you can see how well it works into the routine.

"I Want to Finish All of My Grad Reqs by Spring of My Sophomore Year"
And Why This Is a Bad Plan

Though the labels vary from school to school, there are almost always two sets of grad requirements: general education (that everyone has regardless of major) and major requirements (that vary from department to department). Each involves a prescribed series that looks like a Chinese restaurant menu (take one from column A, two from column B, and so on).

Though they may seem utterly random, both sets of constraints were developed through an agonizing political process involving faculty and administrators. A lot of smart people invested hours of committee time and enormous thought and effort into designing a horse, and in the process created a camel. Every set of requirements has its own implied narrative that aims to take students along an intellectual journey, visiting places that students might not otherwise visit and dwelling in some places longer than students might otherwise stay.

Undergrads tend to have one of two equally bad reactions to general education requirements. Some view them as an insult to be resisted as long as possible and then only grudgingly indulged. Others view the requirements as a game of speed bingo, racing as fast as they can from the dinging of Day One to fulfill the requirements with no thought whatsoever as to the quality of the courses.

Don't be like most students.

View graduation requirements as an invitation to embark on a variety of intellectual excursions that you otherwise would not have taken. As much as you can, grab only good classes as they become available rather than accepting whatever is offered this semester just so you can check off that box. If you choose your grad reqs well, you may be surprised to find, years later, that some were among your favorite and most memorable courses.

Some students take comfort in finishing their grad requirements early but have no idea by the end of them what they are majoring in or where their interests lie. There is no harm in spreading out general requirements over four years. In fact, it might be advisable to save a couple for your last year if that means you will be better able to use the requirements as they were designed to be used—to help you find your major in the early years, to complement your major in the later years, and to broaden your academics throughout. Though there is certainly the danger of having fewer choices if you leave many until your senior year, chances are that you will fulfill more reqs along the way than you realize just by taking courses (strategically) for your major.

You should make it a goal to choose the most vibrant courses possible when it comes time to fulfill a requirement. Go for the best courses, whatever they might be at your school: "Ancient Egyptian Literature," "Social Dance," or "How the Harmonica Shaped the American South." A priority should definitely be placed on discovering your major and possibly using your general ed reqs to do so. We have much more to say on choosing your major—in fact, a whole chapter's worth (in chapter 11)—but for now let's just say that your major is the cake and the general education reqs are the frosting.

> View graduation requirements as an invitation to embark on a variety of intellectual excursions that you otherwise would not have taken.

Plan to take at least one course within your potential and then actual major each semester to build depth. Over a couple of years, you will have banked some considerable knowledge in your field, not to mention discovered some great profs early on so you can spend the next couple of years getting to know them better. However, too much of a good thing can be just plain too much. Don't take more than two courses in a department in a semester except, perhaps, for one intensive semester in your junior or senior year.

"If the Course Title's a Snoozer, I Won't Take It"

Unveiling the Mystery behind Course Listings

If only bad courses came with a truth-in-advertising label, like hot-dog packages that tell us what's actually inside (not that we *really* want to know, right?). It is, alas, not that simple. For one thing, much of what will make or break a course for you will be your personal learning style. We can, however, offer some insider advice.

RECONSIDER SUMMER QUARTER

Be thoughtful about taking summer courses. While we've known our share of great profs who teach in the summer, the courses are typically of lower quality. The top students will most likely be gone doing exciting things for the summer (and don't kid yourself—your peers are an asset in your courses), and your profs may be a little weary from the year. Of course, we recognize that summer classes may be necessary for varsity athletes or students trying to finish early (or catch up) in order to save money. And we recognize that some students like to take their most challenging course, like statistics or a science prerequisite, during the summer when they can give it their full attention. This strategy is not a bad one for a course or two on rare occasions, but we have seen many students fail to get the best out of college by loading up with subpar summer options.

RECONSIDER "UNPOPULAR" COURSES

Beware of sexy titles and convenient times. Sometimes they mask a professor who has difficulty drawing quality students without these superficial attractions, or they may attract so many students that you won't be able to get any face time with your prof.

Take a close look at courses taught at unpopular times as well—very good profs sometimes schedule at these times to weed out the duffers and get only good students. Granted, 8 a.m. (or, worse yet, 7 a.m.!) sounds like a ridiculous time for a lecture, especially when your hall mates were up until the wee hours singing with their good friend Bud next door, but for the right professor, a pair of earplugs and an early bedtime will be a worthwhile investment. Plus, it's only for a semester (and heck, the rest of the adult world gets up at this time or earlier, so at least you know it isn't deadly).

PROFESSOR TBA

Beware of the class where the professor is undetermined. Since you want to take courses *because* of who is teaching them, signing on for a course where they can't even locate a willing lecturer could be a sign of trouble. That said, the scheduling department could, by happy coincidence, land a wonderful professor. But we recommend holding off on signing up until the professor is named—or sign up with it as your extra course to be potentially dropped later.

ALMOST A PROF?

Beware of the class taught by grad students or staff (especially if you are dropping a lot of dough for tuition). Don't avoid them entirely. (We'd be remiss if we implied that there weren't brilliant college staff out there that *we* would be privileged to hear. For that matter, every great professor started out as a grad student.) Do, however, select these courses cautiously. Likewise, don't take too many classes from visiting profs, not because they won't be worth it—they may be fabulous. Take one or two if you like.

One big danger of taking courses from grad students or visiting professors is that they are harder to track down to write recommendations for you later on. Another danger is that standards for entry into the course are generally lower, so the caliber of your colleagues may be lower. It's also tough to evaluate their teaching style before taking the course since no one else may have taken a course from them. That doesn't mean that new profs are bad profs—use your grace window, often called the "drop-add period," during which schools let you change courses easily, so that you can test out if they're right for you.

"LAW SCHOOLS AND EMPLOYERS REQUIRE HIGH GPAS, SO I WON'T TAKE ANYTHING HARD"

If grad school is your aim, you need to do some serious planning early on with an advisor in that department. If you specifically have law school in mind, see an advisor in the law department for suggestions on how to craft your transcript. Some schools hold LSAT scores and GPA of equal value, so it will help you plan your transcript if you know your options.

Ideally you want a 4.0 with a challenging course load. Who doesn't? But don't be fooled by the glamour of a high GPA. Once you are over the hurdle of the minimum GPA, schools will evaluate what went into that GPA. A 3.8 with an array of tough courses is more impressive than a 3.9 with a lighter course load.

The earlier you know you will be applying to law school, med school, or grad school, the better you will be able to tailor your transcript accordingly. However, if you have built a transcript that amounts to an interesting narrative on its own terms, then it probably doesn't matter all that much. Each type of graduate school has its own special requirements, so you will need to research your course-selection needs as they apply to that school. For instance, a senior thesis is important if you want to apply to a PhD program, but it matters less for law school; certain science classes are requirements for medical school, whereas law schools are less interested in what classes you chose (as long as they were challenging) and more concerned with the overall GPA.

Knowing which specific schools you would like to attend and what their requirements are will be your best guide. We feel your stress. This probably seems like a lot to ask of you early on, especially if you are not yet a freshman or sophomore and graduation feels so far away (not to mention that it feels like you *just* figured out what college to attend!). But graduation isn't as far off as you think. These next four years will evaporate twice as fast as the last four did. And your top-choice schools will expect to see forethought on your part when it comes to meeting their expectations.

CONSIDER THE SOURCE

Beware of the course that sounds too good to be true—it probably is. Alex dreaded a particular course requirement, so he took a class because other students told him it was guaranteed to be a breeze. His hopes were confirmed when he saw a substantial contingent of well-known slackers in class the first day. What he didn't bank on was that the professor had also heard her course being called "a breeze." Offended, she set out to regain some respect for herself and the course. It led to an obnoxiously difficult semester. To make matters worse, the prof wasn't even that interesting. Alex admits that he should have considered the source; if a goof-off swears by the course, do a bit more research to be sure it is worth your time and money.

READ BETWEEN THE LINES

Be sure you know the prof's expectations before signing up. He could expect his students to research topics that he can use in his upcoming book, or require that a different student give a lecture each week while he sits back and grades them. Anything is possible. It's best to know a little more about what's in store for the semester. This is what the syllabus is for. Read it all the way through and ask the prof about anything that is unclear. Most professors share their vision for the course in the opening lecture. Pay attention to that lecture and that vision, and talk to him about it. It is not a guarantee—the prof's ambition may exceed his reach—but it will give you a sense of what he expects and thus what you can expect. You are paying good money to learn from this man—make sure he's worth it.

"I Don't Feel Like I'm Getting the Best Out of College, and I Have No Idea What I'm Doing Wrong"
Introducing . . . Campus Resources

Though it may sound like it, the following story is *not* an exaggerated account—honest. (And, yes, it really was a man.) Meet Edward. He refused to meet with his advisor to go over his schedule for the spring term. Meet Edward's advisor, who emailed him a reminder early on that he needed to make an appointment with her so she could give him his registration password. Instead, he ignored her emails and called the night before registration and requested his access number (which you typically can only get by meeting with your advisor in person). He said he needed it right away. He also told his advisor that he didn't have time to schedule a face-to-face appointment, and he didn't have time to talk on the phone because he was on his way to—wait for it—his hair appointment. Really. He prioritized his coif over multiple thousands of dollars he was paying in tuition for courses he wasn't sure he needed to take.

Be sure you are taking full advantage of campus resources, such as the career center (more on that in chapter 9) and especially your advisor. Make a priority of meeting with advisors, profs, or even heads of your major department long before the scheduling rush to be sure you're taking the best courses possible. If, for example, you tell them you're feeling frustrated with your classes, they might be able to find some flaws in your schedule that are leading to your frustration. It could be that you have had really poor luck with professors, or you may discover you have a learning disability that is giving you an unfair disadvantage. Whatever the cause, seek help early—after all, that's part of what you're paying for and thus a big part of getting the best out of college.

Every college offers far more exciting courses than any student is capable of cramming into four years. You are standing at a buffet line of a five-star establishment. Don't settle for beans and weenies. Even if your college seems smaller than most, and thus may not have as many flashy course offerings, don't be discouraged. You may have to search a bit harder, but you will definitely find the WOW courses that will jazz up your personal narrative and make your college experience memorable.

CHAPTER 4

Alliances, Fellows, and Clubs, Oh My!

Engaging in Extracurriculars

No matter how long four years may seem, you won't be an undergrad forever. Sooner than you think, you will become a cubicle junkie or some other freeway-shackled member of the global workforce. We know lots of them, and very few play a round of ultimate frisbee before their workday starts. Even fewer follow up a good discussion on poetics as influenced by Aristotle with a quick scramble up the campus climbing wall, or regularly join eight other voices a cappella, harmonizing in perfect pitch to a dorm of adoring freshmen, or watch anime in their living rooms until the wee hours with five other manga fanatics. What is par for the course for college students will soon enough be only a hazy, happy memory.

Let's face it, the world is practically assembled at your dorm doorstep—convenient, funded, and waiting to tickle your slightest whim. Never again will you be in a setting with so rich and convenient a menu of clubs, organizations, and activities beckoning for your time, not to mention interesting people with big ideas at the ready. And, unless you're hoarding some eternally stocked trust fund we don't know about, you'll most likely have a career, a family, or personal responsibilities that prevent you from joining an unlimited number of clubs after you graduate.

Simply exploring what there is to do outside of class is almost worth the price of admission. Alumni affairs folks recognize what deans and professors sometimes don't: the good times most alums seem to boast about typically occurred outside of class. So plan to have fun. It's one thing to challenge your brain, but if you really want to get the best out of college, plan to challenge your *self* too.

Top Two Ways Extracurriculars Go Awry

Campus extracurriculars offer an endless variety of possibilities across universities nationwide; given that diversity, rather than tell you exactly how to approach them, it would be easier to point out how *not* to approach them.

THE SPARSE SCHEDULE

Afraid of underestimating the college workload, some freshmen eliminate all extracurriculars from their agendas, determined to use that time to study. Because there will always be time to study later, nearly all freshmen who attempt this strategy end up frittering away their time on . . . *what did I do all semester? I don't remember. I have vague recollections of Xbox,* Seinfeld *reruns, and a popcorn fight in the commons. . . .*

Were freshmen truly able to make use of their hoarded time for studies, then arguably it might be time well spent. But experience has shown that to be the rare exception. Besides, it's unhealthy to spend all of your time at your desk.

THE CHOKED SCHEDULE

The second group is just the opposite. They enter the activities fair like a man breaking a fast at an all-you-can-eat buffet, gorging themselves on more clubs than they have time to pursue. Not long afterward, they have more emails about meetings and events than they even have time to read, let alone attend. All too often, these folks discover midway through the first semester (usually right after midterm grades are posted) that the number of extracurriculars that was manageable in high school is ridiculous to attempt in college. We can think of no more than a handful of college students who pursued more than three clubs at a time and did it well. We can think of many who attempted it and failed miserably.

Beyond simply seeking out a happy medium, we actually recommend you set aside less time to study and more time to join a club and play. (Try not to choke on your Coke—it's true, this is one of the few times in life your parents will approve of a book that promotes non-studying.) The fact is that most first-year students should be involved in slightly more extracurricular activities than they think, but less than they want. If attending meetings or completing some other club responsibility frequently becomes a scheduling burden or truly gets in the way of your class assignments, your extracurricular life is out of balance.

Somehow joining an invigorating set of clubs makes what little time is available for study that much more productive. Scarcity of something makes it all the more valuable, and that is especially true of time. Even during the freshman year, students get more done when they have more to do.

At the very least, try it for one semester. Join some nutty club that's only possible in college (medieval warfare, wilderness survival, or Taiko drums are a good start) and tell yourself that you're paying for it, so why not? It will never again be as easy to join as it is now. If nothing else, it will make for entertaining small talk someday while you sit around with colleagues at Friday drinks regaling them with tales of how you managed to survive on pine needles and wild blackberries when you got lost in the woods one weekend with the backpacking club.

How Many Hours Do You Really Have in a Day?
Outlining a Sustainable Work Schedule

Your high-school physics teacher may have told you that there are only twenty-four hours in a day, and that the possibility of expanding that amount of time is nil. While that may be true in theory, in practice time expands in college and shrinks thereafter. You will never have so much unstructured time as you do now. Well, maybe in sixty years if you're retired, but you get the point.

Let's do the math. For the sake of argument, we will assume you spent a solid seven hours in seat time each day of high school. Add to that an hour for lunch, thirty minutes to ride the bus each way, and at least three hours a week spent doing some sort of school activity—let's call it band practice. That brings us to a grand total of forty-eight hours, so far. Now let's add to that two hours of homework a night, at least four hours of homework on the weekends, oh and you had to polish your tuba before the big game Friday night, plus your performance that you planned to write about in your application essay, which totals four more hours. Now we're up to sixty-six hours you spent a week on life as a student in high school. You may have worked a part-time job (after all, you had to save for college), and so we may even be pushing eighty or ninety hours. You letter-jackets get to add extra time for athletics. Now, let's compare that with collegiate living.

Time spent in class: three hours a day, plus two hours in a lab once a week. Time spent commuting: zero hours (ah, the beauty of living on campus). Time spent eating: well, since you eat meals where and when you want to (heck, you can often take your minipizza to class), we won't count it. So far we're up to seventeen hours. Let's assume you spend three hours each weekday in the library studying your notes and readings (most freshmen take fifteen units their first semester, and most advisors figure an hour a unit in study time). And, now that you've officially "arrived," you don't need to join any filler clubs to boost your application. So time spent in obligatory extracurriculars: zero hours. Finally, you might want to take on a part-time job. In fact, this may likely be a part of your financial aid package. This type of work is called *work-study* and is part of a government program. Students are not allowed more than 19.9 hours of work-study per week, with most students actually working around ten. Assuming you work the average, that brings us to a grand total of—tuba toot, please—forty-two hours.

Are we kidding? Nope. High school life was roughly sixty-six hours a week and that number is cut by a third once you become a college freshman. Talk about free time! (Great news! Now you can eat your dinner just a little bit slower and actually engage in discussions with your friends about current affairs between mouthfuls.)

High-achieving high schoolers (and you may have been one of the exhausted many) keep more plates spinning than is doable in college. It's not unheard of for a high-school senior—let's call her Maria—to be VP of her class, editor of the school yearbook, and play a varsity sport—but that just isn't done in college. Maria needs to pick just one club or activity and truly invest in it; then a few months later, once she has the hang of it, perhaps she can add another activity that's a little lighter.

It's not that Maria doesn't have the time. After all, we've just shown she has more than twenty more hours a week than she's used to having. The point is that committing all her time to joining Tiptoeing Tap Dancers and being passionate about it (with perhaps an hour a week spent volunteering on trash pickup in her local park) is far better than being superficially involved in four different clubs. Companies that hire freshly minted college graduates are not as impressed by a smattering of shallow interests as they are with a person clearly following one interest and developing it to its fullest extent. Put another way: a top-performing senior in college will have a resume several pages

> The first quarter of my freshman year, I took a full load (nineteen units) because I thought I could handle it. I also piled on the clubs and joined the African Students Association and the gospel choir. I was constantly off to one meeting or the other and did not have a dedicated time to do work. Everything slowly fell apart at midterm, and I decided to drop out of the clubs and focus solely on my academics. By then, it was almost too late, and I was barely able to salvage my classes. If I could do that quarter over again, I would take only three classes and balance it with one club because, at that time, I was also getting acclimated to the US. In retrospect, I think I packed on the classes and clubs to avoid thinking about how far away I was from home and how homesick I was feeling.
>
> **Onome—junior, Stanford U**

shorter than a top-performing senior in high school. Feel free to let out that voluminous sigh of relief.

While we're on that point of future employers, it's critical to note that the club or organization you choose to join has almost ZERO relevance to your career path. Maria's participation in Tiptoeing Tap Dancers shows little more than how she chooses to spend her time. It does not destine her for a career with the Rockettes any more than joining the Future CEOs Club would guarantee her a seat in a corporate boardroom.

Joining an organization is valuable more for the experience of becoming part of something larger than yourself than it is for developing a technical skill you will later use on the job. After all, you don't plan on spending 24-7 in your office for the rest of your life, right? Your employer doesn't (or shouldn't) expect you will either, so outside interests are more than okay. In fact, in the job interview for one recent graduate—we'll call her Elizabeth—a critical component of being hired was her proving that she had enough hobbies to help depressurize the intensity of her job. Bottom line: they wouldn't hire her unless she could demonstrate she had a means uniquely different from her work to let off some steam. Balance is the sort of thing it's nice to learn early on.

Isaiah is a friend of ours who had a keen interest in law school. However, he preferred singing in an a capella group to joining the Bench and Bar Society (BBS). Because of his passion for singing, his participation in the a capella group actually made him a very strong candidate for law school later on because he excelled in what he enjoyed. In fact, the experience was so influential that he was able to develop it into an impressive narrative in his graduate application and interview. On the flip side, had he joined the BBS out of obligation, he most likely would have been less active in the group since it wasn't as strong an interest, and his boredom would have shown on his resume. And he wouldn't have been able to win his lady's love with such finely tuned vocal cords either.

As always, there are a few exceptions to consider. Students who write for student newspapers or volunteer regularly as a cameraperson on the campus television station do develop marketable skills that may "pay off" in the future. But again, those same students partake because they enjoy it.

Getting involved in extracurriculars is worth the investment of time and pays off with leadership skills—like people and project management—as well as personal development. There are virtually no "adults" involved, as nearly all campus clubs are student run, so this presents a great opportunity to learn how to work with peers.

As you choose a group, consider what strengths it will help you develop and how you would describe them in a job interview. Keep in mind that there are very few clubs that don't pay off with some skill set or another. Even cheerleading, which often takes a ribbing, might be found to teach valid skills like PR, time management, or goal setting. Other than joining a drinking club, you really can't go wrong (and even wine-tasting clubs provide some lifelong benefits). Joining a club is not just a matter of gaining experience or skills; it's about fulfilling responsibilities and proving yourself to be dependable, trustworthy, and recommendable—that last one being especially key.

Maneuvering the Activities Fair

It's electrifying. It's inspiring. It's overwhelming. Long before the first hint of a midterm comes the awe-inducing, schedule-filling possibilities of the annual activities fair.

Despite the hype, it's true that this is one of the most valuable functions you will attend all year. Congregated in one location is a representative from almost every interest group, association, and club on campus—and nearly every one of them is vying for your attention. Depending on the size of your institution, it can be truly impressive, not to mention a wee bit flattering.

However, before you start scrawling your email address on every clipboard in sight—a word or two.

The activities fair is a bazaar where everyone is hawking their wares. While they are selling experiences and not rugs, the same basic rules apply: they are likely to exaggerate how nice their group is;

misstate its true cost, and say they like your hairstyle more than they really do. But it's still the best place to shop.

Don't be put off by the fact that they are trying to sell you on something. EVERYONE in college proselytizes—and this isn't limited to the religious and political groups at the activities fair. The exuberance of ideas and possibilities runs rampant on the college campus. Profs are doing it on their subject, students on their interests or beliefs, and groups on their mission statements. It's how the world works, and to be honest, it isn't that bad a thing. When folks are passionate about something, they typically try to share it with someone else. As a result, the activities fair proves to be a rich sampling of college life.

Beware, however, of giving out your email address too readily. Once you get on a group's list—despite their assurances and good intentions that you can easily unsubscribe—it can be very difficult to get off. And then, for the next four years, you are spammed on a near-weekly basis by people you've never heard of to attend meetings you couldn't care less about.

A sane alternative is to set up a free email account online expressly for the purpose of the activities fair and give your email out to any table you wish. Then use that account to sift emails for the next couple of weeks and decide which groups you like best. Once you've decided, forward your university address to the groups you like, delete the free account, and take a deep, spam-free breath. Voilà!

While choosing an organization to join is an important decision, don't feel like it's carved in marble. Make it clear you don't want to take on any major projects or leadership positions in the first semester as you are still in a courting phase—unless you are certain this is the group for you—and then see if being a part of that group brings out your happy face. Don't worry—these groups are used to flirtation.

Of course, narrowing down which group to join may be the toughest part of all. Typically you will see groups that are sports/fitness oriented, production oriented (newspaper, yearbook, movies), arts oriented (music, dance, drama), issue clubs (save the whales), community service groups, demographic clubs (race, gender, religion, political party), and socially oriented clubs (Greeks). Since you only have time for a couple, try to pick what gives you the most levels of stimulation—such as exercise, an intellectual challenge, a chance to build friendships, and developing new skill sets.

Sound like a lot to ask of a group? Try to look at it this way: A student who has only been involved in a socially oriented club probably misses out in college because he never benefits from the exercise, intellectual challenge, or skills development aspects of other extra-curriculars. A student who has only joined a sports-oriented club is probably a little better off because the social aspect is coupled with some aerobic exercise, but he may still be missing out. Why? Because sports and social interaction can easily be found after graduation. Students who participate only in these types of extracurriculars don't take full advantage of the unique opportunities they can *only* get as a college student (not to mention the fact they don't engage the mind as fully). As part of a portfolio they're fine, but not as the whole thing.

If you absolutely need a sport, choose team sports over an individual sport because it will help meet your quota for social interaction as well as exercise. Try to meet as many of your quotients as possible in one group, or perhaps a combination.

The exception to all this is varsity sports—at the college level, it's a world unto itself of training, leadership development, mental gymnastics, and social skills. As a result, it is all a student has time to do. For those who weren't drafted to a varsity team, intramural athletics are nothing to sneeze at. Shawn was a varsity wrestler in high school who didn't make the cut when he attended a major Division I NCAA school, so he decided to follow the "why not" philosophy and went out for intramural wrestling. He ended up facing a state champion who had decided not to try out for varsity. Shawn says the guy made mincemeat out of him—now *that's* an experience he won't be able to duplicate after he graduates!

One last thought when considering how to while away your time. If you'd like to develop your schmoozing skills for later on in your career, consider signing up for a club such as golf or social dance, which will offer lessons cheaply or even for free. These sorts of lessons tend to be cost prohibitive outside of the campus, and finding the time to develop a new hobby will be easier now than while you are adjusting to a new career.

Why Are There So Many Campus Fellowships and Why Don't They Offer Money?

Christian Groups on Campus

The term "fellowship" applies most commonly to scholarships, but also pertains to religious groups that meet on campus. In this case, we're referring to the latter—sorry, no cash prizes here.

For those who've never been involved in church or religious groups, college is a great time to test them out, primarily because they are so accessible and interested in welcoming new people. If nothing else, it's a worthwhile venture and you might be surprised that what you *thought* you knew about a particular religion just isn't the case.

While the groups may seem interchangeable at first glance, they usually have a distinctive personality. (You wouldn't be the first person to wonder why there are so many fellowships on campus and why, if so many belong to the same religion, they don't just create one big group.) Some may specialize in inward activities (teaching, developing close friendships with others in the group), others in outward activities (community outreach, missions projects abroad). Some may specialize in the needs of athletes while others focus on international students. Some tend to attract folks from similar ethnic backgrounds; others aim to be as diverse as the college itself. In talking with the leaders of various fellowships, ask them how their focus differs from that of other groups (as well as how their beliefs may differ) so you can match your interests with a group you might want to join long-term.

As much as we'd like to offer specific advice on narrowing down the options, fellowships vary by campus and year. What may have been a thriving, engaged organization one year may be in the doldrums five years later, or vice versa. There's no way we can give specific advice (nor even can the alums of the school you are attending), so getting to know the students and leaders within the fellowships as well as learning more about them at the activities fair is really the best way to get started.

Generally there are three sorts of fellowships (also called college or campus ministries) available to students on campus. One is parachurch groups, and they tend to be more active on campus, or at least more widely recognized, because they are nationwide organizations (such as InterVarsity or Navigators) that offer a fairly consistent program from campus to campus and are not connected with a local church or cathedral.

The second type of college ministry is one based in a local church. Though often smaller, these provide a link to the community, which can be nice for getting involved in life outside of campus, getting to know people beyond the college-age group, or building networks of friends should you decide to stay in the area after graduation.

The third is more of a freestanding group of campus congregations that have no direct connection with local churches but offer services on campus under the umbrella ministry of their respective denomination—Baptists, Lutherans, Catholics, Episcopalians, and so on.

If you've been active in your faith or in a parachurch organization in high school (such as Young Life), you may want to get involved in a similar group soon after you arrive on campus. Most religious groups offer retreats or conferences toward the beginning of the school year to help freshmen get to know people quickly, and you can attend without committing to officially joining the group. In fact, many groups anticipate that their retreat is, at a minimum, an initial step in the search process rather than a decision to join. By attending one of these retreats, you'll get to know a bunch of folks on campus at the start of your college career, you'll check out some new scenery off campus, and you'll find out more about the faith of a particular group on campus. There's little to lose. And there's no better time than at the beginning of your freshman year, when your workload is at a minimum.

Over the long run, it will be nearly impossible to sustain meaningful interaction by joining more than one of these sorts of groups. The time required to attend functions, meetings, conferences, and so on can be fairly substantial, not to mention that you'll probably want to build some deep relationships within the group, and that takes a lot of time as well. Fellowships are the sort of extracurriculars that offer deep involvement on many levels, and as such you should limit yourself to only one as soon as you can make a clear choice.

If you can't pick one from the start, that's okay (few freshmen do). Try to narrow it down to two in the first week or so, and set a goal of choosing one by the end of the first semester. Should you choose to

> I got involved with a Christian fellowship on campus and that has been one of the best parts of my college experience so far. They have retreats and lots of fun events that go on year round, and I have also met lots of great people. I'm a shy person in general, so when they announced their fall retreat, I didn't want to go because I didn't know anyone. I went anyway and I made a lot of great friends in the process.
>
> **Brian—freshman, U of Oregon**

join, consider this your deep engagement and do something totally different (go mariachi band!) for your second extracurricular.

You Say Om, I Say Shalom
Other Faith-Based Opportunities on Campus

Of course, there are many other religious traditions that have a strong presence on college campuses, including Buddhist, Jewish, Muslim, Hindu, New Age, and more. These groups tend to be fairly individualized from one campus to the next, and choosing which group is best for you may require some initial sleuthing on your part.

The various religious centers on campus are often a great resource for students looking to practice their faith while far from home. And a lot of faith-based community centers offer resources beyond religious services. We've known religious centers to offer traditional

Seder feasts, celebrations at Ramadan, and meditation seminars, just to name a few. When Ayelet discovered that a kosher meal plan was available through the Hillel House on campus, she said it was a game changer for her and that it made her next four years on campus that much more meaningful.

All that is to say, if your faith has a holiday coming up that is not traditionally celebrated on campus, or if you'd like to learn more about one, swing by your campus religious center. If what you are looking for isn't offered there, make the offer to organize it—they will likely be thrilled to have your help.

The bottom line is that college is a time when many students explore spiritual paths that they ignored or were not even aware of prior to arriving on campus. College expands most people's horizons, and in every direction—intellectual, emotional, physical, and spiritual. As you apply the critical skills you are learning in the classroom as tools, you will likely discover important truths about yourself and your world in the process.

Does Work-Study Count as an Extracurricular?
Does It Require Time Outside of Class?

Absolutely—work-study counts as an extracurricular. While it may not sound as fun as joining a club, if funds are an issue this is an aspect of college life that could be a great opportunity to develop your leadership and time management skills while earning some cash.

Work-study programs are federally subsidized, enabling universities and colleges to hire a student at a lower cost to the university. And students' work-study ratings are based on their financial need. To find out your work-study rating, visit your financial aid office. The typical payment split between the college and the government is 50/50, though some students qualify for a 75/25 rating, which makes them very desirable to be hired on campus (because the college is only paying 25 percent of their total earnings). The bottom line is that your college may be able to offer you a plump hourly wage to shelve books or wipe counters, but it costs them less than hiring someone from off campus. It is, as they say, a win-win.

Work-study is an important element of college life for some 30 to 50 percent of students. Surprised? A lot of students want a job that is confined to a desk and is fairly mundane so they can study simultaneously. In some ways, they're getting a two-fer by getting paid to study, such as the sophomore who reads a novel for class while scanning students' meal cards as they pass by her register for dinner. Other students go crazy trying to study in informal settings and would prefer something a bit more engaging to break from studies, like sparring with the cafeteria chef who's known for his edgy sense of humor while serving hash at the buffet together, or lifeguarding at the campus pool. For some, work-study jobs can turn into permanent positions if the student performs exceptionally well. We know of one sophomore—Jaime—who did a work-study job for her resident faculty, liked it, and six years of schooling later returned to become the resident dean (with her original RF as her employee!). More and more students are doing research with professors and that can be a college-defining experience (see chapter 6). The options for work are nearly limitless for those who start their search early enough to get their pick of the best offerings.

Not to raise your hopes too high, we should add that most work-study jobs tend to be fairly routine (which is a nice way of saying monotonous). These humble jobs aren't without their benefits, though, teaching critical office skills and time management and—most importantly—a personal look at how the "other half" lives. When you're an exec, it will help earn your employees' respect if you personally know what it is like to walk around in their hair net.

Another benefit of pursuing a work-study job on campus—even, dare we suggest, if you don't immediately need the money—is that it can supplement your budget to allow you to take an impressive (yet no-pay) internship over the summer. Instead of going out for wrestling, Jonathan took a work-study job in the performance arts department spackling holes between exhibits, hanging flyers for upcoming performances, and managing the box office every Friday night. (He was a biology and political science major, so he figured some art exposure might round out his experience a little.) As a result of his work in the university's performance art department he was able to afford an unpaid internship on Capitol Hill the following summer because he'd paid for his books the previous semester in spackle.

While no undergraduate believes it, there is ample time to get everything done if time is managed wisely. It is completely doable to carry a full course load, have a work-study job, and join one campus club. Granted, Jonathan probably didn't catch many *SportsCenters* or hold the top score in the dorm on Halo, but he was able to manage two majors and a job, volunteer in a nearby housing community, and join a campus fellowship—plus a whole host of experiences besides, like wooing the girl of his dreams and marrying her after graduation. It's doable.

A big question students often ask on this topic is whether or not it makes a difference to switch work-study jobs over the course of four years. This depends on your personality. If doing the same job will drive you nuts, go for variety. But if you find a good fit early on, there is a real benefit in building up seniority. With seniority comes more responsibility, more interesting assignments, the impression of dependability on your resume, and often better pay. By switching jobs frequently, you return to the bottom of the pay scale with each new position.

A common assumption among students is that there will be a shortage of jobs on campus—to date, we've never heard of one. There always seem to be more vacancies than there are available students, since campuses tend to rely very heavily on student labor. Obviously, as time goes on, the variety of the selection decreases and your idea of a primo job may no longer be available, but a job is always waiting to be filled if the main goal is to make some money to offset tuition.

One semester, Lizzy, due to a schedule snafu, had to work three jobs because she couldn't get enough hours with one. That meant on Mondays and Thursdays she worked at the computer lab, on Wednesdays she checked IDs at the gym, and on Fridays she shelved books in the library. Her employment obligations were so schedule sensitive that she wasn't able to join any organizations that semester. However, the benefit for her was that each job was totally different and the variety made the time pass easily. (On a side note, you won't get rich with work-study jobs.

Federal law allows students to work up to 19.9 hours per week to qualify for work-study pay, and that's it. Hope that didn't burst your bubble.)

If work-study isn't your gig or you're looking for an excuse to get off campus, you can often make more money waitressing (love those tips!), nannying, or working at nearby software companies. The career center is your best resource for connecting with all sorts of off-campus employers who are interested in hiring undergrads. Even if you're looking for an enriching internship off campus (which, by the way, probably won't pay), the career center can help you there as well. For more direction on pursuing valuable internships, be sure you read chapter 9.

Are You a Geek If You Aren't Greek?
How the Greek Alphabet Spells More than P-A-R-T-I-E-S

Rush can make Greek life seem very desirable: brotherhood forever, sisterhood to save the day, cool kids make big bucks, and the added perk of a few Greek letters to get your foot in the door. The founding principles of most fraternities and sororities are scholarship, leadership, community service, and brother/sisterhood; however, for many Greek organizations, only the last of those principles is genuinely prioritized. In the past twenty-five years, Greek life has made some big changes.

One of the most obvious changes has been to the leadership positions in the Greek community, which in the past were reserved for seniors or the exceptional junior. This arrangement provided an incentive for students to join early and prove themselves to be "good brothers" or "good sisters" in conduct, discipline, and service, upholding all four tenets of the organization. This seems to be changing, and it is not unusual to find sophomores who are taking on most of these positions after being a part of a fraternity or sorority for less than a year. Once they reach upperclassman status, they become active in some other organization and remain part of the fraternity or sorority in name only.

As a result, the organization of these groups increasingly appeals to freshmen and sophomores. Many students come to college struggling with leaving home and family and needing to satisfy the strong urge to belong to something. The Greek system meets this need by providing a family atmosphere with a high level of acceptance. However, students seem to outgrow that need halfway through their college career and, consequently, interest in Greek life dwindles. Likewise, the

> Greek life is not a necessary part of college. It's there if you want it, but there are also parties by other groups on campus and all sorts of entertainment aside from the typical party scene. Some of my favorite memories in college are from sitting on the fifth floor landing of my dorm with friends until 3, 4, or even 5 a.m. talking and laughing about whatever comes to mind while eating massive amounts of popcorn, ice cream, and pumpkin seeds.
>
> **Helen—sophomore, U of Chicago**

push to honor the intent of the founders peters out as well, and the integrity of the system begins to flounder.

In response to this trend, several groups have shifted how they recruit students by trying to appeal to students in all four years. Sigma Phi Epsilon, for example, has taken on a more developmental approach by offering the Balanced Man Program, which makes sure all upperclassmen are provided with career advice and assistance on grad school applications. The program has met with some success, and other fraternities and sororities seem to be taking note.

In the past, Greeks used to offer an opportunity to learn from peers: role modeling reigned. Seniors knew their way around campus and could serve as a resource to help freshmen make connections. When Rick Wagoner, former president of GM, was asked if there was anything about his undergrad experience that prepped him for his role at GM, he said it was being president of his fraternity. That leadership opportunity—both difficult and challenging—still exists today. However, since so many upperclassmen lose interest in their fraternity/

sorority, much of the valuable networking and role modeling that took place in the past is lost.

All this might look like we're down on the Greeks, so let us assure you that just isn't the case. What we're saying is this: your time is a commodity and joining the Greek system is a gamble. On the positive side, they can teach group relationships, brother- and sisterhood, and accountability to one another. Most Greeks also encourage social service, like holiday food drives, and serving in such activities can forge the kinds of friendships and networks that will last for decades. Many alums will tell you that the Greek system really does build invaluable connections. Clearly there is potential for reward from the system.

On the downside, there are huge costs in terms of relationships and academics as well as finances. Fraternities and sororities alike are known to foster the kinds of activities that fritter away time on unfocused or repetitive events that can destroy GPAs, and, sometimes, are quite dangerous. It isn't all hype. We certainly aren't pinning all campus evils on the Greeks—not all cases of date rape or death by alcohol poisoning on campus are the result of a frat party; however, being a member probably increases the likelihood of encountering situations where there are large quantities of alcohol or sexual risks on a regular basis.

In most cases a student must be invited to join a fraternity, and quite frankly that's a really big deal. Let's face it: it's a bigger ego boost to be selected than it is to simply join. However, that boost comes at a cost: as much as $500 to $2,000 per year to cover dues, initiation fees, formals, and so on.

In the end, should you choose to go Greek, do so with your eyes open, and consider being involved in another group outside of your house as well. In other words, be a thin member of the Greeks but a thick member of another organization so that you are less prone to rely on alcohol-related functions for your main social stimulus. The other group will offer an easy alternative should you need one. Not only does this provide healthy choices, it will enrich your friendships and provide a more diverse educational experience.

To go Greek or not to go Greek is an important question, especially if your school has a big fraternity and sorority scene. At my school, being "independent" was a little like committing social suicide. Try to sum up the situation before rush season begins—and preferably before you even commit to the school, if you don't think you'll be interested in Greek life.

Hans—recent grad, Duke U

The Best Extracurricular Is You
Healthy Habits Start Now

We realize this sounds like a cheesy Saturday morning special, but it's true.

All too often, it seems as if college students perform the worst of any age group at eating, sleeping, and exercising. The notion of three meals a day at a normal time (or even five small meals at regular intervals), a minimum of eight hours of sleep (many studies show that the undergraduate age group requires ten to twelve hours of sleep), and using exercise as a healthy way to reduce stress and manage weight levels all consistently lose out on the priority scale for many undergrads.

The greatest way to achieve balance in your schedule is to tune into three basics.

1. Choose your courses.

2. Schedule three essential life-sustaining activities (sleeping, eating, exercise).

3. Add extracurriculars as time allows.

For maximum success, it must be done in that order. Students who ignore this frequently battle illness, don't perform as well as they could either academically or socially, and generally aren't as satisfied with themselves as they could be.

GETTING THE BEST MAY NOT MEAN PILING ON MORE COURSE WORK

If given a choice between taking a course overload or joining a club, choose the club—unless you have an unusual reason to sign up for an additional course, such as:

- This course is offered so rarely you will miss it otherwise.
- A prof is retiring and this is the last chance to study with him.
- This is your last chance to fill this grad requirement.
- You need to save money and get out a semester or two early.

The experience outside of the classroom is such a strong supplement to your academic work, not to mention a stress reliever, that it will be worth the investment of your time. That *was* what you wanted to hear anyway, right?

For those parents reading along who question our recommendation, our answer on this goes back to the notion of balance. All work and no play is not healthy. Being active in a club is a necessary part of a healthy lifestyle because it's playtime. This also ties into our belief that it is critical that students join clubs that are interesting (rather than obligatory). These clubs can provide students with much-needed stress relief, a positive energy boost, or a fresh perspective on life on days when there are inevitable disappointments.

However, if a club feels like just one more obligation, it isn't serving its purpose. That's often the tipping point on how students decide whether or not it's worth it. Sure, there will be times in all clubs where work outstrips play and you have to buckle down and do ten more reps, type up that budget spreadsheet, or make a dozen phone calls for donations. We aren't suggesting life will be all cotton-candy sweetness with these groups, just a breath of fresh air.

There is absolutely no shame—not with professors or employers or colleagues—in saying you joined a club simply because you liked it. It's much more disappointing to hear that a student joined a group because she thought she would gain something from it on her resume down the road. Most likely, she won't. Don't join because you think it makes you look brilliant—join because it's fun.

Sleep deprivation is one of the most significant health issues for college students today, one that doctors say affects students' immune systems and enables disease to run amok on campus. Health clinics nationwide are actually quite concerned about the rise of meningitis on college campuses and attribute this to students abusing their bodies (even with simple disuse), which allows epidemics to spread more rapidly.

It's amazing what happens when Mom and Dad aren't around to cook three squares and make you go to bed on time.

Now that you are on your own, begin to develop good habits for a lifetime of mental and physical health. Seriously, it won't get any easier after college when you're working fifty-plus hours a week with many more demands on your time.

Creating a healthy lifestyle is one of the most foundational decisions you can make for yourself as an adult, and there is absolutely no reason to spend the next four years pushing your body beyond its limits. Nope, not even med school. (You won't be much good as a doctor if your brain and body are trashed from years of abuse.)

I really took their point around health and exercise to heart and decided that I wanted to go to the gym every single day. And, for the most part, I have. I feel better and so much more energized after running and lifting weights (and I sleep better too).

Philip—freshman, Virginia Commonwealth U

CHAPTER 5

Memories You'll Want to Remember

Maneuvering the Social Scene with Aplomb

One of the best parts of college is the social scene: new friends, a chance to redefine who you are, and many of the freedoms of adulthood with very few of the responsibilities. What's not to love? It's a once-in-a-lifetime, four-year window where your best and most important subject will be you. While some students take this opportunity to an extreme and go wild, we assume that (since you're reading this book) you're looking to get more out of college than a four-year kegger.

Although this chapter will certainly discuss how to maneuver the party scene like a pro, we take the subject to an even deeper level. This is a chapter about defining who you want to be, how you want to be known, and how your recreational ventures will play into that definition. Rather than stumble onto the college social scene with an aimless, deer-in-the-headlights expression, we want to push you to make purposeful and strategic choices about your future—choices that will have you reaping the rewards from here to retirement rather than paying the penalties.

We believe students who get a clear view of the social scene—its choices, risks, rewards, and consequences—and then create a strategic plan in response will fare better, make fewer mistakes, and enjoy their college years far more than those who simply walk on campus and follow the herd. That belief has been reinforced repeatedly over the years as we have observed the greatest successes come from students who entered college with five principles in common:

- Know who you are.
- Decide what you *want* to do.
- Decide what you *won't* do.
- Envision what types of memories you want to make.
- Identify the personal achievements you want to accomplish.

This is a pivotal time. These five principles—if thoughtfully evaluated and put into practice—will have a greater impact now than they potentially will at any other season in your life.

Ultimately, we hope this chapter will provide enough guidance that you are able to enjoy the freedoms of adulthood in a way that makes your undergraduate years some of life's best, that you are able to avoid the pitfalls that trap so many unsuspecting undergrads, and, in the end, that you are able to graduate without regrets and be proud of your accomplishments.

This One's on Us

Let us be the first to rave about the thrilling buffet of social offerings before you. While a large university may have a more diverse spread, even small colleges have their own unique subcultures that are waiting to be explored. For example, Stella went to a small women's university and started a group that went rappelling off the clock tower as a stress reliever during finals week and organized midnight movie fests projected off the quad walls as an incentive to finish term papers early. At a large public university, Karen was able to persuade her friends (and the administration) to host an open-air French banquet on the chapel roof as a fundraiser for breast cancer research. Many campuses have sculpture gardens, primate centers, marine labs, extended field trips in China, and so much more, so you have before you a nearly endless array of lip-smacking possibilities.

Getting the Best Out of College

All that is to say, aim to do something out of the ordinary at least once a quarter with people who initially may not seem like your type. Should you find yourself needing some inspiration, locate one of dozens of flyer poles on campus and pull a couple to take home for consideration; you'd be amazed how many students walk by those flyers expecting they'll see that show or go on that tour "someday," and then life gets busy and "someday" never comes.

Of course, you could be like some students who ignore their campus's social offerings altogether and go the more traditional route of the undergraduate holy trinity for entertainment (drugs, booze, and hookups). But why be that predictable? Why limit yourself by engaging in high-risk, low-reward activities when you could be creative about your adventures and in the process develop deep friendships? Really, when you come down to it, that's what everyone wants when they graduate: great friends and great memories.

So get slightly crazy as you plan the weekend's festivities. Parachuting over campus, an all-night soccer tournament, a forty-eight-hour marathon viewing of James Bond movies in chronological order, a social dance class that culminates in New York for the weekend—you are limited only by your imagination.

> We believe students who get a clear view of the social scene—its choices, risks, rewards, and consequences—and then create a strategic plan in response will fare better, make fewer mistakes, and enjoy their college years far more than those who simply walk on campus and follow the herd.

Live it up. Enjoy making memories that will happily last you the rest of your days.

Starting Off Strong
Deciding Who You Want to Be Before You Reach Campus

Chances are you've spent more time your senior year pondering the college party scene than the classroom. No parents to ask embarrassing questions, only a few hours of course work a day, and a lot of time to experiment—isn't that what college is all about?

Not really. We won't even pretend that partying doesn't happen on campus on a weekly basis. But what should remain *at best* (within certain legal confines) an extracurricular activity can become a dangerous distraction that undermines students' opportunities to make the most of their college education.

You should know yourself and your goals well enough to know whether, where, when, and how to (or how not to) cross boundaries you have established for yourself. And the clearer you are with yourself about what goes under the categories of "to do" and "not to do," the more you will be able to enjoy the company you are in because you don't have to second-guess the situation.

It may be that the standards you kept in high school will serve you well in college, and, if so, that's great. But even if that's the case, you will need to reevaluate how they apply to the college campus. The first step is to get someplace quiet and sketch out some personal boundaries/standards/goals/values—call 'em what you like, their function is pretty much the same. In a few sections, we'll discuss the most common concerns in more detail to broaden your sketch even further.

Granted, if you are reading this as an incoming freshman, it will be much easier to apply your goals once you have a better idea of how the campus works. What we're asking you to do might even seem like a premature exercise in hypotheticals, but we promise it will pay off. It is much easier to enter your freshman year with momentum aiming you in one direction (which you can alter as needed) than it is to try to jump-start the process once you're on campus. And, if you're reading this after your freshman year, it's not too late. You understand yourself and your campus well enough now to reevaluate your goals and set some new ones.

As you design your goals, aim for a holistic view of yourself on the college campus. While this chapter is largely about creative (and not-so-creative) adventures on campus, even academic goals will have implications for what sorts of parties you decide to attend.

For example, what do you want "studious you" to look like? Are you naturally inclined toward being bookish, so you think you need to limit your study window and set goals to socialize more? Or are you the opposite, and you want to get as much of your work out of the way during daylight hours so you can have a night life? Design your social life intentionally so that the primary reason you came to college (getting an education) doesn't take a backseat to what should remain extracurricular.

A more obvious link in considering how you want to explore the social scene is relationships. Friendships are an easy one—not too many boundaries are required there. Dating, however, is another story. Should you decide to date, how physical do you want to get? Make your standards *as clear as possible* with this one because the fewer gray areas, the easier it will be to honor your goals in the heat of the moment. Chart it out if that helps: how far do you want to go on the first date? Once you're officially dating? Once you're engaged? What would you prefer to save for the wedding night? For each of these stages and topics, consider the long-term effect of each choice and use those potential consequences to help you determine where to put boundaries.

Don't feel obligated to show your final strategy to anyone, but keep a file somewhere. Here are a few other topics to ponder as you spell out your boundaries and develop an image of who you want to be by the time you graduate.

- Health and well-being—goals for exercise, sleep, or a certain diet?
- Studies—scheduled to be done by a certain time each day or at random? What about "borrowing" papers, graduating with honors, writing a senior thesis?
- Religion—regular weekly service, spiritual buffet, or none?
- Alcohol use—at what age, in what settings, to what extent?
- Drugs—if ever, what kind, what setting?
- Sex—activity or abstinence, how many bases and when, what setting, under what influences?

If it helps to query peers, parents, or other folks you respect, by all means do so.

As you begin to sort through their answers, what you will hopefully find is that setting boundaries for yourself doesn't prevent you from exploring the world; if anything, it frees you to be more adventuresome because you've chosen the best ways to do so. To date, we've never heard a graduate say, "I wish I had been more sexually active" or "I wish I had gotten drunk at that frat party," but we have sure heard the opposite. So be willing to set the bar high for yourself; if necessary, it can always be lowered. (The inverse holds true as well: you can always push the bar higher later, though just as is true of gravity and a bench press, it requires a greater force and focus.)

In forming your own standards, the best advice we've heard on the subject is "hold principles tightly and policies lightly," meaning, as you sketch out goals and boundaries for yourself, aim to discover the principles that undergird those boundaries rather than simply listing out a block of rules to follow. Principles allow for flexibility and game-time applications, whereas policies could write you into a corner. "I'm never going to be out after 2 a.m." or whatever arbitrary time will be a very difficult policy to sustain and may not apply. Neither will "I'll never be around anyone who's stumbling drunk," since it will be difficult to control someone else's behavior. Instead, a better principle would be "I'll avoid putting myself in situations where my safety is dependent on the sobriety of others," and how that's applied will depend on the situation.

Having a prearranged agreement with yourself about your limits avoids many regrettable decisions, especially when it comes to sex. By establishing limits with myself, I was able to evade potentially awkward situations more easily and also say no when situations could have gone the other way. Now that I have a boyfriend, I am very glad that I kept to my standards and did not let myself fall prey to a momentary lapse in judgment. Several of my friends wish they had set standards ahead of time too.

Lauren—sophomore, Northeastern U

It's thrilling, really. From the time your parents drop you off and head for home, you will be presented with a host of new ideas and opportunities. No curfew and no serious course work for a few weeks: that's a lot of time for hanging out, exploring campus, and meeting new friends at orientation events, and it all spells fun.

But large amounts of unstructured time make for other possibilities as well. There is a strong likelihood that you will be approached about alcohol, sex, and drugs your first week on campus. The key is to anticipate these situations by studying your campus and how your principles apply. If you feel like you could use some support or, at the very least, a trustworthy listener, we recommend talking to your RA, someone at the counseling center, a religious advisor, your parents, or an old friend from home, since the friendships you will have begun at this point won't have had time to be tried and proven.

Please understand—by asking you to establish boundaries for yourself, we're not suggesting you make up your mind, close it, then lock yourself in your room. While surrounding yourself with like-minded people can help you become the person you want to be, that doesn't mean you should avoid getting to know people who think differently. Every day you are surrounded by people of a similar age with similar goals from all different walks of life. A fabulous risk to take would be asking them to treat you to a new perspective of the world from their eyes. Go to an art show your friend likes but you otherwise would never attend; visit a part of town another friend loves but you've never seen; eat white rice with sugar and butter like she does just to see how it tastes; talk about your childhood and what sort of childhood you hope your kids will have someday. Not only will you broaden your friendships, you will broaden your understanding of the world (which, ironically, makes you a deeper person). And you may surprise yourself by developing new tastes, both for rice and for friends.

In that same vein, we recommend that you look for opportunities to intellectually challenge your values. College is a rich smorgasbord of ideas. Use it as a forum to flesh out your worldview by starting some spicy discussions over dinner. Exposure to other viewpoints is a huge part of your personal growth, and one that will hopefully be ongoing throughout your life. Some of your encounters may simply be for the sake of fun and not so much intellect—that's superb.

So go to that tailgate party. If you've decided not to drink, great (and quite honestly most of your classmates won't care either way). You'll get to relax with new friends and have a blast at the game. Sure, some of the folks will be so sloshed they think they're funnier than they really are. You've got your lines, they've got theirs; it's entirely possible for everyone to still have a good time.

Beyond campus-wide social events, we *do* recommend that you select your close friends carefully. The type of people you spend the majority of your time with—downtime, uptime, or anytime—is quite simply the type of person you will become. Use that to your benefit. Seek out the sorts of people you respect and who will respect you— especially if you feel like your views might put you in the minority. On almost any campus, you will be able to find others who share your ideas and standards or, at the very least, people who respect you for them.

College is not the socially neutral environment that we wish it were. On most campuses, there is prejudice in favor of experimentation, particularly with alcohol and sex. Don't be naive. This is the direction your culture will push, regardless of the school you attend. If you want to push back and stick to your standards, you will need some like-minded friends, or at least friends who support your choice in values. Plus, good friends make college loads more fun.

> Whatever your standards may be, focus on placing yourself *only* in situations where you can stay in control of those decisions.

A final move that will help you live up to your goals will be knowing which parties to join and which to ditch. In the beginning, these distinctions will most likely be blurred and your choices may feel a bit out of control, which should be a yellow flag. Whatever your standards may be (about when or when not to drink, when or when not to have sex, when or when not to do drugs, when or when not to party), focus on placing yourself *only* in situations where you can stay in control of those decisions.

Choose your close friends carefully. Try to avoid the common trap of thinking your freshman hall mates will remain your inner circle. You may cling to each other the first semester, but have the courage to branch out and choose friends based on chemistry and values rather than mere proximity.

Hans—recent grad, Duke U

Risks You'd Want Us to Mention

Part of what makes college so exciting is the fairly accurate impression that your opportunities are limitless. Most undergrads see it as a season of boundless exploration and experimentation—and that's largely true. However, it's not a time devoid of consequences. They may be delayed, but you definitely have to pay up at some point or another. Out of respect for you and your ability to make your own decisions, you won't find us citing the overquoted yet popular "everyone does it," pretending that it won't come back to haunt you later. We're willing to risk a little unpopularity to spell it out like it is so you can make your own best decisions.

The most obvious risk is health related. Some estimates have suggested that nationwide, as many as seventeen hundred college-aged students die each year from alcohol-related incidents. Even if that number is inflated, any alcohol-related death is tragic and unnecessary.

Some would argue students are only posing risks to themselves, but their argument is demonstrably untrue. Sexually Transmitted Infections (STIs) pose risks to future partners, drunk driving can be deadly for anyone on the road, and hazing is debilitating to fellow students. Poor decisions affect us, our loved ones, and even strangers.

Perhaps some students make poor decisions because, when accountability is low, the risks feel low; when risks feel low, students feel invincible and behave as though the logical outcomes of their actions will go no further than the campus gate. If suggesting that students might hold such a belief seems condescending, we apologize. We wouldn't mention it had we not seen that belief played out on campus time and time again: students get caught crossing the law and they are shocked to find themselves being held responsible for their actions.

A case in point is one student who recently made a name for herself by committing a ridiculous petty crime. Jordan was in a rush one morning trying to get to class on time, so she parked in the faculty parking lot. Sure, there were signs posted multiple places as well as a mechanical arm at the exit to dissuade anyone but faculty from parking there. But, like she said later, she was late for class so she ignored the signs and parked there anyway.

Trouble came when she got caught trying to lift the arm of the parking gate in order to leave. Sometimes students get away with it, sometimes it scrapes up their paint jobs, sometimes it breaks the gate mechanism. Oddly enough, she complained to the student conduct officer during the hearing that she shouldn't be held responsible because there was no sign posted stating that lifting the gate would break it. The officer found it a laughable excuse. She was put on probation, lost parking privileges, paid a fine, and now has a *permanent* mark on her disciplinary record—all to save herself ten minutes.

Will this witless story shadow her future success? Absolutely. Will it ruin her future? Probably not—though it made her look foolish and irresponsible. What is worse, for every grad school and job application from here on out she will have to check "yes" when asked if she's been involved in any disciplinary measures. Depending on the competition for the position, she might have an opportunity to explain herself or it could ding her from the list of hopefuls before she's given a moment to speak. There's no way to know.

Perhaps students are willing to cross the law more on campus than they would otherwise because the lax enforcement of the law has given them a false sense of security. Whether or not we want to admit it, it's true that alcohol restrictions are not as rigorously enforced on college campuses as they are off. However, they are not totally ignored either, and "everybody does it" turns out to provide no legal protection should you get caught. Even if drinking laws are loose, the rest of the legal paradigm applies.

Over a quarter of the students entering campus each year come with fake IDs. Melinda remembers first becoming aware of their prevalence when a dorm mate begged for her Oregon driver's license because the background was easier than most states to scan and forge. By the time freshmen learn their way around campus, that fraction of fake IDs grows to half of the matriculating class. Don't be misled. Just because that number is enormous and fake IDs are common doesn't mean the sentence will be any lighter should you get caught.

The Unforgettable Web
As in "World Wide Regret"

"How do I want to introduce myself now that I'm an adult? I've always hated 'Leroy.' Should I go by my middle name instead? Should I hide that I like bluegrass and tell people I listen to Latin jazz? What if I stop styling my hair and go natural and refuse to eat all meat products?"

Part of the appeal of college is precisely this opportunity to write a new chapter. You may have been known as The Nerd, The Cowboy, The Jock, or any number of stereotypes that you might be eager to shed. It's particularly common at highly selective schools to see students go to great lengths to ditch their nerd factor now that it has gotten them into their college of choice.

The trouble is that in trying to earn extra cool points, some people go overboard. In fact, it's part of the reason why so many big mistakes get made in the first few weeks of college. Included among the consequences of having made those mistakes is the reputation that follows. It can be difficult to shake. Whatever your moral standards in high school, if you start out as the proverbial good-time-to-be-had-by-all in college, you'll be hard-pressed to convince others that you're no longer that person later on should you decide to take a step back. Rumors spread across the college campus much like a small town, and tongues wag freely. So take care with first impressions.

We doubt experimentation was ever risk-free, but as our world becomes smaller, the risks become more costly. Nowadays your "worst ever" might not simply live on in your friends' nostalgia. Once on the Internet, always on the Internet—somewhere.

Of course, that's not always a bad thing: As a way to earn some extra cash his sophomore year, Josiah wrote an article for an online magazine about trends on the college campus. A decade later, potential employers still cite the article during interviews. At least it's well-written, but in hindsight he wishes he had tempered his speech.

Online displays of adventure *can* be used to develop networks for your personal and professional future. After growing up as her small town's hokiest dresser (and scaredest scaredy-cat), Evie spent the next four years of college and four more years postgraduation determined to broaden her horizons. She braved backpacking trips that began with the dorm and eventually took her as far as New Zealand. She made a new group of friends at a Korean club on campus and later moved to Korea to learn the language and culture while teaching English. She traveled from the straw huts of Indonesia's jungles to the beaches of the South Pacific, and with each of her new adventures her confidence and character grew. (Thankfully the exposure to a world of style improved her wardrobe as well.) As a result of her thoughtful and engaging online postings, she was invited to write and publish a book by a former campus mentor, which launched her into a career as an author.

On the flip side, that posting Jason listed not so subtly on his blog about the threesome he had on Friday (with one of them being under-age and high) is almost guaranteed to get him in trouble somewhere down the road. What if Jason was smart enough not to post it on his blog, but one of the "other two" did? Misadventures are especially newsworthy, and once it's reported in the news, the story will be forever searchable on the Internet.

Even if you keep your Facebook wall hidden and your online social image impeccable, there is still that less manageable web of *real life* social networks. Should the sister of your best friend be best friends with the guy thinking of hiring you, and should they play the name game of "Oh, you went to that college! Let's see, do you know_____?" your name just might come up.

We sense the need for a disclaimer: we aren't advocating illegal activity and then instructing you to hide it well. If anything, our point is to hold up the indefatigable network of wagging tongues as an incentive to keep yourself out of trouble. Should you make a mistake along the way, be as discreet with that information as possible, apologize to those necessary, and refrain from posting it in an email or online to *anyone*.

Let the Good Times Roll
Maneuvering Your Newfound Freedoms Like a Pro

On campuses larger than many small Midwestern towns, how is an unknown freshman expected to thrive his first year without becoming social hamburger?

FIND A TRUSTWORTHY LISTENER

By definition, a "trustworthy listener" means someone who is tight lipped and who puts you at ease. Someone you are in fact so comfortable with that you could have conversations like, "I'm really worried I'm going to try crack when I get on campus, but I don't think I should" or "I lost my virginity and I wish I hadn't." This should be someone you can respect to help you through difficult choices without having to worry about being judged or, conversely, pushed farther into an activity you are seeking to avoid by condoning it. (Preferably this trustworthy listener is someone you have known for years or who is professionally bound to confidentiality) It could be a counselor, a former teacher, a spiritual advisor, a parent, or someone you have met on your campus. The point is not to go it alone. Have someone to call anytime for backup—especially that first year while you are still trying to lay the groundwork for trust in your new friendships. Remember all those goals you sketched out in the "Starting Off Strong" section? It helps to have someone cheering you on as you excel in them or offering a hand should you veer off course. That being said, it will take months or even years to test and prove which of your peers on campus are trustworthy with deeply personal information, so you might prefer a professional on campus or a trusted friend off-campus until then.

SAVE BIG DECISIONS FOR DAYLIGHT

As a junior, Ellie opted to live in a campus apartment with her room-mate instead of a dorm and was excited at the prospect of having her "own place." Her visions of homey serenity were dashed, however, the night she came home late from the library to find her roommate asleep and the kitchen a cooking disaster: cold pasta stuck to pots, burned remnants of what must have been brownies in a pan, oil splattered on walls, and dirty dishes left scattered around the small living area. (Was that the box of brownie mix she had been saving for her study group on Friday?) Worse yet was that none of the delectables were left. Ellie, understandably, was furious. She reached for a Sharpie, soothing her-self with the idea of broiling her roommate with a fuming note that she would leave taped to the fridge. But wisdom got the better of her. For a shred of a moment, Ellie realized that harpooning her friendship over thirty minutes of cleanup might not be the best plan, and that a better idea would be to get some sleep and tackle that conversation tomorrow. The next morning, Ellie was relieved she had hidden the note—a quick read with fresh eyes showed her how immature it was; she headed to the kitchen to grab some cereal and talk things out with her roommate.

Initially this may not seem like a life-altering decision—but it is. When it comes to choices around friendships (or, really, relationships of any kind), career moves, personal goals and standards, and experi-mentation, the best plan is *always* to delay a decision for daytime, when you are more likely to be clear-headed about the matter.

LEARN FROM THE VETERANS

Try to connect with upperclassmen in a mentoring sort of relation-ship. Since they've been on campus for a while, they probably have (or know someone who has) made all the rookie mistakes. Why repeat them? What could take a year or two to discover on your own about what to do or not to do at your particular college is already well known by someone else out there. Plus, then you get the added benefit of sto-ries like, "I once knew a guy in college who . . ." without risking your precious reputation.

Even If You Don't Get Caught . . .
Newton's Third Law Will Find You

Drugs, alcohol, and sex get lumped together for discussion purposes, but they should really be addressed separately. For that matter, they shouldn't be lumped together in any situation.

Alone, they bear a weight that is difficult to manage, but where they become extremely dangerous and where the risks become magnified exponentially is in combination. It's one thing to experiment physically in your relationships within clearly drawn boundaries. It's a completely different beast when you combine it with alcohol and find yourself reeling from loss of self-control. At best, you won't stick to your lines; at worst, you could find yourself surviving a real nightmare. Combine that with drugs and you're someplace you may regret for the rest of your days.

We are tempted to end this topic at that, but it would be negligent of us to do so. Despite the continuing evidence that fewer students are involved in drugs, alcohol, and sex on campus than most would assume, for those readers out there who plug their ears and plow toward the danger zone with abandon, we feel obligated to map out a few escape routes to help minimize the risks.

So we continue . . .

Alcohol tends to be the stimulant of choice on college campuses, but drugs cannot be discounted. We treat them differently here because society treats them differently. Because illegal drug use is disciplined far more rigidly than the occasional beer, you therefore need to be far more wary about experimenting with drugs.

We're not just talking about pot either. Campus administrations note an increase in prescription drug abuse among students. The average reader of the sports page would generally agree that it isn't fair for athletes to use steroids to boost their performance and that steroid use should remain illegal. Yet somehow that same reader, when confronted with the option of "borrowing" a friend's Ritalin to stay up late in prepping for an exam or to have a greater sense of focus when finishing a paper under the wire, doesn't see the ethical dilemma. Worse yet, she doesn't see the physical threat.

Were that student found to be taking prescriptions illegally, her integrity would be brought into question. Setting aside the possibility that the student conduct office would penalize her were she to get caught, this student runs an enormous risk to her personal future should employers learn that she self-medicated to artificially boost her work capacity. Even greater is the risk that her health history may disagree with this pharmaceutical exploit and she wind up in the ER (or worse). College is all about laying a groundwork for your life as an adult—ask yourself if you really want to make your success drug-dependent, and if that's something you will be able to sustain throughout your professional career.

Because of Peter's work for the government, students frequently query him about wanting to get security clearance, often asking how that process is affected by past recreational drug use. His advice is this: admitting to a *single* experimental use of marijuana is not necessarily a deal breaker for getting security clearance, but it's a red flag.

Admitting to drug use? Who would be that dumb? (We actually know of someone who admitted during her interview for the FBI that she tried mushrooms once—that was the end of her dream career with the FBI.)

Actually, dumber still would be lying about it. The security clearance process is looking first for honesty and second for a narrative that demonstrates how you have matured beyond repeating that mistake. As you sit on that splintered park bench or squishy subway cushion reading this, you may not be planning for a future career in defense, so this may seem like a moot point. The trick is, you never quite know where your future will lead you, so why limit yourself? There are a great many careers out there that consider drug use a sensitive issue and require a clear break in your lifestyle choices in order to be hired. The longer that break is, the better. Obviously, the best case is avoiding drugs altogether.

Even if you are absolutely certain that you will never want security clearance, we still advise against experimental drug use. It's best to approach any sort of experimentation—bungee jumping, eating live baby squid, asking the homecoming queen for a date—this way: watch, learn, then (and only then if your sources come back on it being a worthwhile and relatively risk-free experience) do. Maybe.

It's vastly more dangerous to push your limits on the first night of freshman orientation than it is to play designated driver for a while to get your bearings. The parties won't be going anywhere and this front-row seat will give you a big picture of what the party scene is all about. Once you've seen more than an eyeful, you'll be able to apply your standards that much more accurately, and hopefully you'll decide not to drink. If you feel like the social lame duck, keep in mind that at most schools nearly 10 to 20 percent of students don't drink at all. (Now you can tell your folks you're in the top 10 percent of your class!) With the current trend in thought being "everyone is entitled to their own opinion," no one worth mentioning will think less of you. In all probability, you may become Mr. Popularity for being the designated driver for all your friends.

Since this is a critical section, allow us to recap.

1. Don't drink underage, get drunk, or do drugs. That's a period right there. If you agree, feel free to move on to the next section. If you insist on ignoring this invaluable wisdom, consider the next point.

2. Before jumping into an experiment, watch and learn. Measure the consequences as far down the line as you can. There will always be risks, and if they outweigh the rewards, avoid.

3. If you choose to take on these risks and experiment, do not combine the new variable with another control-altering influence. And if you are caught, don't lie about what you did to school officials.

The bottom line is if it's illegal or if it poses health risks or if it has other negative consequences, find a better hobby.

I came to college when I was seventeen, which is not a legal drinking age in the US, though it is in Nigeria, where my parents let my sisters and me drink wine and champagne on occasion. However, I decided not to drink in college as a freshman when I saw that I was surrounded with people who drank for the sake of getting drunk rather than for social enjoyment. I quickly became the one that every one of my friends tried to get drunk, but I always had my apple juice and a ready excuse at hand.

Onome—Junior, Stanford U

"But I Wanna Drink"
What "Drinking Responsibly" Means

In writing this book, we have to be honest: each of us made very different choices as college students. We swung on both sides of the line, two of us by never drinking and one definitely drinking. Despite our personal choices, each of us admits that it was nearly impossible to avoid being in the presence of alcohol while on campus. It was definitely doable to choose not to drink (in fact, some parties offered alternative beverages that looked like their alcoholic counterparts), but whether it was a drunk roommate stumbling in late one night or a party down the hall, we would've had to go into hiding to avoid alcohol altogether. (On a side note, however, it *is* more doable to avoid exposure to drugs.)

Most students will say they drink either to alleviate stress or as a social lubricant, both of which are an entirely different proposition than drinking with the goal of becoming drunk. College is a time to explore your world, and we stand by that notion. But challenge the premise that your college experience is lacking if you haven't crossed every line and experienced all.

Exploring issues that conflict with your values doesn't mean you need to test them out on yourself like some supersized guinea pig. It just means you should encounter them fairly by listening to an intelligent voice on the matter. In other words, it's listening to your roommate's spiel about why he thinks it's okay to drink underage, not taking a swig to find out for yourself.

RESPONSIBLE ACTION #1: PICK A GROUP

For the sake of discussion, let's assume someone around you is drinking. How are you supposed to handle that "responsibly"? To start, let's set up a few safety nets. Assume that you are the only person looking out for your best interests. Should you decide to attend some of the larger parties on campus, go in groups and make sure beforehand that you are going home in those same groups. Where students most often get into trouble is when they go to a party alone, or their group dissolves and no one has their back. It's dismal. As much as we wish it weren't so, the whole notion of trusting people because it's a community of scholars is a farce. One would expect to be safe, but if scholarship made people trustworthy, you wouldn't need a bike lock on campus.

> While drugs, sex, and alcohol are quite prevalent on most college campuses, if you do not feel like engaging in these activities, it is not that hard to avoid them. Another solution, as unimaginable as it may seem, is to still go to parties (even at fraternities) and just not engage in those activities. Other people will care less than you may think. I, personally, have been to countless fraternity parties where I have danced and had a blast without even feeling the temptation of alcohol.
>
> **Helen—sophomore, U of Chicago**

RESPONSIBLE ACTION #2: GET YOUR OWN DRINK

Sometimes the pressure to push boundaries is obvious, and sometimes it is deceptive. Whether you fill your Solo with a nonalcoholic disguise or partake in the punch dipped out of a garbage pail, under no circumstances should you swig a drink handed to you by someone else. Let's face it, unless you've known the person for years, everyone there is a stranger. This is true especially for women. It doesn't matter if the guy handing you the drink has been the nicest guy in the dorm since you moved in last week—even if he was the one who helped you lug your heaviest boxes up three flights of stairs. Get your own drink. You need to know exactly what is in your cup, and the easiest way to do that is to fill it yourself.

Date-rape drugs are far more prevalent than most students realize, and it doesn't take many sips to faze a woman—especially if she's slim or new to the party scene. The amnesia brought on by these cocktails is temporary and over time, via flashbacks or nightmares, the woman who was abused remembers all. It's very real and very disturbing. We hate to be the ones to crush any remaining innocence you may have about the world, but we'd rather crush an illusion than sit back and watch *you* be crushed because you didn't know.

RESPONSIBLE ACTION #3: GIVE YOURSELF SOME TIME

The most vulnerable time for students is first semester of freshman year, and the risks seem to diminish by senior year as students find more creative ways to entertain themselves and have a better handle on their boundaries. Until then, be wary. Students are vulnerable anytime an event involves alcohol. Whatever the cause, the cold numbers remain that victims of date rape tend to be freshmen (male or female) between orientation and Thanksgiving break. At the high end, some groups estimate that one out of four women on college campuses today will be sexually assaulted, with 80 percent of these assaults being committed by an acquaintance.

> The most vulnerable time for students is first semester of freshman year, and the risks seem to diminish by senior year as students find more creative ways to entertain themselves and have a better handle on their boundaries.

Even with our recommendations, you can't bank on the residence hall guaranteeing sanctuary. Not even the group you came with to the party can be depended on to save you. It's delusional to think rape doesn't occur in dorms or that it won't happen the first time you get sloshed. It's one of the big reasons we suggest you wait as long as possible before engaging liberally in the party scene. Get to know what else there is to do on campus. Over time you will learn (via the rumor mill, the campus paper, and observing peers the morning after) which parties are safe and which are not. It could be that in that time you'll discover more fascinating outlets on campus, and the party scene may lose its appeal.

RESPONSIBLE ACTION #4: ENJOY COLLEGE FOR THE UNIQUE EXPERIENCE THAT IT IS

On her second night on campus Shauna decided to do her own thing and attend an off-campus mixer with some upperclassmen. She was invited by a friend she had known for years who happened to be a senior on campus, and she took her roommate as backup. Before heading out, she and her roommate also secured their own ride home. Smart, on both counts. In that respect, she played the game well. However, what she gave up in attending that party was a chance to interact with her new classmates during a campus-sponsored (aka FREE) event during what is a critical and brief window for forging friendships on campus. Assuming for the sake of argument that the event she missed was the most boring function of the week, for some reason the shared misery of those inane events can bond people faster than the best night on campus.

The good news for Shauna is that no one got hurt. The bad news is that she lost an opportunity to build key relationships with her own classmates. In a year or two, those upperclassmen she met will be gone, and, should she continue with the off-campus scene, she will have few friends remaining on campus.

RESPONSIBLE ACTION #5: SAVE YOUR LIFE (OR SOMEONE ELSE'S)

Should you decide to drink, the single and only absolute point we will insist upon is this: don't drive. Driving buzzed is driving drunk. And, please oh please, don't take a ride from someone who's been partaking either, no matter how well they hold their liquor. In a split second, you (or they) could kill or maim someone, be seriously injured, or be killed. Most campuses have some sort of escort service to ensure you get home in one piece. (And they won't be taking names either.) Or call a cab. Some schools have even contracted with companies who sell pre-paid taxi rides. Sure, you may have to wait ten minutes for your coach to arrive, but what's ten minutes when compared to a DUI or spending the next six months in traction?

It's Just Sex
Really?

You've known there are no birds or bees involved for some time now and you don't plan on doing anything stupid. But have you decided what you *do* plan on doing? Remember to ask yourself, "Am I prepared for every possible consequence, not just the ones I think are manageable?"

The major complaint we hear from men and women seeking counseling about sexually related emotional or health issues is that they didn't take their options seriously enough from the beginning; that they always assumed they wouldn't be THAT statistic. They wish someone had sat them down early on and suggested they put pen to paper and actually spell out their sexual standards—especially while out of a relationship—so they knew ahead of time how far they really wanted to go. So here we are.

Like we said earlier, the grimmest statistic out there says that one of every four women will be sexually assaulted during college. That means that taking precautionary measures up front doesn't make you a conspiracy theorist, it makes you logical. We've said this before and we'll say it again—don't accept drinks from people you don't know. Go out in groups, and come home with the same people you left with. And always remember that adding alcohol to an already risky social situation can cause an avalanche.

Laws state that in order to give consent to sex, both parties must have the capacity to do so—meaning they can't be drunk. And catch this, guys: if both parties are drunk, the burden is most often on the man to put on the brakes. Whether or not you agree, a woman can take legal action even *years* after the incident (depending on the state). So don't put yourself in an emotionally, physically, and legally dangerous situation by combining alcohol and sex.

But what about sober sex or mutually consensual sex?

In the media, the consequences of sex are often minimized. (I mean, when was the last time you watched a *Friends* rerun where a lead character complained they got hepatitis?) We're in the midst of a great social experiment that is questioning the beliefs society has had for years about the consequences of premarital sex on emotional well-being and physical health (the theory being that those consequences don't merit discouraging the activity).

The questions about the implications are endless. And for good reason. It's a complicated topic, no matter how featherweight society would like it to seem. Setting aside physical consequences for a moment, does making less of sex actually make it less? Another recent social theory is that the most intimate act we have as human beings can be done casually without long-term emotional effects. How disappointing. Sex used to be "the ultimate" as an expression of love, hence the term "making love." What seems particularly odd is that our culture elevates the significance of saying "I love you" above the act of sex so that people are willing to make love but not verbalize it. Now *that's* strange, if you stop to think about it.

Before hooking up, give some thought to how this relationship will affect others in the future. Consider the "first law of sexual dynamics": the physical limit where you and your last girlfriend or boyfriend stopped is where you will get to in a fraction of the time with your next. What would you hope your future partner or spouse is doing or not doing? Are you expecting more of that person than you do of yourself?

Finally, consider the health implication of your decisions, and ask yourself, are you financially, emotionally, and physically prepared to deal with your own potential STI risks? Take a stats class sometime and review the odds of STI calculations. Because we figure you've heard them before, we'll keep this simple: it only takes once. Regardless of what you think of the odds—if STIs were rare, do you think drug companies would be running herpes ads on prime-time television?—your maiden voyage could permanently mark you with a disease that would leave you uncomfortable at best. Some lead to sterility and others lead to cancer. Most critically, some can be contracted even with a condom or other protection. So run those numbers and weigh your risks. You could play the odds and bet you won't end up a statistic, but is it worth your health?

One assumption we want you to reconsider is the one that claims "everyone is doing it." No matter what the graffiti on the stalls may read, the bottom line is that there is much more talk than action. It may seem like everyone is doing it, but really everyone is *talking* about doing it. Students continue to buy into the notion that they haven't lived or had the all-American college experience if they haven't been wasted or sexiled their roommate—or both. However, national statistics consistently show that far fewer students are doing it than students *think* are doing it—meaning whatever the collegiate average of escapades, it is lower than what people assume.

Okay, well what about those who decide to wait?

Hollywood loves to mock virgins as being regrettable social outcasts, but in all our conversations with students about sex we actually haven't heard one complain that his conscious choice to abstain was a waste. On the contrary, we've heard a lot of students lament that they gave up their virginity too easily. If you still have yours, guard it. If you don't but wish you did, give yourself a second chance to build relationships without adding the complicated physical dimension of sex.

> It may seem like everyone is doing it, but really everyone is *talking* about doing it.

Oh sure, now we're suggesting the impossible. Or is it? Autumn is a recent grad who arrived at her wedding day with her virginity intact, her diploma on the way, and the satisfaction that the guy she was about to marry was the only man she had ever kissed. Her groom had his too (his virginity, that is) and was a college grad. They had known each other four years and, no, it wasn't an arranged marriage.

Her secret to success? Autumn says that she applied the Law of Diminishing Returns—which says that it's very, *very* hard to experiment with going one step further and then continue to find the same satisfaction from the previous step—early on in setting physical standards for their relationship. She set the bar incredibly high from the start to help keep the physical aspect of the relationship simple. Essentially she told her boyfriend she wouldn't kiss him until they were engaged. Sounds like it worked.

College creates a very real possibility of starting a new chapter in your life. Even more so than high school, there is a significant shift that takes place at the beginning of each term. It's never too late to make a change. College allows for new beginnings with every season, though it takes a great deal of willpower and accountability with friends to hit the brakes and alter course.

The advice in this section applies to relationships of all kinds, whether of opposite or same sex. Spend some time on your own thinking through the ramifications of all your decisions and how they will affect whom you want to become. Get advice from friends, parents, mentors, and peers. If you find yourself needing support thereafter (either because you are experimenting with your sexuality or because you are looking for input about those who are), seek out the friends we mentioned before (the ones whom you respect and who respect you) to ask their advice so you can be intentional about your decisions with the fullest support possible.

Thanks for Playing

Given the content, this may have, at times, been a difficult chapter to read, so thanks for sticking with us to the end. For you, we were willing to risk unpopularity and perhaps redundancy in the hopes that you would find a few gems that would not only help maximize your college experience but also would propel you into a more successful future. Heck, you can't have enough good advice.

And so we leave you with this parting encouragement: have fun. Your undergrad years only come once. Consider them an animated version of the Choose Your Own Adventure books you may have loved as a kid. Be intentional about choosing the best adventure possible. Graduation probably feels a long way off, but it arrives in half the time you expect. So hurry up with that chem lab so you can get out and have a good time.

CHAPTER 6

What Professors Wish You Knew

Paying Attention to the Person Behind the Curtain

They are the ones with the power to ruin your vacations with untimely assignments. They are the ones you lauded as your reason for choosing this college in your application essay. They are the ones who may bore you with a monotone that defies caffeine. Or perhaps, if you have chosen wisely, they are the ones who switch on some inner lightbulb that makes the world and your place in it suddenly clearer. Professors.

Getting the best out of college means, in part, getting your money's worth out of your relationships with the professors who are paid (largely by you) to provide a product you are buying: an education.

By now you may have heard that every session of class at your standard university tends to be around the price of a front-row seat on Broadway. Unfortunately few lectures actually live up to that kind of billing. Don't take the Broadway metaphor literally, expecting your professors to be entertainers. They are, after all, only educators. (Hey, if they could do improv, they would be making a lot more money working on *Saturday Night Live*.) Some star professors manage to be entertaining educators, but more often than not even the good professors are simply adept at conveying the mysteries of their subject—minus the stand-up comic routine.

You don't need your professors to be stand-up comics. You *do* need them to be stand-up academic citizens. And here is a secret. Most of them want the same thing from you. If you can match up these two realistic expectations, you can build relationships with your professors that will make college an incredibly rewarding experience, one worth your time *and* money.

Whether you attend a mammoth state university or an intimate-sized college, your goal should be to know two professors well enough that they are able to write strong, personal recommendations for you. Even better, you should seek to establish a close mentoring relationship with at least one professor during your undergraduate career.

> Seek to establish a close mentoring relationship with at least one professor during your undergraduate career.

To build these relationships, you must understand the three open secrets about professors.

The first is that profs are human. Not a shocker, though there are some who seem determined to prove otherwise. Look past the quirks and eccentricities and you will discover that professors have fears, foibles, and personality glitches like the rest of us. As we will explain later, if you can keep this simple truth in mind during your interactions, you'll be more successful in getting to know them.

Second, professors are generally quite good at providing you with quality instruction in their courses, but you can get a lot more from them than a lecture. If you just take what's given to you (that is, the course as it is offered) you won't get as much out of it as you would if you were proactive about interacting with the professor.

The third secret—and professors cannot be persuaded otherwise on this one—is that they believe their time is more valuable than yours. The smart student will strategize around this inconvenient view, finding ways to build relationships without becoming a drain on the professor's time.

As obvious as these points may seem, it's amazing how many students behave as though they do not understand them. Internalize these revelations, act upon them, and watch the doors begin to open.

This Isn't High School, and We're Not Nannies
Understanding a Professor's Role

One of the biggest differences between high school and college is that in college most teachers won't come looking for you if you miss class or fail to turn in assignments. (Okay, if you miss too many classes the prof might turn you over to an academic dean who will come knocking at your door—don't misread our point here.) Perhaps you are counting on this. Perhaps the greater freedom is precisely what you are looking for in college. There is, however, a fine line between being given free rein to roam and being ignored.

Frankly the students who never get noticed by their professors are probably not making the most of their education. But getting noticed (that is, getting the right kind of notice) is difficult because relating to students is only a part of the professor's job—and in many research universities, it is a very small part.

In nearly every college and university in the United States, professors are hired with the understanding that they will divide their time among three baskets: research and publishing, university service, and teaching. Their salaries depend on success in all three areas. The baskets are prioritized differently depending on the institution, but at many schools, research and publishing take precedence. If you are not sure whether or not that is the case at your school, mention the phrase "publish or perish" and see if your professor exhibits a nervous tic.

Beyond that, the urgency of university service often competes all too effectively for the professor's attention. University service refers to a long list of faculty responsibilities such as serving on multiple administrative committees, advising student groups, developing department policies, and reviewing and evaluating the published work of their peers, to name only a few. Most profs have a fairly small appetite for this sort of thing and are force-fed much more than they can stomach.

The third basket, of course, is prepping for and delivering a lecture (or seminar) and grading the polished gems of academic work you and your peers generate by the bushel.

We all know that people have lives beyond their day job, so figure at some time these profs are also going home to raise kids, grow their marriage, care for elderly parents, or often all of the above. The point is not to make you feel sorry for professors (you shouldn't—they generally enjoy what they do and no one forced them at gunpoint to follow this career), but rather to explain why they may seem distracted when it comes to teaching and relating to undergraduates—why, in other words, they might be harder to approach than the teachers who helped you finish high school so successfully.

A key distinction between college and high school faculty is their degrees. A bachelor's degree (which your high school teacher likely had) suggests that a graduate has mastered a subject and is capable of passing it along; a master's degree suggests an even deeper command of that knowledge.

Most college professors have a doctorate degree (called a PhD, which someone once said stands for "piled higher and deeper"), and that degree confers the expectation that graduates not only have a deep understanding of their subject area but are also expanding the field of knowledge in some way. Their standing in the field and at the university is determined by how much "expanding" they accomplish during their lifetime.

So what is the relevance of this to you? Due to the constraints placed on a professor's time by the university, it is of utmost importance that *you* assume the responsibility of pursuing the professor rather than expecting the professor to discover the genius in you. Make yourself memorable by showing an interest in the material and class discussion as well as a dedication to learning outside of class. And consider responding graciously when your professor inevitably makes some error either in miscalculating your grade, losing your paper, or mispronouncing your name for the eighth time in a week.

Matt recalled his ordeal attempting to contact a prof in the hopes of networking. In his naïveté, he called the professor once and, finding she was out, left a message assuming the ball was now in her court. Needless to say, the days passed into weeks and still no response. He happened to mention his predicament to a friend, who chided him on his laziness, insisting Matt find some other way to track her down. "Pursue her with the same dedication you would show if you were trying to borrow her car for spring break," he said. "Figure she's too busy to return your call. Understand that you need to see her more than she needs to see you, so you have to work at it more. Don't take no answer for an answer."

We are not recommending that you stalk your professor but that you do the math: several dozen or perhaps several hundred students per lecture times multiple lectures a term plus a few seminars of twenty-five each. Your face is part of the blur. It will most likely require some extra effort to get your prof's attention.

Our advice so far has been tailored to students at universities where the student-faculty ratio makes it a bit harder to establish a connection with the professor. If you are at a small college, these tips will apply even more so, since there is a greater expectation among faculty that these relationships will emerge and they are primed to participate.

No Sycophants or Hecklers Allowed
How to Interact with Profs in Class

Professors want students. Real students. Not students who sleep in class—that's frustrating. Not students who hang on their every word—that's embarrassing. (Okay, maybe it is flattering, but it gets old quickly.) And not students who put up their verbal dukes at the slightest provocation—that's disrespectful and downright annoying.

Professors want students who interact professionally in both behavior and appearance and who show at least a minimal interest in the topic—a student like you.

Profs are astounded at how often students behave in class as though the audience were invisible. Perhaps it is a weakness of the TV generation, subconsciously behaving as though class were a plasma screen. Regardless, professors frequently lament how too often students are disengaged from the lecture, such as the prof lecturing on financial collapse in the developing world who looks up to see students laughing at someone's Facebook update or students who prove their true intent by bringing a pillow or wearing pajamas to class.

If I'm Not Prepared for Class, Should I Still Attend?

Most definitely you should attend class even if you are unprepared, but—we quickly add—depending on what type of class it is, you may need to make a preemptive strike.

If it is the sort of class where you might be called on, such as a seminar or a small lecture, then you should absolutely contact the professor before class to explain the situation. Apologize that you have made a mistake but don't make excuses. Be clear that you will not be making this a habit and that you promise to be prepared from here on out. Most profs are gracious enough to let you get by without damage; however, they might toss you a question in the following class just to be sure you're tracking.

Of course, if the class you are unprepared for is a lecture, then the odds are very much with you that you can sneak by unnoticed. It is still a mistake to be unprepared, but there is no reason to compound the mistake by skipping the class as well. Remember, every class is about as expensive as that front-row Broadway ticket and consistently coming unprepared is like watching the performance from a soundproof booth. Even if you haven't read the material, you may still get something out of the lecture if you take notes. And those notes will make more sense when you review them after having completed the assignment you originally missed.

Life is not without its obstacles, and if there is an unforeseen circumstance that has genuinely made it difficult for you to keep up with class (that is, a death in the family, a chronic health issue, a financial burden, and so on), make the effort to speak to the professor about it before the term progresses any further. There tends to be a rash of plagues that mysteriously coincide with due dates each term, making some profs a bit jaded. However, most faculty should be willing to help (either with extensions or by reworking assignments) if you give them enough advance notice.

In very small doses, the professor may be amused and might play along. One instructor preempted an incorrigible napper by pulling out a copy of *Goodnight Moon* and reading it to the dozing student (much to the hilarity of the rest of the class). Others like to sneak up on their snoozer and jostle him awake. One in particular—and this is probably an urban legend, but it is one professors share wistfully among themselves—wielded a permanent marker on a sleeping student's forehead, giving him a Zorro-like Z. More commonly, some give an instant class-wide quiz or even an extra term paper assignment to punish a student's apparent disregard.

Sleeping in class is only the most obvious and infamous classroom mistake. The more common error, and the one we want you to focus on avoiding, is failing to make a positive impression on the professor.

By a positive impression, we don't mean bringing the prof a piping hot pizza after class or tattooing her lectures on your bicep. We mean engaging in class. Practically it would look like this: As you read through packets for Thursday's lecture, make notes to yourself of questions you have in response to the text (yes, you should actually write them down). If one or two of your questions are big enough that they might lead into an actual conversation, or are important enough to warrant a response before you complete your readings, raise them with the prof in advance (preferably during her office hours).

Either way, come Thursday you are sitting in class (list of questions in hand) with a goal of finding those answers as you listen to the lecture. This will help you pay attention and look alive.

Chances are that if you are confused about the text, others are too. If the professor is willing to take questions in class, take advantage of that time by picking some tough ones from your list (as long as you remain sensitive to the fact that she needs to finish her lecture). In high school, this sort of preparedness would have been considered sycophantic, resulting in ridicule by your entire table at lunch. But there is more at stake now than your reputation with prepubescents in new sneakers: your education, your student loans, and, ultimately, your career are on the line.

To look at this another way, it may help to consider your title. When you fill in the blank on DMV or doctor's forms, what do you list for occupation? Student. You are a *professional* student. As such, it makes sense that you would approach your relationships with faculty and the administration (not to mention your forty hours a week of study) as a professional.

> During my freshman year, I had a class in which I received a slightly lower grade than expected and, after consulting the grading rubric, realized I had been docked points for class participation. This came as a surprise since I had attended every class, been attentive in class, and actively taken notes—in high school, this would have been sufficient. Afterward I made it a goal to raise my hand at least two times per class, which gained me points, but also helped my professors remember who I was. This helped build important relationships as well as further my education by heightening my engagement in each class.
>
> **Lauren—sophomore, Northeastern U**

Help Me Help You
Getting Profs to Agree to an Independent Study Request

You might be asking why in the world someone would sign up for an independent study. After all, there is no way to hide if the assignment isn't complete and skipping class is nearly impossible. Don't give in to such reasoning. Many graduates, when asked their most valuable college experience, cite some sort of independent study or research as the pinnacle.

An independent study (IS) is a unique opportunity for a student to craft a semester around a subject that interests him, and then follow through with readings and assignments alongside one of the finest minds in the field on that subject—all at no extra cost!

Unfortunately, at most institutions, there is also no extra pay for the faculty member; so what is a great deal for you is usually worse than a so-so deal for the professor. Before drafting an independent study proposal, find out if the university will be crediting him for his time by asking any department administrator. Even if there is an incentive for the prof, don't assume you are doing him a favor. With all the demands a prof has on his time, an independent study proposal needs to be attractive to the professor in order to get off the ground.

Above all, remember this: an independent study should be the culmination of a relationship that you already have with a professor, not be the beginning of one.

Practically this might mean taking an introductory course freshman year and discovering you connect with the prof and his topic during office hours, offering to be a research assistant the following term, perhaps taking another course that is closer to your area of interest sophomore year, and finally finishing up with an independent study as a junior—all the while looking for opportunities to get to know the prof outside of class.

Because of the way course scheduling and publication deadlines work, some semesters may be fuller for professors than others. There is an advantage to seeking out independent study opportunities early on in your college career. The process of finding good faculty mentors can begin in your first year so that you will have time to adjust. If a professor is booked the first time you request an independent study but he invites you to return next year, you have more flexibility to fit it into your course schedule. Not all faculty relationships require this much time, but preparing yourself now for that possibility will give you the most options in the long run.

Should you decide to offer your services as a research assistant for a term, recognize that you may not get paid. If that's the case, consider it an investment in furthering your education and your relationship with this professor. Showing an interest in what a professor is already researching communicates to him that you are dedicated to the subject, willing to give as well as take, and respectful of his time. All three will bode well as points in your favor when it comes time to request an independent study (not to mention the fact that being a research assistant can be an incredible learning experience).

Desirable as an independent study opportunity is, we should warn you that it is also rare. Don't agree to being a research assistant expecting that it will automatically earn you an independent study with this professor. It is probably also wise to refrain from mentioning your interest in an independent study until you have proven yourself to be diligent in the work at hand and superb in achieving positive results. (Otherwise it gives you an unfavorable "entitlement" shine that can damage the mentor relationship.)

As with anything, there are exceptions. Some profs have been known to sponsor a student in an IS after the student has taken only one course with them. It will be up to you to discern the individual prof's various obligations and weigh them against his interests.

A common pitfall on this topic is requesting an independent study as an alternative to taking a regularly scheduled course. Let's say Dr. Rothstein is teaching Innocence Undressed in Sixteenth-Century Literature in the fall term. Sonia wants to take the course but thinks she would learn better if she met with the prof individually. Should she propose taking the course as an IS, she will most likely get an immediate no.

What if Sonia wants to take the course but can't because it interferes with her chem lab? That seems like a valid reason for an independent study, right? Again, Dr. Rothstein is likely to turn her down and suggest she sign up for the course in a later semester. Why? Dr. Rothstein is not an ogre. He simply can't afford to add multiple sections of a course to his already full teaching schedule.

However, if, after taking Innocence Undressed, Sonia wants to further her own study of sexuality in *The Faerie Queen*, Dr. Rothstein will be more inclined to agree to this independent study request because Sonia has proven herself to be an excellent student in at least one term and is interested in pursuing a subject that he does not teach but that is considered part of his field.

The key here in successfully choosing an independent study topic that is attractive to your prof is to pick one he knows well, one he is also interested in researching, or one he is already actively researching.

An independent study is not essential to getting the best out of college. For most students, it may not even be a realistic option. Despite the size of the college, the student/faculty ratio makes for too many students should every one of them apply for a sustained, individual tutorial with a professor. But it's worth a try. At worst, the work you put into the failed request could rebound to your benefit in other ways in your relationship with the professor, and, at best, you'll be one of the lucky few who get a spot.

We're Never Wrong, Just Mistaken
How to Disagree without Torpedoing Your Prof's Respect (Not to Mention Your Grade)

Every subject has its unknowns and unanswerables, and no one is above them—not even professors. The first step to intellectual growth is discovering how little you know about a topic. One professor observed that as an undergrad he figured he knew about 60 percent of his topic area; after several years as a grad student, he scaled his estimate back to about 30 percent; now that he is a world authority on several aspects of his field, he figures he knows about 3 to 5 percent of what there is to know.

Nevertheless, in almost every case, the professor will know more than you. That is why you are paying her and not vice versa. However, knowing more about a given topic does not mean that every opinion the professor holds is authoritative and infallible. The trick is to find the distinction between what your professors know and what they think.

To do that, it's important to go to class with two things: an open mind and a sifter. An open mind is required because professors have thought long and hard about their topic and a core part of their job is to convey that knowledge to you. That said, always sift what you hear. All ideas contain some bias, even those that are loudly proclaimed to be fact. Merely calling it a fact makes it *seem* that there is no room for bias—however, don't check your brain at the door.

All professors believe it is their job to challenge you. Expect to be provoked—relish it because it is what sharpens you. Many professors believe it is also their job to convince you, if not of their own ideology then at least of their own means of evaluating competitive ideologies. Don't be afraid to push back against a professor's bias; but don't feel like you must resist every attempt either.

A large part of your education will revolve around these conversations, because they will stimulate your thinking and either galvanize your own convictions on a topic or lead to a revelation. The important thing is not to view a challenge to your own opinions as an abuse of professorial authority. It isn't. Instead, treat it as an opportunity to exercise your brain as well as your backbone.

Should you find a point where you disagree with a professor, keep the fanfare to a minimum. A well-handled disagreement with a prof need not cost you your grade. In fact, it could even help it.

There are two kinds of disagreements you may have with a professor: academic ("I disagree that the world is round," "I think the argument in this assigned reading has a fatal flaw," and so on) and personal ("I think this seminar reading is boring," "You miscalculated my grade," "You looked at me funny," "You stood me up during office hours"). In dealing with both, be professional and speak to your prof *before* telling the story to anyone else. Too many students have bungled that point and regretted the consequences.

One such student, after disagreeing with a point in a mythology lecture, called the department chair, the career guidance center, and the administration to complain *before* speaking directly to the prof about the incident. The complaint was a relatively small misunderstanding that could have easily been addressed. However, because Andrea spoke to nearly everyone but the professor, it made for an awkward situation for both her and her professor for the remainder of the term.

Be conscious of your timing in presenting your argument. Some profs are exhausted after a big lecture and are not up to sparring, while others may seem eager to talk while the lecture is still fresh in their thoughts.

Most profs don't mind a challenge or two during a lecture, and almost all earnestly desire such engagements in smaller seminar classes. But be sensitive to the professor's plans for the course. A brush-off response may be a sign that he has other material to cover, and not necessarily that you have him flummoxed. For sustained challenges, speak to your prof apart from the crowd and offer to come back at a later time if he prefers.

Perhaps even more fundamental than timing and directness in handling conflicts is this: have a sound argument and at all costs articulate it clearly. Merely emoting passionate thoughts only reinforces the professor's original prejudices and makes the next debate with him even harder.

If the disagreement is not academic but personal—such as you want to question a professor about your grade without appearing to be a grade grubber—approach the professor during what will be an appropriate time when she can fully concentrate on your conversation (such as office hours). Consider the following to be an example of a great opener: "Dr. Veith, I'd like to speak with you about the grade I earned on my last paper. I'm not sure I understand the rubric that led to this grade and I'm hoping you can help me understand what I could have done better so that I can improve in the future." There. You've said it with respect and clarity. There is no accusation, no begging, and no defensiveness. You are showing yourself to be teachable and in want of improvement while finding out what went wrong with your grade. If, after hearing the professor's explanation, you think you deserve a better grade, say so, and be ready to give specific points as to why, your sincere desire for a higher GPA not being among them.

The question of the hour is how far to take a challenge. The answer depends on the issue and how much it is personally worth to you. One student told us of a critical moment in her degree program when a disagreement with her professor resulted in a lower grade. Though Veronica approached the professor with proper timing and professionalism—and the professor even recognized her point—it led to one grade lower than she had hoped to earn that semester.

The disagreement was an academic one; Veronica argued that a book on the syllabus was inappropriate for a student discussion group.

She invited the professor out to coffee and explained her concerns, asking for his advice on how to approach a book she found clearly offensive and unsuitable. He suggested the importance of reading books that are offensive in the hopes of learning something new; she agreed but asserted that the value of what could be gained from this book was not worth the cost.

In the end, she admitted to him that, out of principle, she would not read that book for the course. She would attend class and take notes as usual but would not be a part of the discussion. He understood and chose not to call on her, since it would have been a pointless exercise. After the week of discussion for that book, she resumed course work by reading the next novel and became involved in class as before.

Where this plan backfired was on the final exam, when one of the essay questions dealt with that book directly. Did the professor intentionally give a question from a book he knew she hadn't read, or was it mere coincidence? It was probably coincidence, but she didn't consider it worth a fight—after all, taking a stand means taking a risk. The definition of a principled stand is "one for which you are willing to pay a price," and it is critical to evaluate the cost before approaching any potentially risky conversations. But the story doesn't end unhappily. As a result of her integrity and professionalism, she retained a valuable relationship with this professor, who went on to write a recommendation leading to her first postgraduation job. In the long run, she earned the points where they mattered most.

If you're looking for a moral to this story, it would be that pursuing a discussion with a professor may or may not have the immediate expected results, but that it is a privilege to engage with a professor on this level. When done so appropriately, it can lead to a rewarding outcome.

Of course, not all professors will be as congenial as this one. In fact, student naïveté on this could be dangerous. There are certainly incorrigible types who are imperious and vindictive if challenged. If you discover your prof to be of this species, do all you can to avoid confrontation—it will only end poorly.

Contrary to Popular Belief, We Do Have Lives

How to Relate to Profs Outside of Class

Before going much further, let us offer this caveat: each professor is unique. The guidelines we provide are just that—guidelines. The odd professor (and there will be more than a few odd ones in your college career) may well break the mold and have his own style of communication. That said, there does seem to be a pattern.

Samuel was a young man from a small town in the Midwest who, upon arriving on campus as a freshman, made it his goal to take advantage of faculty-oriented social events that students usually skip so that he could get to know some of the great minds on campus. Much to his surprise, he met another student on campus—Nicholas—who was interested in doing the same.

Together these young men took over the campus by attending as many events, panels, and speaker presentations as possible. Through a few stints as research assistants, they got to know faculty well and made it a point to mingle with professors at campus-wide gatherings as often as possible. Being a dynamic duo enabled them to stay abreast of happenings around campus, and it nearly always ensured at least one familiar face would be attending the event if they felt entirely out of place.

They were not sycophants or even bookworms; they were genuinely interested in enjoying all their university had to offer. They had active social lives and knew hundreds of students on campus, largely because they hung out at a wide variety of campus events. They took care of their bodies (which meant no bacchanalias), bedded and woke early, and four years later graduated with top honors—one a Rhodes Scholar heading off to Yale Law School and the other to Harvard Medical School. The only thing fictional is their names.

What is most unusual about Samuel and Nicholas was their perceptive realization that meaningful student-faculty interaction can happen outside the classroom. They were also discreet in their selection of events: gatherings were campus wide, were large enough for them to blend in, and welcomed students. By carefully selecting events professors were already making time to attend, they had the opportunity to mingle with some of the great minds on campus outside the classroom while not infringing on the professors' time—a brilliant solution.

Consider this radical take on getting to know your prof—a little something we call "dead time." Simply put, "dead time" makes use of mind-numbing tasks a prof might have ahead of her by turning them into opportunities for individual face time. Express to your prof an interest in discussing a few course-related topics and offer to staple packets, file papers, or address envelopes while you chat.

Throughout history, the greatest leaders in the world cultivated disciples and mentored protégés by inviting them to be a part of everyday tasks, where diamonds are mined in simple conversation.

We aren't suggesting this merely to provide free labor to faculty. It's that we are painfully aware of the many pulls on a professor's time and how few professors are able to find the time they'd like to interact with students. If you happen to have some media savvy, you might offer to help make the professor's notes into a PowerPoint presentation, update his website, or download software that could be a timesaver to his research. (If there is enough of this sort of work, you might offer to become a technology assistant for his research, which might lead to an independent study opportunity later on.) Free up pockets of time for your profs so they are more inclined to find time for you. As an alternative to "dead time," consider taking a stroll while you chat and walk your prof to his next appointment even if it is not on your way. It's easier to follow your prof where he wants to go rather than convince him to stay where you want to be.

Recognize that any time you spend with a professor outside of class is *not* meant to improve your grade. It will prove a sour experience if that is your goal. If you are genuinely interested in hearing her thoughts on a subject, explain your interest and be sure to follow through by arriving on time, or, dare we suggest, even a little early. Few things will drown your chance at success faster than being late. To a prof who considers herself busy, waiting for a student to show is a lot like being held underwater—it can only be tolerated for so long.

Of course, being the thoughtful person you are, you are now aware of the pressures placed on professors' time. You also recognize they are not required to make time to meet with you. Any extracurricular conversations should be considered (and treated) as generous.

If you don't go the "dead time" route but prefer to meet in a more traditional manner, be sure to suggest times that are appropriate for the real world. A 10 p.m. pizza party might not be the best way to encourage a prof to meet with you if she has been up since 6 a.m. The best way to find a time that is convenient for her is to offer a selection of two or three times, or to ask outright if she has a suggestion.

If you are aware of a professor's involvement in an area of research or responsibility that interests you, make it a point to help in whatever capacity he needs and be sure to express your hope of being involved further.

> As a student at a small school, it is a lot easier to build relationships with my teachers. One of my middle school teachers used to tell me, "I am not your friend; I am your instructor," and I feel like that is most untrue in college. I have found many of my professors helping me outside of class to figure out everything from which other profs to take to their opinion of local High Point cuisine. I even have a teacher that I tweet back and forth to on Twitter. I have found that in building good relationships with my profs, they can be a real help to me because they know the system.
>
> **Billy—sophomore, High Point U**

Just Because We're Busy Doesn't Mean We Don't Care

Office Hours—What They Are and How to Use Them

Before the days of email (gasp!), there were office hours. And despite the presence of email, office hours still exist on campuses nationwide—college is a medieval institution and so it tends to hold onto quaint traditions a long time—though they may not be as popular as they once were.

Were you to poll professors on their biggest frustrations, being stood up for office hours and confirmed appointments would definitely be high up on the list. Being inundated with incoherent, overly familiar, or inconsiderate student emails would also have a prominent showing. Interestingly these two frustrations are related, and both can be distilled to one cause: personal convenience.

From a student's perspective, it is far more convenient to email a question to a professor than to leave the comfort of a dorm room and walk across campus for office hours (particularly when temperatures are extreme). However, consider the professor's perspective: recall for a moment the number of students packed into her lecture hall, or the multitude of seminars she offers, and imagine each of those students sending an email to her every week.

Email is a recent enough invention that many professors are still overwhelmed by it, never having progressed past the two-finger typing method (and this applies double to Facebook, texting, and tweets). Add that assumption to their three-basket workload we discussed earlier and it's not surprising that it takes some professors days to respond to email, if they respond at all. Tack on that multiple students send emails with variations of the same question and it's easy to imagine why email can drive professors batty. Even more than the quantity, it is the quality that bothers them. Properly done, email can be an efficient way for managing large classes. But when students send emails that read like a text to a high school chum—or worse, a foul-mouthed rant on an angry blog—the system breaks down.

Email is a generational skill. Younger professors may actually prefer to answer your question via email rather than in office hours. We are by no means giving an ironclad rule banning email, just suggesting that you find out your prof's preference and do your best to stick to it.

Whether or not email is acceptable to the prof, it is to your advantage to make use of office hours because they provide more meaningful contact: now your name is finally linked in her mind with your face. Genuine face time can be a valuable exercise in developing rapport with your prof. It is an opportunity to interact with one of the leading minds in a field—perhaps by asking questions about recent news events or soliciting opinions on a text as they relate to her research. It is also a great opportunity to ask clarifying questions about class work or lectures, and to get an immediate reaction to the thesis of the paper you plan to write for class next week. Some professors offer individual office hours, while others make the time open to as many as can fit in the room—but there are some general principles that hold in both scenarios.

> There is a significant increase in the professors' helpfulness when you meet one on one. I had a teacher for a freshman writing class who during office hours would not only answer my questions but would also help proofread my drafts, expand my ideas, and comment on my progress. By meeting with her before the deadline of each paper, I found it nearly impossible not to get a good grade, plus I gained a valuable and close relationship.
>
> **Lauren—sophomore, Northeastern U**

First and foremost, come prepared with something relevant to discuss. Unless you know college basketball is your prof's favorite subject, asking her about the recent playoffs may be a waste of time. You could ask something like, "What is your take on the recent study about X that appeared in the *New York Times*?" or "Could you expand upon the point you made yesterday in class about Y? I'm not sure I fully grasped it."

Most profs typically welcome relevant chitchat, done in moderation, toward the beginning of a semester before crunch time hits, and will be happy to clarify yesterday's point (assuming they didn't see you surfing the Web when you should have been taking notes).

If you are looking for conversation starters, you might want to dig up her resume online to learn more about her expertise. Or check out articles or books she has written from the campus library. Don't be fawning about it, dropping hints that you loved what she said on page forty-seven. There is a fine line between stocking up on conversation topics and simply stalking.

Second, and this almost goes without saying: show up. Once you know your course schedule, walk yourself over to the sign-up sheet and pick a time (please, oh please, don't email the prof and ask her to do it for you), make a note of it on your calendar, and be there.

Pretend this is a job interview, where timeliness counts. In a way, it is. You may want to ask this professor to write your recommendation at the end of the term, and the little details of your meetings will play a big role in how professional she believes you to be.

Third, take advantage of off-peak times to cultivate a relationship with your prof, such as the beginning of the term when most students are taking it easy before grades become a threat. On the flip side, try to avoid busy seasons for relationship-building encounters (such as right before grades come out) unless you have a time-sensitive question to address.

As we mentioned earlier, profs are human and thus fall shy of perfection. It may be the case that you have done everything right and that, upon arriving for office hours, you find the door locked and the professor nowhere to be found. Try to be understanding—it happens to the best of us—and leave a note or send an email that looks something like this: "I had hoped to meet with you today to discuss Y, but something must have come up, since the door was locked at X:XX. Please let me know when you'll be hosting your next office hours so I can attend." This is not the time to roast the prof. In fact, there is rarely ever a time to roast the prof.

If your professor doesn't even offer office hours, let him know after class that you are interested in coming by and ask to schedule a time. You may need to pursue him a bit on this one, but most profs will kindly agree.

Once you have secured an appointment, come dressed for the occasion. We are not saying "no suit, no tie, no service," but that clothes generate conclusions about character and intelligence whether you want them to or not. Dress professionally for the reputation you are hoping to earn.

Developing relationships with professors takes persistence and a thick skin. I remember walking into a star professor's office hours and trying to spark up a conversation—he spent the entire time typing emails on his computer, only managing an occasional filler comment. They are extremely busy, and sometimes they can make you feel pretty small. Pick up on whatever signals they're sending you when you try to engage them. The trick is in not getting discouraged.

Hans—recent grad, Duke U

You Want Me to Say What?
How to Secure a Glowing Recommendation

We will assume you are a student worthy of an excellent recommendation. Being worthy is a start, but it is only a start.

A fabulous letter of recommendation should not be the highest goal of your academic career, but it is a pretty good sign that you have gotten closer to reaching your goal. (Reality check: the goal of an academic career should be an excellent education that prepares you for a lifetime of growth and learning.)

Earning a glowing recommendation is a process that takes about two to three years. Sadly, many students never get close enough to a professor to even get the filaments warm. Though you may be extraordinarily diligent, realize that you can probably only achieve this sort of relationship with a couple of professors, due to constraints on time as well as personal chemistry.

A glowing recommendation flows out of extended intellectual interaction, much like the progression of working your way up to an independent study proposal. The capstone of your work is a letter where the professor honestly knows you and can speak to your integrity and intellectual development.

What makes this sort of letter so exceptional to graduate schools or potential employers is that it has the unmistakable ring of authenticity. The recommender really knows the recommendee, and so the letter carries more weight.

A good recommendation evolves over time, but that doesn't mean you should wait until the end of your academic career to request one. As soon as you have finished a course in which you did well (and in which the professor got to know you, which may not necessarily be possible in large lecture courses), ask the professor to write you a letter of recommendation. Feel free to wait for grades to come out if you like, though that's not necessary. Email *and* snail mail a letter to your professor saying you really enjoyed the class (add a few specifics here), that you're thinking of following up with more work in this area (add some more specifics), and would he please write a letter of rec *for your file*. Then mention how you intend to return in a year or two to request that that letter be sent to a specific file or location, such as a grad school or a think tank.

> The key is to get the professor to write the letter of recommendation as close in time to the class as possible, rather than close to the due date when you actually need the letter.

Though most professors are willing to store (and perhaps even update) your letter in their computer, if he is a visitor or is likely to leave the school, it would be better to ask that a hard copy be sent to some third party, like your academic dean. Since recommendations need to be confidential to retain their full impact, the third party is critical. (More on that in a moment.) The career center or your academic dean will most likely be prepared to store student recommendation files, which can be updated by depositing new letters as needed.

If you take a subsequent course with the professor (and we hope you will), then ask him to update the letter after you finish that course. The process repeats as often as you complete a "season" (for example, research apprentice, independent study, follow-up course) with that professor. The letter grows in length, but even more importantly, it grows in depth.

The key is to get the professor to write the letter as close in time to the class as possible, rather than close to the due date when you actually need the letter. Every professor has horror stories of barely recognizable students coming back years after taking a course to request that she write a letter. Even if the student was wonderful, chances are the memories will be hazy and the letter will be vague. However, if all she needs to do is change the date, add some final details, and print out the glowing, detailed, personal letter written several years before, you are in great shape.

If you're reading this book for the first time as a college senior and feel like all hope is lost because you didn't ask for recs earlier, some hope remains. With a little apologetic politeness mingled with your request and—at the very least—a month's notice before you need the letter, your prof may be more understanding about it.

In these cases, do try to meet with the professor in person so as to help trigger memories. If you have to do it long-distance, send a picture or two (preferably dated to the time you took the course) and include in your letter several of your own recollections to help the professor situate you.

Let's return to the big question about whether or not recs should be requested as open or confidential. We hate to sound brutal, but any recommendation requested as an open letter is virtually useless. Confidential letters are the only kind with credibility. Since profs are human and don't want to hurt an eager student's feelings, open letters tend to be bland. Even if it seems nice to you, the people reading the letter are far more experienced at sifting through the niceties and will wonder if the professor was simply avoiding conflict.

University career centers and preprofessional advising offices (such as medicine, law, and business) recognize the need to preserve confidentiality and are willing to maintain student recommendation files upon request. You can request that these confidential letters be sent to whatever program you wish at any time, but you won't ever be able to see them.

Now the question is whether or not this professor will actually write that *glowing* recommendation you need. After all, if you agree to let him send it confidentially, how can you be sure it will be all you hope?

You accomplish this simply by asking—but might we suggest using a little artful diplomacy that you probably mastered in the days of asking a crush to the junior high dance. Do not ask, "Will you write me a glowing letter?" Do ask, "Do you feel like you know me well enough to write a strong letter?" That way if the prof (or dean or whomever you are asking) doesn't think she can wax eloquent about your many virtues, it gives her room to respond with, "I don't think I know you well enough" or "I know you somewhat," which signals that perhaps she would be unable or unwilling to write the recommendation you have in mind. This little song and dance will require that you read between the lines of her response, but at least you'll have a fair chance to find someone else if she seems less than enthusiastic.

Most profs welcome the opportunity to beg off writing letters of recommendation for weak students, those they don't know beyond a name and grade, or those who performed poorly in their class. No matter how desperately you need a letter, you cannot be so desperate that you are willing to ask for one from a prof who dreads the idea of writing a letter on your behalf. Trust us, it won't be pretty.

Profs understand that writing recs comes with the job, so don't feel like you need to approach them on bended knee. However, some students have made the fatal error of *not* recognizing the inconvenience of such a request by forgetting to show gratitude—or, worse, by giving very short notice (less than a month). Good profs won't retaliate by slamming you in the letter, but they are human; your prof might rush a bit, not adding that extra touch of glow to your letter just because you didn't give him enough lead time. So timely, polite requests *with follow-up thank-you notes and a final quick note letting the professor know the outcome* of the job search or grad school application are not just courtesy: they are self-preservation.

The general rule of recommendations is that you want the best recommendation from the most distinguished people you can get. However, if forced to make a trade-off, go with the recommenders who know you best rather than the famous people who barely know you. Few things are as worthless as the bland letter from some bigwig saying, "Nancy was a wonderful intern in my office for six weeks and I would not recognize her if I ate dinner with her at a table for two."

This is especially true with applications that require personal recommendations as well as academic (such as the Rhodes and Truman scholarships). The more demanding the program, the more closely the recommender must know you to make the letter any good for your purposes. For these sorts of applications, read the instructions weeks or even months before you hope to apply to get an idea of what sort of campus personalities (such as deans, coaches, or advisors) it will expect to see in your fan club.

I do not plan ahead very well. I did not ask my professors for recommendations ahead of time, and so when I had my sights set on a great job that required some rec letters from them, I had to wait. And wait. And then, I waited some more. My professors felt rushed, I was impatient, and the application deadline was approaching at a worrisome speed. It led to a very uncomfortable email in which I begged my superiors to hurry, a very uncomfortable conversation with my potential employer explaining why my application had not yet been submitted, and an altogether, you guessed it, uncomfortable situation. For heaven's sake, listen to the advice in this chapter and ask for recommendation letters before you even know that you are applying for a job.

Rebecca—recent grad, Point Loma Nazarene U

We Make Awful Wallflowers
Getting Profs to Attend Your Event

"One of the last functions I ever attended for my students was at the invitation of several of them to be a part of a student-faculty mixer at their sorority," a tenured professor at an elite university tells his advisees. "I arrived on time at the hall where the mixer was hosted, and much to my surprise I was the only one there. It was a cavernous room, a well-stocked veggie platter, and me. After a few minutes of getting to know the various tastes of broccoli, a student finally walked in. Not one of my students, it turned out; just the faculty interaction chair for the sorority. She did her best to make me feel comfortable, but it was painfully obvious she knew little about me. My students never even showed, and after a period of desultory conversation which rarely rose to the level of superficial, I gave up. I couldn't wait for class the next day and the chance to single out these students for special recognition."

This particular professor actually doesn't mind chitchat and he enjoys meeting new students, but that was not why he agreed to attend the event. He attended as a courtesy to his students as a way of extending the educational experience beyond the classroom. The prof held up his end of the bargain, but his students failed at theirs (though they didn't fail the course—let's not lose perspective here).

Such student-faculty interaction can be even dodgier if the professor is not the gregarious type. A professor who might be quite animated when discussing Shakespeare in a seminar could become quiet and withdrawn when turned over to small talk at one of these mixers. Add to the batter that most profs are a generation or two older than their students, and you have a recipe for a very dull social event.

But this is not the end of the matter. There is hope. With a few well-chosen steps, you just might persuade your English professor to read love sonnets to the cafeteria on Valentine's Day or goad your biology prof into playing his trombone for your club fundraiser ($10 for a five-minute serenade, $20 for him to stop after two minutes).

The first well-made step is to play to the prof's strengths—some area of expertise where she will feel comfortable pontificating should the need arise. The second is to be sure the event is something students will be interested in; you may think sonnets over meatloaf is romantic, but if the rest of the student body would rather chat with a stranger than listen, it could be a very awkward occasion for both you and the prof. Save yourself, and him, the embarrassment. If you're unsure if your event would be professor appropriate, ask yourself two questions: Is the event hosted by a university-sponsored club, and is it something I could invite my roommate's parents to attend? If the answer is yes to one or both, you're off to a great start. The third step is to be sure you (or the person inviting him) actually know the professor.

Once the first three steps are under way—and this is most critical—invite your professor in person *at least a month* before the proposed event. The personal touch will show your genuine interest in the humanity of your professor as opposed to another faceless email asking for something.

If you're only interested in grabbing coffee with a prof after class, telling him at the beginning of the week is fine and he may be able to work you in before Friday. But when it comes to a specific slot on the calendar, and especially one after normal work hours, nearly a month's notice is needed.

Once the professor has accepted, your work does not end there. You should keep him informed of any important changes in the program (not an hourly ticker of trivial details, but say an every-other-week reminder and update).

Several days in advance of the event, offer to meet your prof a few minutes beforehand so that you can attend the event together. If you happen to have a shy prof on your hands, this will alleviate any fears of being forced to make conversation in a room full of strangers, since you will be there to protect him from boring small talk and general silliness.

An added plus—if you are really trying to make this work—is to invite the prof's spouse or significant other and offer to arrange for babysitting, if needed. By doing so, you have turned your event into a kid-free date for the professor.

When inviting faculty members to a function, be sure you are clear about the length of the function and any specific expectations you may have for them during that time. It is not unusual for professors to get invitations to "come speak at our house meeting" with no reference to how long they should speak or what in their vast field of study they should expound upon.

Worse yet, some students try to arrange panels of multiple speakers at once—meaning that all the profs who attend have to sit through each other's minilectures. Students love these, especially if they can throw together a couple of faculty who they suspect will disagree with each other about some topic of the day. Smackdown professorial wrestling is great sport for students, but professors are usually less keen to participate. The more profs on the slate, the less likely any of the profs will want to be there. To them, it promises to be nothing more than sitting through a tiresome litany of superficial summaries of points they know all too well.

If the event absolutely needs a range of perspectives, then by all means try for it, but be creative. Realize that if the idea occurred to you, it has probably occurred to other students as well, and yours may be the nth invitation the prof has received. Teaming up with all the other invitations to have one major, well-attended event is probably your best shot, especially if you strategize with those other clubs about ways to make the event more attractive to your key speakers.

One last note: be sure to send a thank-you note (old-fashioned snail mail is best) within a week of the event, perhaps relaying a favorable student comment or two. A wise man once said, "Writing thank-you notes is an art form, and anyone who desires success must become its eager student." Get yourself some professional stationery; you can never seem too grateful.

University Email Belongs to the University
Standards for Professor/Student Exchanges

Professor Stevenson tells of a student who approached him during office hours with a genuine concern that some psychological issues (for which she was being treated) were interfering with her course work. It was a perfectly appropriate conversation and they were both quite professional about it. Then arrived her apologetic email gushing gratefully about how understanding he had been and how his words had really meant a lot to her; then she expressed some concern that she may have revealed too much.

Given the context of the situation, her email would seem to be appropriate. But since their original conversation wasn't recorded, this email, if read by the wrong person, could incorrectly lead someone to believe that the professor was pursuing an inappropriate relationship with his student.

Dr. Stevenson admitted to us that he is certain the young woman meant no harm in sending the email, but it left him quite limited in how he could respond. University email is university property and may therefore be confiscated at any time: a terrifying thought for most professors.

As a result of the semipublic nature of email, many profs limit their correspondence to terse replies, and some don't reply to personal emails at all. Email is fabulous for arranging appointments and clarifying class assignments; it is serviceable for follow-up clarification about something said in a lecture; but it is dangerous when used for deep, personal revelation. If you are the sort of person who sends emails to colleagues without giving them a quick scrub, consider your reputation (and theirs); invest the time to review it from the perspective of someone with the *worst* intentions before hitting "Send." (This advice also serves well for all emotionally charged email conversations.)

As for texting, Facebook, and other social media, some professors are adept users (especially if they have kids of a certain age), but many will view it as an inappropriate way to interact with students. On these as on other related generation-gap issues, our advice is to adjust to what the professor finds most natural rather than trying to impose your generation's customs on him.

THE STUDENT'S ROLE

Since we've already spoken about the professional nature of your job as a professional student, we won't belabor the point about modest attire and minimal cologne. However, you may want to sharpen your Jedi sensitivity meter for this last point—guys especially.

Sexual overtones apply to both genders, so for the male readership who were already planning on changing out of their spaghetti strap halter tops before meeting with their female profs, you're not off the hook just yet. Women professors want to be treated as authority figures equal to men professors, and many have struggled in a man's world of academia to make their place. Guard your signals carefully lest you inadvertently disrespect her authority by being either overly familiar or combative—not only is it inappropriate, it could trigger an unfortunate result.

THE PROFESSOR'S ROLE

But what if you have done your part and it is the professor who is acting inappropriately? It does happen; perhaps less often than Hollywood would suggest, but more often than university administrators want to admit.

If a professor is indeed giving you unwanted looks, favors, or flattery, you have every right to put a stop to it. The law is pretty clear on this point. But as it is still a very delicate issue, might we make a few suggestions should you find yourself in that improbable situation?

First, be aware that any accusations you make about a prof will be a *permanent* part of his record. Or her record. These matters are not gender specific. Were you to visit your academic dean even to ask for advice on how to handle the situation, she would be required to report the prof for inappropriate behavior, whether you were certain he was ogling you or not. Out of deference for his career, be sure the professor's attentions warrant this sort of strong response and consider keeping his name out of the discussion until you are certain it is necessary.

If it is as simple as a misunderstood gesture or comment made by the prof—say he made a crack about "sorority girls" after you made a less-than-brilliant contribution to class discussion—schedule a time during office hours to explain that his comment or actions made you uncomfortable and interfered with your learning experience. Calmly state that you would like it to not happen again. No threats are necessary.

That you had the courage to speak to him directly already communicates that you will have the courage to expose him should the behavior continue, without you needing to bully him with ultimatums.

And, in keeping with the power of paper trails, send *yourself* an email after the meeting explaining the situation and what happened. It will automatically be dated and you can store it for reference should the inappropriate behavior continue.

However, if the prof's attentions have clearly crossed the line into the inappropriate, you should absolutely make a beeline for the office of either an academic dean or a resident advisor and explain the situation. Both will know what to do from there. Fortunately this sort of case is quite rare and most professors are more petrified of a misstep than you are; very few are willing to risk what they have worked a lifetime to achieve. So breathe a sigh of relief and attend class unconcerned.

My TA Will Be Happy to Help
Learning from Grad Students

Nearly all of the advice on professors in this chapter also applies to your TA (whether grad or undergrad) in terms of how to manage that relationship. All of your professors started out as graduate and undergraduate students once, so it's not as though TAs are an alien species.

However, they are in some sense a breed apart and that can alter the professor-student dynamic somewhat. You should be sensitive that TAs may have less experience from which to draw and so will probably make more mistakes or be slower to adjust to awkward situations than your professor would be. On the other hand, TAs will likely be better able to read the latest cultural cues and may therefore have a better intuitive feel for social improprieties.

If you have students (grad or undergrad) as your TAs, you should treat them in the same professional manner that you would treat a professor—and you have a right to expect the same professional treatment in return. What should drive the relationship is the professionalism behind your roles (teacher and student), not the age difference.

In large classes and especially lab courses, students often work more closely with a graduate TA than with the actual professor. In those cases, you should not hesitate to get a letter of recommendation from the graduate student. The rule of thumb that personal authenticity trumps distinguished signature still applies. Of course, best of all would be if the graduate student could write a couple of paragraphs of personalized evaluation that would be inserted in a longer letter written by the professor. It is worth asking whether or not both would be willing.

Let's Not Relive That Nightmare
Profs' Top Pet Peeves and How to Avoid Them

Throughout this chapter we have given a variety of tips on how to cultivate meaningful relationships within the academy. On the flip side, here is a series of professorial pet peeves that reinforce the basic point.

Being stood up. One professor claims that in his many years of teaching he has never hosted a meeting involving more than three or four students outside of class where every student showed up as promised. What an awful record!

Unprepared and unmotivated students. There are few things as disheartening as devoting your life to a topic only to find that someone who, after paying thousands of dollars to study with you, considers it so worthless that he doesn't even review the notes you labored to provide.

Techno addicts. You may think you're being discreet as you type a quick message into your cell phone or catch up on your favorite team's final score, but your facial expressions give you away. That glazed expression or that odd look of glee that doesn't relate to anything your prof just said are clear ringers that your body may be in class but your brain is elsewhere. Be aware that you are being watched. Come exam time your prof may be less than sympathetic if you can't recall large chunks of the course material because even though your face was in class your mind clearly was elsewhere for most of the course.

No-search research. After a full day of lectures and meetings, it is not uncommon for profs to return to their inbox and find students asking them to do their homework for them. "It drives me nuts that students email me asking me to help track down a book as if I were their personal librarian, while others want me to decide their research topic for them," said one professor expressing a commonly heard complaint. Unfortunately, modern search engines seem to make the average student even more dependent on the professor for cues than he was a generation ago. "I have no problem offering suggestions for summer reading if a student is looking for extra material on a subject, and I'll help students puzzle out a research topic if they come in for office hours to ask. But for students who are just plain lazy and ask me over email, no way."

Late rec requests. With scores of students flooding through a professor's life each term, it's no wonder she gets a bit stressed when one from the masses requests a recommendation months to even years after taking the course; even worse is when that student needs the letter in a hurry.

Scantily clad office hours. There's nothing quite like trying to keep eye contact with a student whose neckline is less than modest, or attempting to breathe through the fog of cologne without keeling over.

Email dumping. One student went so far as to generate the following email correspondence with her prof:

Student: Do you have office hours this week?

Prof: Yes, the sign-up sheet is posted outside my door.

Student: What days?

Prof: Wednesday and Friday; the sign-up sheet is posted outside my door.

Student: Do you have any openings on Friday?

Prof: Yes, see the sign up sheet posted outside my door.

Student: When are they?

Prof: From 12 to 1 and 3 to 4. The sign-up sheet is still posted outside my door.

Student: Would you mind signing me up for 3 on Friday?

Prof: I would most certainly mind.

Though this student thought she was being polite, ten emails prove that she was clearly more interested in saving herself the hassle of walking over to the prof's office to sign up than respecting her professor's time. Do your own grunt work.

Time sappers. No matter how hard they try, some profs feel as if student demands are insatiable. Even the most accessible professor will get complaints on end-of-term evaluations about how he could have done more to help students enjoy the learning process (such as come to the library to help with research or attend a cram session to help students prep for his final). The students who make these complaints have no idea about the pulls on a professor's time and have clearly not read this chapter. We're glad you aren't one of them.

Wrapping Up

If after reading this chapter you're a little overwhelmed by the professor-student relationship, don't be. Of all the areas in your undergrad experience where time invested is directly proportional to maximum value, your relationships with your professors is at the top.

CHAPTER 7

Getting What You Came For

Studying Smarter (and Why It Shouldn't Be All That Hard)

If you're like most students, you've made it to college with a few academic tricks up your sleeve. The cram session over a bowl of cereal before your first period French test; the cram session over a pizza slice before your fifth period chemistry test; the cram session walking between sixth period and seventh period mumbling the Gettysburg Address—they may have worked then (though even that is questionable), but they are unlikely to work now.

Most freshmen figure out too late that very few of those habits are suited to the unique and intensive challenges of collegiate course work. Then they either find themselves settling for mediocrity and hoping that future employers won't ask about their undergraduate GPA (sorry, almost all employers check) or, even worse, they risk their reputation and college career by handing in work that isn't theirs.

The good news is that a college admissions board tends only to admit students they believe are capable of making the grade. If you are smart enough to get into the college, you are smart enough to thrive there.

The Easy Way In
Confessions of a Cheater

But what if the whole reason you performed well in high school (and thus got admitted to college in the first place) is because you *did* cheat? Don't you need to cheat to keep up the performance? And since college is often so much larger, isn't it true it's less likely you'll get caught? Well, no and yes.

No, you don't need to cheat to get the grade you want. Regardless of what stunts you may have pulled for the last four years, you—and every other freshman—are starting over. You are *all* back at square one in terms of learning how to study, how to take effective notes, and how to learn (and it may be the last time in your college career that you get a fresh start, so take advantage of it).

Yes, it is true that the likelihood of getting caught is lower in college than it was in high school, but in that same breath let us add that the consequences are far, *far* greater. There is *little to no grace* if you are caught cheating—many schools have a "one-strike" policy, meaning a cheating conviction can get you expelled. Every job and grad school application will see that pockmark on your transcript from here until your teeth fall out. That's no exaggeration. Learn to be master of (rather than be mastered by) your course load.

"Toto, We're Definitely Not in Kansas"
How College Differs from High School

The most significant difference between college and high school is that you aren't required to be here. So if school isn't for you right now, you might talk with your parents about some creative ways to take time off. Seriously. College is an expensive proposition, and it will be here when you are ready. If this sounds in any way tempting given your situation, be sure to check out chapter 10, where we discuss taking a gap year in detail.

THE SYLLABUS

Assuming you decide to stay, one of the biggest differences in course work is that from the first day of class your college courses will be governed by a syllabus. With the exception of a few slacker profs (oh yes, they do exist), every professor will hand you a syllabus on the first day that maps out what you will read, discuss, and examine for the whole semester. Cool, no? Overwhelming too.

It can be daunting to see an entire semester's worth of work listed on a few pages. On the upside, it will be rare that your weekend plans are soured (as probably happened more than once in high school) by a professor giving you a surprise massive assignment on Friday that is due Monday. In this scenario, if your weekend is ruined, it will most likely be because you failed to plan (and work) ahead.

Because of the syllabus, you will have more power than ever before to structure your academic life, as opposed to just reacting to it. We recommend the following strategy to help you get the best out of it: Start off by buying a month by month calendar (either paper or digital; the medium doesn't matter) and fill in all the major reading and writing deadlines, as well as any labs or course meetings listed on your syllabus. Next, backtrack from each of those deadlines and figure how long it will take you to prepare for and complete them, and build a couple of your own milestones for each. For example, if you have a fifteen-page paper due halfway through the course, fill in a date by which you'll have all of your research finished and another to have your annotated outline completed. If you really want to crush it, plan to have your paper finished a couple of days *early*.

Whoa! We know that sounds like nerddom and insanity talking, but if you have never experienced the "done early" high, you shouldn't knock it. It's a fabulous feeling to look at a beastly deadline and know that you were finished long before the midnight hour, especially when you see your colleagues slaving away at 2 a.m. in a state of panic while you head out for a Playstation tournament instead. Plus, in case something goes wrong—"Ack! It's harder to write a fifteen-page paper than I thought and my laptop just died!"—you have a little breathing room.

ACCOUNTABILITY

The second huge difference between high school and college is that no one will be checking up on you (unless you commit some sort of heinous crime). Whatever support props you used in high school are gone now, and though assignments might be daily, they won't be monitored on a daily basis, if at all. Profs rarely even check if you attend class unless you're at a smaller school or in a smaller class, so you need to set up some sort of artificial monitoring to alert you if or when you're falling behind. Practically that means that if you are expected to read a novel a week, it might help to create a reading schedule for a while until you've learned to align your reading pace with that of the college level.

It is also worth probing the professor's expectations about readings listed on the syllabus. For many courses, especially in the social sciences and humanities, there may be some readings that are required and others that are only recommended. Few (if any) students do all of the recommended reading, but the very best students *will* do the recommended reading for particular weeks or topics that seem especially interesting. Supplemental readings are designed to reward the student whose curiosity has been piqued.

Every syllabus, no matter how vast, really just skims the surface of the topic. Some profs underscore this with a lengthy list of recommended readings to prevent students from getting smug thinking they have mastered the material prematurely. At some point nearly all of us have promised ourselves, "No pressure, I'll just read the recommended readings this summer," but we don't believe we have ever met someone who actually did that. So if you think it's worth the read, carve out the time now while the subject's fresh in your mind. Beyond just passing a class, getting the best out of college means educating yourself well.

ANALYSIS

The third major difference between college life and high school will be that you are expected to analyze more. (This is largely why your rote memorization strategies from high school won't work.) By and large, the expectation is that students begin to internalize and synthesize what they're learning as opposed to just regurgitating facts. You will be expected to go deeper with the facts and to make meaning of them. A good way to test whether or not you are really analyzing the material as you learn it is to try to interact with what you're reading—ask yourself questions at the end of each section to see if you were actually paying attention. The ultimate test after you finish reading is not only your comprehension of the material but your ability to communicate what you learned. If you don't know it well enough to teach it to someone else, you don't know it well enough.

Upper-level courses take analysis a step further in the direction of critique. Master's students go even deeper and are expected to master, synthesize, and thoroughly critique whole subfields. PhD students dig down to bedrock by making original contributions to knowledge in the field. The very best profs at the very best schools in the very best courses will try to expose students to all of these levels—analyze, critique, contribute—and you should enroll in a class like that before you graduate (but rarely in your first semester).

In keeping with this, students will definitely be expected to analyze resources more. A quick Internet search will no longer be sufficient. See this as a great opportunity to develop a more astute grasp of the Web. Just as you wouldn't use the "journals" by the grocery checkout as sources for a science paper (tempting as the two-headed pig story may be), you can't use everything your search engine lands upon either. Real research involves reading a lot of sources and evaluating their credibility, seeking to understand whatever biases may lead a source to its point. Ultimately you will learn which sources can be trusted and which require some skepticism.

To help plow through the avalanche of hits you may discover on any given topic on the Web, it would be wise to talk with your TA or professor about respected sources in the field and start there as a point of comparison. The point is not to bad-mouth search engines, but rather to say that they are a very sophisticated instrument that most students mishandle. By itself, searching doesn't lead to good analysis. Entire books could be written on how to weigh the value of sources, so we can't delve into it here as much as we would like. If you assume that the sources listed on the syllabus or in books on the syllabus are reputable, then build your own web of sources from those references and you'll be off to a good start.

Beyond that, see your college librarian. Reference librarians are the secret weapons of successful research, and far too few students use them. Some colleges have sought to remedy that oversight by offering workshops on navigating library databases and websites. So stop on by for a chat.

He Who Procrastinates Is Lost
Studying Smartly

Making the most of your education has a lot to do with how well you manage your time. However, we are NOT suggesting you study all the time. In fact, it's just the opposite. If you are studying smartly, you should be studying only a few hours each day, as opposed to feeling crushed by deadlines in the wee hours when your brain feels like porridge. For a resource chock-full of tips on how to study, check out *Study Smart, Study Less* written by our very own Anne Crossman; you may find it to be a significant time saver, not to mention grade booster. In the meantime, a few pointers on time management.

MAKE USE OF SMALL POCKETS OF TIME

Establish a realistic yet "stretching" routine you can follow from week to week that maximizes small pockets of time in your schedule.

One possibility is to start your workweek on Sundays in order to lighten your load for the remainder of the week. Alternatively you could study during the typical workweek of 8 a.m. to 5 p.m., Monday through Friday, and have the weekends off. The most successful students take advantage of that hour here and there by reading, studying, meeting with a tutor or professor, or exercising to refresh their brain cells with a new supply of oxygen. Those measly one or two hours between classes can turn out to be a gold mine that adds up to a lot of free time later if you use them to get your work finished.

The best way to discover those valuable wedges of time is to map out your weekly schedule for the term with all the immovables in your calendar—class, labs, your work-study job, rugby practice, etc. From there, look at all the unused portions of time and be intentional with how you use them, scheduling breaks or study sessions where needed.

Something else to consider as you construct a study schedule is that most readings are paced with the lectures, and as a result will make the most sense if read on schedule. If possible, read the assigned material on the day of the lecture (or, most definitely, within a week of the lecture) so it is fresh in your mind—yet another reason not to schedule all your classes on the same day.

When I studied music in college, I was required to practice at least seven hours every week. It was a daunting task. Freshman year, I often dragged myself into the practice room dungeons at 10 p.m., trying in vain to get that German aria off of the pages and into my voice. One semester, though, I had forty minutes of downtime between my classes several days a week and started using that time to squeeze in a practice session. I was amazed at how it improved my abilities with the music, as well as freeing up my nights for socializing or other studies. Now I love it when there are gaps in my schedule; I make full use of them.

Rebecca—recent grad, Point Loma Nazarene U

STUDY WHERE YOU CAN BE STUDIOUS

Most important of all—and this one you shouldn't ignore. . . please—don't make your room your primary place to study. Go to the library or discover some special study location the rest of campus has overlooked (tip: it probably isn't at the table near your friendly neighborhood barista), but *don't study in your room.*

Despite your best intentions, your room is nothing but a small area packed with distractions and visitors who aren't interested in watching you read. It may have worked at home, but this balance shifts now that you are living with your friends. You need to go somewhere else in order to focus, and it's good to make that distinction early on.

> Even though I had been advised repeatedly that my room was not a good place to study, I ignored these warnings my freshman year. One night, when I was writing one of my papers, I felt like I needed a break and before I knew it I had actually watched an entire season of *The Office* on Hulu. Realizing I had just wasted the past several hours, I packed up my stuff and moved to the library where I found a somewhat secluded table in the corner and cranked the paper out in less than two hours.
>
> **Lauren—sophomore, Northeastern U**

DEVELOP YOUR OWN STUDY GUIDE

So now that it's your designated time for studying and you are in your designated space, how do you study? A basic tool we find to be highly valuable is the outline. It sounds bland, we know, but give it a chance.

The idea is to limit yourself to one sheet of paper and, after reading your material for class for the week, to construct some sort of outline or logic chart that concisely summarizes what you read.

Tempting as that extra ream sitting near your elbow may be, keeping it to a page will not only force you to test whether or not you understand the information well enough to simplify it, it will also provide you with a handy study guide. Believe us, it is *much* easier to review a single page than to go back through all of the handouts, class notes, and highlighted text in your textbook only hours before a final exam.

You can take this one step further and distill your weekly pages onto single index cards, and then at the end of the term summarize all of your weekly cards onto one or two pages. This may be some of the most intense analysis you will do all semester, but as a result it will make your exams that much easier (and, hopefully, successful).

The bottom line is that if you have studied the material properly throughout, there will be no need to cram at the end of the term. Even if the information doesn't seem connected naturally, there is a connection of some sort since your prof saw fit to link it all together in one course. Sitting down to search out the course theme with the TA or professor during office hours partway through the semester (so you don't have to fight the frantic crammers at the end of the term) may prove to be an invaluable exercise.

Most material can only be mastered over several weeks of sustained study, so start early and keep it up. Since most courses are cumulative, with later material building on earlier material, the better you learn the early stuff, the easier it will be to master the later stuff.

One Is the Loneliest Number
Using Peers to Your Advantage

When it comes to getting the best out of your education, why go it alone when there are tutors, comrades, profs, and campus resources ready to come to your aid?

TUTORS

The most common mistake we have seen in this regard is with students who assume that only dummies need tutors. They wait too long to admit their confusion and when they finally do, the tutor sign-ups are full. There is a sort of stigma or humiliation that goes with needing a tutor, especially for those who are used to *being* the tutor. The best advice we can offer is this: get over it. Tutors are in high demand campus-wide and to get one, you need to sign up early. LOTS of people need and use tutors. In fact, most big league universities frequently run out of tutors because they are so popular, especially by the last three weeks of the semester. So should you find yourself needing a tutor, you can assuage your pride by reminding yourself you aren't the only one.

Most schools provide at least some free tutoring for some students (such as athletes) or the equivalent of a generic help desk at a study center. Depending on the department, some tutoring may even be offered free to students within that major.

Check with the department's main office to start your tutor search. Academic deans may know where to find them, as well as RAs—and just because these people haven't heard of a tutor in your field doesn't mean one doesn't exist.

> In my chem class, when I didn't quite understand the material, it snowballed until I got farther and farther behind because each new chapter built on the last. I let it get to a dangerous point where if I didn't do something quickly, I was going to fail the class. So I finally got help from a tutor. Going over the material a couple of hours a day with someone else helped me understand it better, and I made enough headway to salvage my grade.
>
> **Brian—freshman, U of Oregon**

STUDY GROUPS

If tutors aren't your gig or you would like to get help beyond a tutoring service, study groups can be a great way to go. Depending on the subject, four or five people is often the ideal number. Dividing work among you can be an effective means of getting more accomplished, but be aware that input/output is a critical element of learning. That means you need to be handling all of the information yourself at some point in order for it to sink in.

Most people learn better with peers in an interactive setting because—let's face it—it's fun. Heck, most anything is fun in a group. And it's been proven time and time again that the best way to learn a topic is to try to teach it to someone else because you reinforce what you already know and quickly figure out what you don't. It is a paradox: study groups can be a good place to learn if you go there prepared to teach other people.

Where a study group tends to go wrong is when its members rely on it too heavily, such as a student attending her group expecting to take more than give. The most effective groups are those that require some sort of advance preparation from each of the members so that coming together is an opportunity to resolve, clarify, or synthesize what each has found. The group can also be effective for brainstorming questions that may be on the test or drilling each other on certain concepts.

Of course, sometimes groups can be less than helpful, being more pooled ignorance than shared wisdom. Most students get in trouble with their study groups by not spotting difficulties early on. One solution is to arrange meetings from week to week (as opposed to promising to meet for the entire semester) so that there is more freedom to change or leave the group as needed. Just remind yourself that the study group isn't some twisted popularity contest and that everyone needs to pull their own load if they want to stay—which includes you as well as the guy everyone thinks is hilarious but always has a convenient excuse for not doing his fair share.

I had a study group for all my math classes and believe me when I say that it's a lot easier to understand a peer than a professor or TA since they are more likely to be on the same intellectual level as you. However, a couple of my study groups have gone awry and ended up as time-wasting avenues since all members of the group were really good friends and we ended up talking rather than getting work done.

Onome—junior, Stanford U

FACULTY

Let's not forget the profs. While we covered the topic of getting help from them extensively in chapter 6, there is one final point we can add here. If you are lost, before seeking out a tutor or even your study group, the first person you should consider speaking with is your professor. A simple visit during office hours to say, "I don't get this" and a few minutes of help will illuminate whether your problem will be easy to solve or if a tutor will be necessary.

UNDERUTILIZED RESOURCES

Our final tip is to ask campus resources for training on time management and study skills—it may be that there is an afternoon course or weekly session you could join "free" (aka, part of your tuition). Your best bet is to seek out an academic resource center or counseling center.

Libraries are also rich resources—the reference libraries especially. Most staff are knowledgeable and eager to help (particularly for research papers or projects) and are not well utilized. It isn't against the rules to ask a librarian for help searching out sources or recommending materials, and she may be more helpful if you visit during nonpeak library hours and before closing time.

Some campuses also offer writing studios where peers or instructors can help you with writing a specific paper or even writing in general, while others may have an alumni "expert" program through which alums can advise you on specific research topics.

Every college offers a host of resources to help you learn better. It may require some perseverance to sort through the offerings to find the one that best suits your needs, but you'll be glad you did.

"Did I Do That?"
Cheating, Whether You Meant to or Not

Everything we described in the previous section is legitimate help. But we don't have to tell you that there is equally illegitimate help out there. "I regret to say that we have seen more plagiarism in recent years than we ever wanted to imagine," said an ethics board member at a prominent university. "Without question, there are two causes of plagiarism that dominate. The first is the act of desperation. This is the student who waited until the last minute to write her paper or lab and now has to throw something together. It's 2 a.m. and the class meets in six hours—she simply panics. She cuts and pastes from the Internet and it's destined for doom.

"The second type is the truly ignorant act. This is where a student doesn't fully understand what the college expects in terms of citations when writing a research paper. In many schools, improper citations equal plagiarism. *The intent is irrelevant!* The student who commits plagiarism out of ignorance is as guilty as the one pasting from the Internet. This second student probably has limited experience in writing a research paper and really doesn't know what is expected, but it still appears as though he is trying to get away with something. Ignorance is no excuse.

"Both students then face not only a failing grade but also major sanctioning or a period of separation from the school. Tuition is not refunded for the time of their absences (depending on the school and the situation). The good news is that if a student doesn't know how to cite a paper, most schools offer writing clinics they can take *in advance*. They can ask their professor for information on citing as well, but few students do this because they are either afraid of appearing stupid or they are just lazy; then they wait until the end and don't have the time they need and we're back at the beginning with student number one." Thus says the expert.

Let's face it, most students don't bother to read their university's guidelines on plagiarism—seriously, it feels a lot like reading the manual to your parents' dishwasher—but you should. Those same students who didn't set out to plagiarize but did (more out of ignorance than deviousness) were found responsible because they erred on the side of inadequate sources. Enough students have failed to read their school's definition of plagiarism that a growing number of universities are now posting it as required reading before students can register for courses. Take it from the ethics board member mentioned earlier: "It is much better to have a prof say to you that you footnoted too many times rather than not enough. The first is annoying; the second is a major violation that could get you thrown out of school."

Most cases of cheating begin with the research paper, when a professor reviews the bibliography and finds the sources to be either inadequate or imaginary. It should be obvious that every source you use must be genuine. Beyond documentation, where most students inadvertently trip up is in researching information on the Web and then cutting and pasting more than they should.

Like we mentioned earlier, the best investment you can make in covering your hide is spending the time to develop a paper trail. Mistakes happen, and you never know when you'll need some backup. A friend of ours—Bob—was accused of cheating in organic chemistry when he had only been following the instructions of the TA. The problem came when the course rotated TAs a couple of times. By the time they got to the third TA for the course, she thought he was academically out of line and sent him to the ethics committee to be reviewed. Fortunately for Bob, he had a paper trail of notes from the original TA advising him how to proceed with his course work, so his name was cleared. Phew. That was a close one.

While you won't want to seem like an insensitive conspiracy theorist assuming every course assistant is out to get you (meaning, don't send an email after every conversation saying, "You said this and then I said that"), you *will* want to highlight the critical conversations and follow up with appropriate emails. Possible ways to follow up would be to say, "Thanks for your time after class yesterday. Just to review, so I'm sure I understood your instructions, you suggested I review this and then talk to so-and-so and then use his suggestions as one of my sources," or whatever the conversation may have been, so it sounds like you are being grateful rather than preparing for a witch hunt.

Some profs make past tests available, and even though it seems like cheating to read them, it isn't. In law school, some profs encourage their students to go to the reserves in the library and use old tests to study. The prof may not ask the exact questions, but the format will be similar. Just knowing how the test will be structured can be comforting. The bottom line is that it's always best to ask—if the prof doesn't mention his policy on consulting previous tests, be sure to ask permission. Don't rely on explicit instructions and then look for a loophole.

┤ BUSYNESS IS NOT A VIRTUE ├

Going Easy on the Extracurriculars

Most freshmen study well for the first few weeks but distractions frequently take over and—when they float by on the lack of immediate penalties—they fall behind. The first week is not wasted, but the first month often is; and, no matter how extreme your efforts to salvage the semester, you cannot make up in December what should have been done in September.

For the first two to four weeks (or longer!), it's possible that you won't have any assignments due, particularly if you're not taking any math or science courses. As a result, a couple of things tend to happen: as a freshman, you enjoy doing zero work and build an unrealistic mind-set about college life, or you begin to fill your time with other activities.

Some students go crazy on that second one. Because they were involved in a zillion clubs in high school or did dozens of hours of community service each week, they continue in that habit. Then, once the semester gets rolling, they find themselves either having missed the boat in what they were supposed to have learned in class or terribly overcommitted.

The key here is to get involved early on but not at the expense of your course work. Take your current free time as a very brief gift, and enjoy it as such.

The student conduct defense process can be painful, so permission and a paper trail are critical.

The coaches of well-respected collegiate sports teams tell their players that it is better to take a lower grade—even an F—than to plagiarize. The risks just aren't worth it. Professors are darn smart, and there are a number of clues that tip them off to a paper being a fake. (We'd love to list those here, but we might have to go into hiding as a result.) It may not seem like they catch many students, but figure that every student taking a course is writing in her professor's area of expertise, so he will be able to sniff out inaccuracies or misappropriations faster than she realizes because he will be incredibly familiar with the material. Profs didn't get their degrees—or their posts—for naught. Some of them know their field so well they can even tell you in which chapter of what book a "borrowed" quote was published. Borrower, beware.

Even if your professor isn't as savvy as some, many universities now have various forms of software that detect cheating. All a prof needs to do is have his assistant send the stack of papers through a scanner and an hour later—voilà! —a printout of any papers that appear on the Internet.

If you can't get the paper done and need more time, ask for an extension. If you don't get it, take your lumps. But don't cheat—it's a quick ticket out of school for a while, if not permanently. Some schools show on transcripts an X rather than an F to indicate when a student has been suspended or failed a course due to discipline. And that means your future employer will have some hefty questions should he even be willing to consider you for an interview.

To future employers and graduate schools, flunking is an immaturity that one can grow out of—or, at worst, a skill limitation. Cheating is a sign of something far more serious that may make you too risky to hire.

"Wait, I Thought You Were Going to Teach Me How to Cram"

Ninety-nine percent of the time there is no reason to cram.

If learning is managed properly, students should not find themselves needing to cram and pull all-nighters—which is why we devoted so much time at the beginning of this chapter to setting up structures for studying properly. Occasionally there are exceptions—where the prof will throw something in that you didn't realize you needed to know or a minor emergency arises and your carefully crafted schedule doesn't work as planned: accidents happen. But for the most part, if you establish priorities and stick to a schedule, there is no need to cram.

An hour spent reviewing organized notes is worth four hours of looking at information for the first time and trying to shrink-wrap it into your long-term memory. We would even add that an hour of studying in the first month of the semester is worth two in the second, three in the third, and so on because you are laying a foundation in a. very time-sensitive manner.

Certainly there will be times when you need to focus only on an upcoming exam and it looks like cramming. But what it will really be is just focused review. A tiny fraction of students can successfully cram in college, to be sure. Yao is a friend who would skip a third of his classes, reserve all of his reading for the last week of the semester, then lock himself in his room and read nonstop. And more often than he deserved, he was able to make that strategy work. But many who tried to follow his example failed miserably. What they didn't realize was that Yao was gifted with a certain and very unusual genius that enabled him to store large quantities of information quickly and temporarily—it's rare, and we recommend that you don't risk trying to do what he did.

There are certainly times in real life when cramming becomes necessary, especially in the business world with project deadlines. Prior to the deadline, team members do all that is required, which may mean getting very little sleep. The ability to perform at a high level on little sleep is a valued skill exercised in countless careers to be sure, but it is an emergency plan and not a daily habit. Companies are far more interested in you having good time management skills so as to avoid unnecessary emergencies, and as a bonus quality, having the ability to fly into emergency mode if necessary.

Should you find yourself in desperate straits with an impending deadline, here are a few tips (what kind of help would we be if we didn't at least throw you a rope?):

Look for course themes. Start with the syllabus and look at the texts that have been assigned with a view of the course as a whole. Is there some sort of theme or big-picture argument the prof is trying to get you to understand? What is the perspective of each assigned reading and how do they differ? Your familiarity with the thematic structure of the course will be helpful should you need to write any essays on the exam, and your ability to cite some of the assigned readings will go a long way—even if you haven't read them in their entirety.

Recharge your brain. Consider taking power naps to help recharge yourself. A twenty-minute nap can go a long way in helping you push yourself an hour or two longer. You may want to experiment first to see if this strategy works before depending on it at crunch time.

Reorganize the workload. Break an unmanageable amount of work into chunks to make it more manageable—it's hard to memorize a chart of diagrams when your adrenaline is pumping and your brain is in fight-or-flight mode because you're super stressed. Break the job down, saying, "I'll work on this half of the page for the first hour, the second half of the page for the second hour." When the project is manageable, it has a calming effect which enables you to focus.

Refuel your body. Eat snacks—the healthier and more nourishing, the better. Think protein. Think carbs. Your brain needs all the help it can get, so go for nuts and cheese and fruit and skip the jelly beans. Refined sugar may give you a temporary high, but if you are pushing yourself without sleep you may crash to an unrecoverable low.

Avoid artificial highs. The latest craze is to borrow prescription medications, especially attention-related meds, to get that extra edge to focus. These drugs often allow students to work through the night, and some perform fine, so students see them as an effective way to get their work done. Of course, whatever works becomes a habit and popping an occasional pill "for emergencies" eventually becomes more routine. There are huge long-term implications for this sort of drug abuse that are dangerous and, frankly, frightening. Rather than abusing drugs in college, use the time to develop healthy lifelong habits that don't rely on artificial means to get the job done.

Get some fresh air. Take a hike. Really. If you've got a lot of work to do, next to a nap and a snack, a quick stroll around the building can do a lot of good—especially if it's cold outside. But even if it's late summer and positively sweltering, getting out of your chair and allowing the blood to circulate a little faster will have your synapses cheering. A quick fifteen or twenty minutes of cardio should do the trick.

Make time for creative study breaks. Knit a beanie. Practice karaoke. Paint your toenails. Essentially find some other means to relax if you find yourself anxious and sweating through your shirt. The more relaxed you are, the more successful you will be in transferring short-term knowledge into long-term memory. Plus, your feet will look pretty.

Take it easy. Don't expect much of yourself the day after (and for some people, two days after) a major cram session. Meaning, don't schedule two all-nighters back to back. The body needs a fair bit of time to recover, so be nice to yourself.

Learning how to manage my course work was, for me, the most helpful part of this book. When I mapped out my schedule for second semester, I arranged a set number of study hours into my weekly schedule for each class. Two good things came out of this: I was done with my work way ahead of time and, if I had time left over, I was able to put extra work into classes I really enjoyed (which, in my case, was drawing).

Philip—freshman, Virginia Commonwealth U

CHAPTER 8

You're Not from Around Here, Are You?

Advice for International Students and Their Domestic Friends

Increasingly, college students come from all parts of the world to be part of the American college experience. Some only drive two hours across state lines while others fly two days across multiple bodies of water and mind-numbing time zones to get here. Together "domestic" and "international" students form the most diverse population ever to pursue higher education together.

The international student faces distinctive challenges in getting the best out of college and, we believe, has a vital role to play in helping others maximize their college experience. This chapter is written not only for the international student who gives up the comforts of home to study in the States but also for the domestic student who stands to gain a wealth of meaningful interactions from another's experience. In our rapidly globalizing world, ambitious universities are eager to welcome international students to campus as a means of increasing diversity and the range of voices who take part in the academic dialogue. So if you are one of these prized international students considering relocating for the next four or more years for the sake of education and adventure, we congratulate you—and we encourage you to pay close attention to this chapter. If you are a domestic student, read this chapter anyway because what you gain indirectly could help you form vibrant global partnerships in the future, not to mention the intrinsic benefit of forming close friendships with interesting people.

Why are universities so eager to attract international students when, in all honesty, it means a lot more work for campus staff to help those students find their niche? For starters, international students enrich the community intellectually; bringing in students from around the world is inviting the world into the classroom.

Discussions around the economics of gender become much more interesting when students from majority Muslim countries are invited to the table; the same is true about discussions on postcolonialism in literature with students from India and South Africa, or copyright and patent law with students from Germany, Japan, and China. And you really don't understand American politics and history until you have talked about it with someone who sees the United States from the outside looking in. Suddenly what seems like a straightforward conversation becomes a very rich forum with a tantalizing blend of ideas.

Universities are also excited to welcome international students because they may bring a unique degree of maturity to campus. Given all they (and their families) have sacrificed to be here, international students may be a little more focused, determined, and dedicated than the average freshman. In general, international students tend to be more savvy about the world. Of course, they also face unique pressures as they familiarize themselves with American social mores, ranging from gender relations to interactions with their professors.

Given these pressures, our advice in the previous chapters applies doubly to international students, for whom college *and* American life are totally new. However, it is necessary to highlight how international students can enhance their education with a few wise decisions early on, and how domestic students can reap the benefits of being educated alongside some of the greatest minds from around the world.

I Was Born in the US—
Why Should I Read This Chapter?

If you are a domestic student, thank you for being culturally astute and reading this chapter. As you do so, we encourage you to make the leap and join an international club. Just as it's important for international students to assimilate into the campus culture, it is equally important for domestic students to get out of *their* comfort zones and get to know new people and explore new cultures that have landed on their doorstep.

Who cares if you're as home-grown American as they come—join the Korean Students Association. Sure, you don't speak Korean, have never tasted kimchee, and don't know who Sejong the Great is or why there is a statue of him in downtown Seoul. All the more reason to join. That's what Kip did. Four years later he found himself taking a job in Korea by happenstance, feeling very grateful that the culture, food, and a bit of the language were familiar. So keep reading.

I Never Should Have Come
When to Brave Homesickness and
When to Just Stay Home

Culture shock is, in part, homesickness magnified. However, for international students, the sheer distance from home can make the feelings especially intense, particularly around the holidays—and particularly around holidays that are not celebrated in the States as they would be back at home with family and friends.

Universities do their best to make special preparations for international students during holidays when most students will be away from campus. Their absence can create deep feelings of loneliness, but holidays and breaks can also open up opportunities for you to delve further into American culture, develop relationships with families off campus, and take your educational adventure to a new level. It's a reasonable goal to befriend an American and be invited to join them for

Thanksgiving, religious holidays, or even spring break. Professor James tells us that when he was growing up, his family always had an international student living with them; his parents considered it helpful for the student and even more helpful in broadening their children's global perspective. This note is for domestic students: Be aware and hospitable. Sharing a holiday with an international student and hearing about his own country's freedoms and heritage will give you a renewed sense of appreciation for the liberties you have, and the shared cultural experience will turn what may have become a stale tradition into a feast.

Culture shock is, in part, homesickness magnified.

Like most international students who come to study in America, you are probably well aware of the potential homesickness, not to mention being absent from many of the traditional celebrations back home. The trade-off for academic opportunities not offered in your home country is worth the cost. Yet the costs can be high.

You know the old joke: all generalizations are false, including this one. All generalizations are also risky, including this one. But in our varied and lengthy experience, we have seen a disproportionate number of international students struggle with mental health issues around depression and severe anxiety. It's hard to know if these challenges existed prior to coming to the States and were simply exacerbated by the stresses of being here, or if it is the stress of culture shock, homesickness, isolation, and academic pressure from home blending into a toxic cocktail.

If you are one of those readers who is particularly prone to such pressures and internal darkness, establish some support systems for yourself within your first week on campus. Make use of academic advisors when you are feeling overwhelmed by classes; campus counselors when you are feeling alone, confused, and stressed; office hours to find clarification in your course work; and resident faculty when you need a wise, listening ear. Bottom line? Ask for help—and lots of it. Knowing yourself well enough to accurately weigh your strengths and weaknesses—and knowing how to ask others for help so that the latter does not engulf the former—is a sign of strength.

Being asked to see a counselor is almost like being told to go home. I never met with a counselor prior to coming to America; neither did I meet with a dean during all my years in a British-styled school. It was simply not part of the student experience, unless a student had committed a serious crime or was failing all his courses. Someone must explain the role of an advisor, a dean, and a counselor to incoming internationals—and stress the importance of using them as *allies*—or international students will rot in their dorm rooms, fearing the thought of approaching what is considered a terrifying group of people in their own countries.

Joshua—sophomore, Duke U

So back to that question we asked earlier: how do you know whether it makes sense to attend an American university and, if so, which university to attend? One way is to ask questions before you decide to study in the United States. We recommend that you pose the questions listed below to each of the universities that you seriously consider attending. Unless universities suggest otherwise, email these questions directly to the admissions office; the staff will help you weigh whether or not attending their school is in your best interest.

First and foremost, locate a university that is particularly strong in the field you plan to pursue; should two or more universities stand equal on this first question, the following questions will help you narrow down your choices. Relative to academic pursuit and the opportunity to find a job and build a life in the US, many of these issues are minor by comparison—but they still matter. Ultimately, if you are happy in your choice of university, everyone is happy; your college wants to make sure this is the right fit from the start.

1. **Are there other students from my country attending this university, if not as undergraduates then as graduates?** (If no, ask yourself whether or not you are willing to be a pioneer and seek out potential alums or members of the community who may share your native country.)

2. **What special support services does the administration offer international students?**

3. **Do you have an international house, and what sort of support networks, advice, and resources does it offer students from my country?**

4. **Will the school have a special orientation for international students like myself, and what does that entail?** (Some universities allow international students, along with their parents, to come to campus nearly a week early to recover from travel and jet lag, explore the area outside campus on university-sponsored field trips, and especially to connect with other international students and develop a base of friendly faces in a more intimate fashion before other students arrive on campus.)

5. **What arrangements will be made for me during holidays while residence halls are closed?** (This is a key question, since, for security reasons, many campuses close residence halls entirely during winter break. They may, however, open a block of rooms for the few students who remain on campus during the break.)

6. **Is it possible to stay at the school during the summer to take classes or pursue internships?**

7. **What extracurricular activities does the university offer that are related to my culture?**

8. **Are there alumni or social networks off campus that are dedicated to helping international students feel welcome, especially when school is not in session?**

As you weigh the answers to these questions and use them to select your school of choice, consider this last point: life as an international student requires a special level of maturity. While domestic freshmen who are immature are likely to have a difficult time their first year, the situation is even more difficult for an immature international freshman. Make time to consider this decision carefully.

Part of the maturity needed involves your ability to weigh not only the social realities of studying in the US but also the financial costs. You need to consider more than just tuition and books; you will also face international phone bills, expensive flights home, and the ever-changing currency exchange rate. Because of the potential financial challenges, take the time to investigate carefully the extent to which financial aid is available to you.

Talk about Jet Lag
Managing Homesickness

In the past, international students had little more than letters mailed back and forth, the occasional care package, and phone calls reserved only for special occasions to stay in touch with people back home. Skype, Internet-based phone services, and email are an invaluable resource for international students. Although in earlier chapters we cautioned undergrads against calling home too frequently, we relax that advice a bit for international students. Likewise, unlike domestic students, we encourage international students to bring special items from home to help make their rooms, as much as possible, a familiar place of safety and retreat. Where we cautioned domestic undergrads from developing too extensive a network off campus in the early years at the risk of losing their network on campus, we encourage international students to occasionally visit neighboring schools that may have more students from their home country. Relationships on and off campus are a worthwhile investment of time that create a sense of home, which will be of great importance as you establish your new home here.

ACADEMIC ADVISORS

Because homesickness is so prevalent for internationals, universities have developed an extensive support system for them. Often the university will do its utmost to pair international students with hand-picked academic advisors who will be sensitive to the unique challenges and opportunities that international students experience. So ask your academic advisor about what resources are available to you now that you are on campus.

> I wish international students were blatantly told that they should expect to be a minority in America. Yes, it sounds obvious but, frankly speaking, it comes as a shock. I frequently found myself among people who, in most cases, had no idea who I was and, inasmuch as they were interested in knowing and learning about me, their approach was often completely wrong. When I was at my lowest of lows, I shied away from people who might ask me silly questions, such as if there are lions in my backyard. On my better days, I've come to realize that I should expect all kinds of conversations—the good as well as the bad. Inasmuch as it is up to me, I will communicate effectively and try to discern between mockery and humble inquiries that are simply shadowed by ignorance.
>
> **Joshua—sophomore, Duke U**

We know of one student, Katrina, who came from Russia to study in the States and had a particularly rough time. In fact, by Christmas she was so homesick (not to mention getting Cs and Ds in nearly every class) that she was ready to leave permanently. Her academic advisor was able to persuade her to at least finish out the school year and take the summer—when she would naturally have a couple of months off and was already planning to be home—to think about it. Katrina agreed. That next fall, she was back. She announced to her advisor upon returning that she was excited to be back on campus and was staying for the remainder of her education. Why the sudden change of heart? Katrina told her advisor that she went home hoping to reconnect with friends, most of whom had stayed in-country to attend local universities, and found those friends to be immature and trapped in the rut of their high school relationships. It was in that moment that she realized how much she had grown and changed during her time away in the States. She decided that, while it would be easier to stay in

Russia, she would miss out on too many opportunities to explore the world; she returned refreshed. And her change in perspective gave her the extra boost she needed to reapply herself to her course work and improve her grades. If there's a moral to this story, it is to listen to academic advisors and campus counselors (more on counselors below). They have seen international students face a vast array of experiences, and they will provide wisdom and guidance for your journey.

COUNSELING CENTERS

If at all possible, go to the counseling center when you first arrive on campus—and go often during the academic year.

Counseling centers seek to provide counselors who will resonate with students from a wide variety of cultural backgrounds. You will likely find someone there who's had similar experiences and can relate to what you are going through. As an added benefit, counseling centers can often give you the names of families in the area who have expressed interest in opening their homes to international students to share meals or holidays. Whether or not the host family has a background similar to yours, you may find that being welcomed into their home as part of the family will be a refuge all its own. The bottom line is, don't wait to be at your lowest low to visit your advisor: go early and go often.

INTERNATIONAL CENTERS

The final element of a typical university support system is an international center. Many international houses offer movie nights with subtitled films from various countries, meals from cultures around the world, dances, and other creative ventures for making the campus feel more welcoming. You may be the only student from your country, but being together with other international students will provide you with a sense of community as you share in your "foreignness" together.

As comfortable as the international house may be, however, we don't recommend you make it your primary haunt. Continually challenge yourself to pursue your adventure in the US instead of trying to recreate home. Remember, you can go home eventually—your country will always be there—but you'll only have this opportunity to experience the life and culture of the United States on a campus full of peers for four brief years. So as much as you are able, make the most of it.

My Parents? It's Like They're from a Different Country
Managing Expectations Back Home

As far away as home is and feels, the expectations of those who love you are, most likely, ever present. As an international student, you may find yourself trying to keep everyone, including yourself, happy. You long for home and try to please the people back home. You also try to maintain your old cultural identity and, at the same time, find yourself developing a new identity as a result of the new culture in which you find yourself.

We cannot overstate the pressure that most international students express when asked about expectations back home. You (and your parents) may expect perfection in all areas and be unwilling to compromise a little academically so you can explore extracurriculars or alternative majors. In order to reduce potential misunderstandings about academic expectations, discuss these with your parents before leaving home and try to reach a healthy, shared goal (or, at the very least, a compromise).

The other great expectation beyond academics you will want to discuss with your parents before leaving home is the concept of dating while overseas. Not all cultures expect their children to marry within their culture, but often it is a hope and sometimes it is much stronger than that. If you do not know where your parents stand on this subject, some conversation—even if awkward—may be warranted. We are not telling you how to meet their expectations or even whether you should do so. We are merely suggesting you tread lightly and be aware of the fullness of their expectations ahead of time.

And now a message for parents: Be willing to let your students learn. You have sent your students thousands of miles to better themselves, push themselves to the limit, and create a future that rivals your own success. You have done so out of love. Now trust your sons and daughters to make wise choices; they have worked hard to get here and will continue to work hard. Trust that they will learn from their mistakes; we all make mistakes, and if students seek wise counsel at their universities, they will continue to succeed. We recognize the difficulty of what we ask, but we also recognize the consequences of what happens when parents are unable to give their students this freedom. Simply put, parents who do not let their children grow up end up with children who are not grown-ups.

Saris and Ultimate Frisbee
When to Assimilate and When to Congregate

International students typically cite two main reasons for pursuing higher education in America: (1) it is generally considered to be the best education in the world, and (2) the value of the cross-cultural experience and all that it entails. Once on campus, your academic involvement is a given: you are enrolled in classes and are held to the same academic standard as everyone else (more on this in the next section).

Getting the full benefit of the cross-cultural experience may be a bit more difficult. On the one hand, you have come here to be part of the American melting pot. On the other hand, you miss home and may be inclined to recreate much of that sense of home here so that you are able to cope and pursue your course work.

Our advice, at its core, is to spend enough time involved in activities related to your home culture that you take the edge off your homesickness, but not so much that you form your social identity solely by congregating with students from a similar background. If we were to risk putting a number on so delicate an equation, we might suggest that, at the very least, 75 percent of your interactions be campus-wide and at most 25 percent be related to your culture back home. In other words, spend enough time within your culture group that you are able to escape the American strangeness from time to time, but not so much that you miss out on the full collegiate experience, which, in America, is a twenty-four-hour experience. If you've never had a 2 a.m. debate on the international responsibilities of the US government, you're missing out. Do your best not to hide out in the lab or library as your safety zone either. As important as your academics are—remember, this is a professor saying this—they are *only one piece* of your college education.

That being said, knowing your comfort zone as you teeter between campus culture and your home culture (and how to find that reenergizing balance where you feel relatively secure in both) is equally important. We know: it seems like we are talking out of both sides of our mouths here. But it really is a matter of fine-tuning your decisions about which groups to join and how to spend time outside of class across your various expectations of what you hope to get out of college; finding the right balance depends on the individual.

We have seen international students who miss out on the best that an American college has to offer because they never leave their group of friends who hail from the same region. They lose something when they fail to fully embrace American culture. And, frankly, the American culture loses out as well. Whether or not it is right, the rest of the student body expects international students to assimilate to them. Rather than wait for the university to create an official campus-sponsored group that highlights your culture, go out and create one. Help raise awareness about your home culture, such as starting a new campus fad based on your local dance, dress, or cuisine.

Again, colleges admit international students like you because they want you to influence their school in a distinct way; they want your culture and values, and those of other international students, shared, explored, and discussed. University deans are quick to point out that they want domestic students to extend themselves to learn more about what is going on in the cultures and countries of international students, not only in the classroom but also—and especially—outside the classroom. Those same deans recognize that the greatest influence will come *relationally* as opposed to programmatically. They can offer international fairs and enough workshops to wallpaper the student union completely in neon flyers, but little will be as effective as domestic and international students simply hanging out over bad pizza until the wee hours discussing how the world began.

My Professor Barely Knows Me and I Don't Think He Likes Me

As eager as the university is to welcome you to campus, the classroom can be a very daunting place. Potentially even more intimidating is the professor-student relationship, which takes its own cultural twist in America that may be a startling change from how you interacted with teachers in the past. For some international students, that they are expected to interact with professors at all may be terrifying, and as a result they are likely to assume the worst about some gesture or comment their prof might make, completely unaware of its value in their culture. For these students, developing professional relationships with their profs may seem like their greatest challenge.

With all this going on in the background, it makes sense that international students might exhibit additional nervousness about course work. We commend you for doing university-level academic work in a second language because it *is* an impressive feat. You may find the sciences (where there is a bit more memorization) or mathematics (with the international language of numbers) somewhat less challenging than courses that require a lot of reading or writing. We've heard many bright international students say that the amount of reading in their political science courses is insurmountable, and that writing papers for their English courses is harder still. While you might instinctively want to avoid the humanities entirely, general education requirements probably won't let you. And should you figure some way around those requirements, it would be unfortunate for you to go through college without having written a full English paper. Even if you shape your courses toward a more technical degree, find manageable ways to challenge yourself: look for at least one course to challenge you on your reading and writing, and schedule it strategically during a lighter semester. We suggest this same approach for domestic students.

WHAT YOUR PROF THINKS OF GRADING STANDARDS

As if the quantity of reading material were not enough, international students seem to be particularly surprised to learn that they are held to the same standard of writing as domestic students. In other words, a professor expects that an essay you write will be written with the same clarity, accuracy, and insight as that of a domestic student, to the extent that if the paper were turned in anonymously, the professor wouldn't know simply by the writing style whether the student was domestic or international. That seems unfair. After all, as an international student, you face a greater challenge in writing than domestic students do simply because you are not a native speaker (or writer) of English.

Okay. The professor may not fully expect perfection, but she will likely demand it—meaning, she will likely give little to no grace or grade advantage to the nonnative English speaker.

Consider it from your professor's vantage point. Her job is to educate. By awarding you a grade for her course, she is, in essence, testifying to the world (with her name on the line) that you are a certain caliber of student and have been educated to that level. Group four years of professors and courses and grades together into an American degree and your institution is putting its reputation on the line, saying you are capable of functioning in an American university at a particular level and that the grades you received are representative of all students from your university. As tough as it is for *you* to be held to the same standard as the domestic students, in actuality that immovable bar is fair for all.

> Find manageable ways to challenge yourself: look for at least one course to challenge you on your reading and writing, and schedule it strategically during a lighter semester.

If professors are willing to lower the bar for you, it weakens the authenticity and respectability of the system. The good news for you is that universities have accepted and graduated international students for decades based upon the merit of their work; those who have preceded you have successfully competed at the same level and done well, and your university would not have admitted you if they didn't believe you could do the same. Many campuses have English as a Second Language

(ESL) offices, which specialize in helping nonnative English speakers navigate language comprehension challenges.

Profs are not ogres. Most recognize the challenges you face, and will be willing to work with you during office hours (or have their TAs give you some extra assistance) to make sure concepts are clear. Since office hours are available to all students, this is not an unfair advantage but is a way for you to get extra help.

> Frequently we [international students] will commiserate about the challenges our peers and professors have understanding us through our various accents. In my case, my accent is very heavy and sometimes it makes me not want to talk. My accent has nothing to do with my intelligence, and even with much practice, it is very hard to overcome. Some of my American friends have been very encouraging, though. From the first time I met them, they acknowledged my accent, saying "the way you speak is so cool." I think they realized how embarrassing it is to have someone say "I don't understand you" time and again. That they were patient and willing to understand me through my accent made me want to be their friend.
>
> **Joshua—sophomore, Duke U**

WHAT YOUR PROF THINKS OF OFFICE HOURS

While we're on the topic of office hours, on average we recommend that you take advantage of them more than domestic students, especially if you're enrolled in a course with a heavy reading load. Office hours are a great way to be certain you understood the material from the lecture. Meeting with your professor during office hours may potentially help you understand the final exam structure early enough in the term so that you can begin studying with the exam in mind even in the first few weeks of class.

That said, we recognize that office hours are beginning to fade out of existence. While we still highly recommend the value of a face-to-face conversation (especially for nonnative English speakers, since much can be lost or misunderstood in email), we encourage you to speak with your professor in whatever modes or media he makes available. Request a meeting if he does not offer office hours, and if he (and his TAs) are unwilling to do either, find any way to talk with him that you can. At a minimum, you can always approach a professor at the end of lecture. Even if the professor is unable to stay behind to talk then, you at least can ask him face-to-face for a chance to meet again.

Let's be explicit: professors expect you to have questions. A contented mind is rarely a learning mind. As any student—domestic or international—encounters new material, that material raises questions, inspires discoveries, and hopefully provides answers. True, your professor will expect you to ferret out as many answers on your own as you can, but if you can't determine the answers or potential answers (which happens to all of us), ask for help. Questions are not viewed in America as a sign of weakness. A student with questions is seen as one who wants to do well, one who wants to master the material, and one who strives to learn it properly.

In our experience, international students tend to show up as the outliers in professor/student interactions. Either they are painfully shy or they don't read cultural cues and nonverbal communication with much accuracy and as a result come across as pushy, and crowding the professor's personal space. The remedy, of course, is to be sensitively aware of what your typical tendency may be and to try to balance it accordingly.

WHAT YOUR PROF THINKS OF SEMINARS VS. LECTURES

While international students often see their relationships with their professors as their greatest hurdle, where we notice a more important (and often unrecognized) challenge is during class discussions. It is not uncommon for international students to assume that, as long as their test scores and essays are up to par, it doesn't really matter how often they speak up in class. While that may be true of larger courses, it is not the case with seminars.

"Oh good," you might be saying to yourself, "then I'll just avoid seminars." Before doing something drastic, please consider this point:

while it may be easier for you to hide in a lecture hall, seminars offer a unique, rewarding learning experience to engage with the material and your peers in a way you could not at home and, likely, will not be able to after college. (Oh, and by the way, seminars might be unavoidable if a certain number are required for graduation.) Professor Marley has taught courses on international law with transfer and international students in the mix and notes that their involvement has made the classroom experience that much richer. In fact, during a section on copyright law, Ling, a student from China, was able to offer a truly unique perspective that Marley admits he could not. Bonus points for Ling.

Part of the reason you may find discussion seminars to be so daunting is the free-flow structure of the course conversation; this may be very different from the learning format used in primary and secondary education in your home country. For many international students, it's a new way to learn. Consequently, many international students stop contributing or only contribute marginally to classroom discussion. As a result, they rarely speak during the seminar because they are waiting for the perfect moment in the conversation to present their ideas; sometimes that moment never comes.

Our key suggestions concerning seminars are these. First, if the structure of a seminar is new or overwhelming, tell your professor about this at the beginning of the course. Ask her to help you identify themes in the material that you should look for as you read so that you can make thoughtful comments in your notes and have more material for discussion. Second, having read the material and prepared your notes—not so you can read from your notes, but so that you will feel more confident when you *do* speak—ask your professor to call on you, if it seems as if you are being too quiet. Please understand, we are not suggesting that you put *your* responsibility to participate onto the professor. You should still attempt to join the discussion as often as you can, and hopefully having thought about the themes in advance will help you do that. At the very least, the prof will know you want her to prod you a little when it seems you are disappearing from the discussion.

Relational expectations from our professors are a challenge. Whereas in my former school system professors were unreachable and the relationship was very formal, here it is completely different; I am expected to meet my professors for coffee and debate ideals openly. Additionally, back home, asking questions was a sign of intellectual weakness or a lack of studiousness, and yet in American schools, the smartest student is the one who asks the most questions in class. It has taken me a bit of time to subscribe to that philosophy of education, but I can wholeheartedly say I now do. Of course, it is one thing to agree that I should ask questions in class and hang out with my professor, and an entirely different thing to feel comfortable doing so.

Joshua—sophomore, Duke U

WHAT YOUR PROF THINKS OF PLAGIARISM

While you may have absolutely no intention of plagiarizing or committing any academic dishonesty, the rules that apply in America may not be the same as those that apply back home. As a result, you will need to learn what academic honesty means in the American education system. (See chapter 7 for more on academic honesty.)

Failure to take this matter seriously can lead to disastrous consequences. We know of one case where a group of international graduate students from Asia were caught cheating on an exam for business school. They saw their "collaboration" as nothing out of the ordinary, but the university disagreed sharply and there were serious consequences. Some were even expelled from the university.

You can do three things that will help you in the area of academic honesty. First, attend your university's orientation session on plagiarism at the start of the school year. Second, if you are struggling with any sort of assignment that should be original (such as writing an essay), ask your professor and TA for help before asking anyone else. Third, avoid peer help on what is expected to be original work. There is often an inclination, particularly among Asian international students, to work in teams and to support each other. And, at times, the whole notion of attributing credit to someone is somewhat foreign—it's a very practical difference between cultures. While that peer support is good from an emotional standpoint, we suggest you use extreme caution in helping each other with assignments.

A study group is quite different from unauthorized collaboration. Generally, being part of a study group means that you are studying together, such as quizzing each other, clarifying class notes, and anticipating what might be on a test. This is generally permitted and encouraged. Collaboration, on the other hand, normally refers to students helping each other to complete an assignment, such as a test, paper, or lab report. Ultimately, students should follow the instructions given by their professors. If the professor indicates collaboration is not permitted, then students need to complete assignments without anyone else's input or assistance. It doesn't matter if you are the helper or helpee; the university will hold you both responsible. A good rule of thumb is this: when in doubt, ask a prof.

What's That Necktie Doing on the Doorknob?
Culture Shock, American-Style

Americans are strange. They have an uncanny preoccupation with personal space, they tend to own a shocking amount of clothes, and they are likely to be the loudest talkers in any crowd. And if they meet someone who does not understand English, they will respond by speaking even louder. We've heard we're an odd bunch, and now you are living surrounded by that strangeness 24/7. It will make for a good novel someday, no? In the meantime, international students have shared with us some of their top culture-shock moments and advice on how to make the best of them.

SHOCKER #1: ALCOHOL

International students tell us they find domestic students unnecessarily focused on alcohol. While it may not come as a complete surprise (after all, you've seen American movies and you knew this was coming), the widespread use and celebration of booze seems a little ridiculous, especially to students from European countries where moderate consumption of alcohol is an unremarkable part of the culture.

That being said, in their attempts to make friends and join the culture, many internationals will take part in the "festivities" as freely as Americans. We've seen international students bungle their educational dreams too easily when alcohol comes into play; no one has a free pass to drink underage, not even if you are able to do so in your home country legally.

We talk a fair bit in chapter 5 about setting personal standards before arriving on campus, and that advice applies to you twice as much. Since even the simplest things about your daily life in America— from food to colloquialisms to fashion—will be foreign to you, it's key that you identify your goals, preferences, and personal limitations *in advance*. Just because the Americans are doing it doesn't mean you're missing out on the college experience if you don't. A big part of your happiness on campus will result from having a sense of self-respect and being secure in your values.

SHOCKER #2: FOOD

Hamburgers and pizza are great, but if you're used to *nasi padang* or piping hot *gomen* for breakfast, you'll be sorely disappointed at the campus eatery. No matter how cosmopolitan the setting of your university, it's unlikely that your comfort food will be offered (and even if it is offered by name, it likely won't taste the same since the ingredients won't be completely authentic). Again, this is where the international house comes into play. Frequently the house will open itself up in the evenings so students can congregate to cook and share meals. You might also take advantage of any opportunity to give feedback to the dining hall staff. They are often willing to occasionally add students' favorite foods from home to the menu.

SHOCKER #3: HOLIDAYS

Who knew that the campus would become a ghost town so people could go home to eat turkey, snooze on the couch, and watch football? It's true that during winter break, spring break, and potentially Thanksgiving break many campuses have major parts of their dorms and buildings locked up for security purposes. But if flying thirty-six hours to get home for the weekend sounds unreasonable, what are you supposed to do? Check with your resident faculty early on to see what your options are. With enough lead notice, sometimes they can arrange for you to spend holiday meals with families in the area who are connected to the university (and who very much enjoy opening their homes to international students). Most campuses offer housing on a single part of campus and all students relocate to that point until classes resume. It's worth planning ahead; that way if your options on campus seem a little dismal, you have enough time to organize a road trip with a few other students to explore more of the US during the break.

SHOCKER #4: COMMUNITY SERVICE

It's one of the great dichotomies of American campus life—on Friday night freshmen are doing Jell-O shots till dawn in their dorms, and by Saturday afternoon they are volunteering at the local children's hospital. Sure, they drink, but they also give back. If you're looking for a positive way to get off campus, meet other students, improve your frame of mind, and help someone in need all in a single activity, community service can be a great opportunity. Your RF or RA will most likely know where to direct you to find more information.

SHOCKER #5: LOST IN TRANSLATION

The confusion here is less with speaking English and more in understanding the nonverbal cues that are rarely discussed in textbooks and vary from culture to culture. A finger raised in one nation means an entirely different thing than a finger raised in another (depending on the finger). Even more enigmatic is the sigh, the pause, the step back or forward, the tongue click—how do you read those? Why don't people just say what they mean?

It's hard enough to understand what your professor means by "sure," but what about the girl you've taken a liking to who sits two rows over in class? Dating someone from a country different from your own can be a very rich relationship. Of course, those differences also require a special measure of thoughtful communication around what you (and your special someone) are expecting from the relationship.

Strive for the best verbal communication and rely as little as possible on the nonverbal. You might also want to pay special attention to the sexual harassment lectures during orientation so you can calibrate the university's expectations and laws with those of your home country. Each country has its own definition of verbal abuse, domestic violence, and consent for engaging in sexual activity, and it is wise to know those laws ahead of time. Summed up, the laws emphasize that parties should be freely and willingly participating in whatever sexual activity is taking place. What's very important to keep in mind is that someone cannot *legally* consent to sexual activity if she is intoxicated. Your RA will have more information and specifics to guide you through your university's dating rules and state's dating laws if you ask.

"It's a Small World after All"
Building Campus and Alum Networks to Your Benefit

That little jingle becomes truer with each passing decade. Thanks to globalization, you may meet someone at college and ten years later find yourselves working together on the other side of the world. Whether or not you are pursuing an international relations degree, you can almost bet on seeing many of your college classmates again.

Even if you plan to return home after graduation, your undergrad years are a fantastic opportunity to develop a network of friendships and acquaintances that you can foster in the coming years. Most major foreign corporations are international, and given your experience in the States, you will likely be called upon to mingle with American foreigners in your own homeland. Then you play the name game of "Do you know so-and-so" and the world becomes a whole lot smaller in a hurry. Building upon these networks broadens your opportunities and career choices and also brings the far reaches of the world into your daily life, along with a variety of personal and professional possibilities. The more elite your academic degrees, the smaller the world becomes. Consider your networks one of the most valuable investments you can make as an undergraduate; do not neglect building and maintaining them.

That said, allow us to clarify further that we are not suggesting that you befriend people for the sake of their wealth or how much you think they can enrich your network or career. Get to know people for who they are, for their passions and goals, for their talents and gifts, and one day watch how your paths overlap in the most unexpected ways. There is always the intrinsic value of a new friend.

Your easiest personal connection on campus will be your roommate. While we generally caution students against devoting too much time to the roommate relationship, in this case we encourage you to get to know your roommate in the hopes of meeting other domestic students (assuming your university has paired you with one); in turn, introduce your roommate to any international friends you have made.

Be Sure You Try the Pecan Pie
Experiences Not to Miss While You're Stateside

The location of your university will determine an even greater number of experiences that you shouldn't miss than what we have listed here, but below are some surefire winners to start you off.

COMMUNITY SERVICE PROJECTS

Community service projects are a multifaceted experience. You get to meet new people unlike yourself with a common goal (and it makes small talk easy while you're all nailing siding or pulling weeds or digging ditches). You are able to get off campus and see more of the surrounding area (for free!). You potentially get some exercise. And, of course, you get the benefit of feeling good that you have helped someone else. A timeless bit of wisdom is that when you feel low or glum or sorry for yourself, do something nice for someone else—it gets your attention off yourself and improves your outlook on life.

TRAVEL

As much as your visa, time, and finances allow, travel. America is diverse in its flavors, seasons, natural beauty, accents, and people. New York, Dallas, and Seattle are all large cities but incredibly different places. Perhaps you can take a work-study job on campus to save money for one adventure per year. Or perhaps you can join a choir or dance troupe that tours the country as part of its regular schedule.

LOCAL COLOR

Explore the community outside of campus by going to local restaurants, performances, and even community libraries. Don't stay on campus all the time, if you can help it. But—and this is very important—explore safely. Be savvy about your environment. There are certain places to be and go and certain hours—alone or with others or not at all. Know them. Unfortunately, it is all too common for international students to be victims of robbery, so learn what you must do to stay safe. If you live off campus, take special care when leaving the lab or library at night. Most college campuses offer free self-defense courses that only take an hour or two as well as free escort services at night; couple that with some safety devices that fit on your key ring, and you're a less attractive target.

FAITH AND SPIRITUALITY

Many local religious organizations help international students and are eager to provide rides to and from the airport, move-in assistance, lodging for parents, and meals and accommodations over the holidays. Unfortunately many international students don't know this sort of community connection is available until they are near graduation, and as a result don't take full advantage of it. We discuss this more in chapter 4, and your religious resource center on campus as well as local churches will be able to supply you with more information.

Because of the extraordinary religious freedoms in the US, the influence of religion on culture both historically and currently, and the diverse array of belief systems mingling in America from all corners of the globe, it's worth checking out. It would be tragic for international students to come all this way and never step foot in a chapel, never have a conversation about faith with someone whose faith is different than their own, or never grab lunch with a rabbi or have dinner at a Christian family's house. Many religious organizations make an effort be available to university students and are eager to help if students express an interest.

> One of the biggest challenges my friends and I have had while in America is growing in our faith. We find our religions are modified in the United States, and, depending on the depth of those distinctions, that may make it difficult for us to make that faith our own while here. I encourage international students to meet with their campus faith leaders before making any assumptions about religion here. At times I have seen students avoid anyone from their religion on campus because they fear being corrupted by those who do not believe in the same way they do, and it has been a very isolating experience. My hope is you will be able to grow your faith even while you study here.
>
> **Joshua—sophomore, Duke U**

GUIDEBOOK

When all else fails, get a guidebook. If you're in a metropolitan city, get one specific to your city as well as your state. Read it carefully and strategically select a diverse offering of sights to take in.

Best of Luck on Your Journey

We find that many (though not all) international students view the college experience as purely academic and see the extracurricular side as frivolous. In contrast, the American philosophy of education, if summed into almost too neat a package, maintains that a great deal of education occurs *outside* the classroom, and sometimes this is the most *meaningful* element of an education. Life for international students is exhausting because nothing is simple: not conversations, with all those cultural nonverbal cues or accent issues waiting to trap you; not running an errand to the grocery, because all the labels and brands are different (not to mention the public transportation challenge of how to get there and back); not studying, because you're studying in a language that is not your own; not relaxing in your room, because you share it with someone very different from you. The list goes on. The heightened sensory nature of the international experience can be exhausting, but also exhilarating. Take it day by day. Every outing is an adventure, with lots to tell the folks back home. It's worth it. But when the adventure seems like more than you bargained for, give yourself a break. When you are overly tired, give yourself the freedom to sleep more. Your whole world is a classroom, and unlike your domestic counterparts, very little about your day is straightforward. Live it up. Pat yourself on the back. Be proud of yourself and this amazing adventure that you will spend the rest of your years remembering. We are confident you are capable of doing so with great success.

One of the reasons we selected Joshua from Zimbabwe to speak throughout this chapter on the challenges confronting international students is because of the strength of his personal academic choices.

His journey beautifully illustrates this notion of finding a balance—a megatheme of this entire chapter. After being identified as premed, Joshua came to the university early so that he could take the prep courses he needed to enroll fully in the fall. He readily admits that his accent is so thick that he is, at times, difficult to understand. He has a host family here that has been tremendously supportive of him, and he is absolutely committed to becoming a doctor. Since arriving in the States, he has grown to love basketball—a sport he was entirely unfamiliar with before he came. His greatest challenge since coming to the States is the food; when he first arrived, he lost twenty pounds simply because he found American food exceedingly strange. The university and the dining staff were able to take him off the meal plan so that he is now able to cook for himself, and he is much happier. He loves it here and says he would love to stay after graduation. He has not been home in the last year and a half since he arrived on campus, but as a result of reaching out to the community both on and off campus, he has been able to make a true home for himself here.

Joshua is a fantastic example of a student who has done all that we are suggesting in this chapter, and then some—he has maintained his identity while taking advantage of the culture of his new surroundings; he has challenged himself in his academics but not at the expense of exploring new sports and interests; he is applying for summer research fellowships at other universities to prepare for medical school, making full use of his free time on his student visa; he is developing relationships with university professionals, members of the community, and students both domestic and international. We respect him greatly for the way he is handling his college experience, and we think he is worth mentioning in the hopes that you will be inspired to do the same.

CHAPTER 9

"I've Never Needed Help Before . . ."

Navigating Campus Resources

The question of the hour is not "Do I need help?" but "What kind of help do I need and where can I get it?" The typical freshman arrives on campus having managed high school well and largely without professional help, and as a result assumes it's time to prove his independence by relying only on himself for the next four years. Then stress begins to pound away—deadline after deadline, decision after decision—until the pulls of campus life are enough to unhinge him. The result is often sleeping disorders, eating disorders, roommate conflicts, relationship issues, substance abuse, and personality dysfunctions.

Don't panic. And don't place your therapist on speed dial just yet. We're merely saying that it is common for students to be unaware of the scale of the challenges confronting them in college, and many fail to take advantage of the extensive professional help that is available.

Everyone in college needs help. In many cases, that help can be provided informally by the wise peer, the sympathetic prof, or the alert RA. Help could be as easy as getting some advice on how to balance a tough course load, how to use search engines properly for research, or what not to wear to the Bare-All Ball at Halloween. Then again, you could take an unforgettable weekend course on study tactics that changes your college career. Or you may find you need some more structured help, such as personality or interest tests at the career center, or a session with a counselor to suggest strategies for managing stress or to provide a listening ear while your parents work through a rough patch. Alternatively, getting outside help could be less about you and more about learning how to support your roommate who may be fighting depression.

It comes back to getting the best out of the resources available to you. This sort of help comes once in a lifetime—for free, anyway—and it comes at a critical moment in your personal development. Since they're part of the cover charge you pay as tuition for the next four years, you should get your money's worth here as well.

Better Late than Never?
When Help Is No Longer Helpful

Though it may be true that any help is better than no help, we've found that all too often students who get help get it too late. The dreaded F (or even dropping out) can usually be traced to an earlier denial of the need for timely help. Students who get help early rarely see their situation get worse. In fact, it's so rare that, after over fifty combined years in the biz, we could probably name from memory the times that has happened. When in doubt, get help sooner rather than later. Crossing your fingers and hoping things will pan out works about as well as pixie dust.

It is common for students to be unaware of the scale of the challenges confronting them in college, and many fail to take advantage of the extensive professional help that is available. Everyone in college needs help.

Needing help takes a lot of different forms. Certainly, we could start off with flashier topics like depression or eating disorders, but those are fairly easy to spot. If you are in the midst of one of those scenarios, you probably know it and should get help immediately. What is harder to get a handle on is why you can't seem to pass stats class even though you aced math in high school and you're working your tail off. So let's start with that one: feeling clueless.

INTERNAL STRESSORS

What typically happens in the first week is that a student, such as Cassie, will feel a little confused and may not understand the material. The second week she is a little more distracted and confused, but she has a lot on her plate, so she doesn't want to talk to the prof just yet. After all, the F-wave on the normal curve—which right now sounds like a lot of gibberish—might just start to make sense come Friday. Cassie doesn't want to look like an idiot by needlessly running to the prof for help. This is college. It is supposed to be challenging. The third week comes, the fourth week goes, and Cassie decides she may as well hold on to see how the midterm pans out. Who knows, it could be that she's being too hard on herself and that everyone feels just as lost, and so she will beat the curve (see, she *does* understand *some* statistics). Of course, it takes two weeks to get grades back since the class size is over a hundred students, so by the time Cassie gets her grade the semester is half over.

And it isn't pretty. The midterm confirms that she Doesn't Know What She's Doing with a big D+. Strangely enough, even at this point a remarkable number of students in Cassie's situation don't ask for help. Cassie figures she'll make it up on the next midterm, or she'll encounter some magical elf who helps her ace the final. Of course, by this time she is fully engaged in the rest of collegiate life, so she has a whole lot of other pulls on her time. The futility of this exercise becomes apparent when she sits down to study a few days before her final and doesn't even know where to begin. Desperate emails to the prof and TA ensue. We'll spare you the crash ending, save to say that there is very little the prof can do at this point to bail her out. She's in too far over her head. Had Cassie approached her prof during the second week of class, she could have arranged for a tutoring session or met with the TA or worked out some solutions with the prof during office hours. At least she would have been able to demonstrate to the prof that she cared and that she was trying diligently to improve her performance.

This same story can be retold for group projects that go awry or research papers that write themselves into a brick wall five pages away from the minimum requirement.

Most of the problems you are likely to face in college are easier to solve the sooner they are confronted. The earlier you seek help, the sooner you can go back to not needing it.

Whether or not you have proof that you're flunking the class or flailing helplessly, if you are feeling stressed about the course, always approach the professor first. Sometimes he is part of the problem. We have known enough professors in our time to know that some have unrealistic expectations of how much their students can either manage or comprehend, so it's best to provide at least one data point on his radar that says, "Hey, this isn't working for me." With enough data points, the prof might *hopefully* get the message. (We did know of one ogre who insisted on teaching grad-level stats to his first-year undergraduate statistics class. The fact that his office hours were bursting at the lintels with scads of confused and panicky students delighted him. He was one of those unusual sorts of academics who took a perverse pleasure in making others squirm in their ignorance—but this type is a rarity.) Of course, the shoe fits on the other foot, too. We're assuming you're keeping up your end of the bargain and at least cracking the book nightly before attempting to tell the professor that his expectations are unreasonable.

> Most of the problems you are likely to face in college are easier to solve the sooner they are confronted. The earlier you seek help, the sooner you can go back to not needing it.

As a general rule, professors are in the business to educate, so they won't be surprised if somewhere along the way to becoming smarter someone gets confused. That's a natural part of learning. They won't lose respect for the student who approaches them early feeling lost. Sometimes profs will suggest that the student come back in a week or two to see how he is managing the material. Despite what it may feel like, it isn't a brush-off. The prof is most likely tracking the student's progress and wants to give another week for the information to seep in.

Where a student *is* guaranteed a professorial brush-off is when the professor recommends he do A, B, and C and he doesn't—and then comes back a week to six weeks later wanting the prof to spend one-on-one time explaining more.

In the unlikely case the student has done all that the professor asked but the professor still ignores her requests for help, the student should pursue other options. Out of frustration, she may want to focus all her energies on red flagging this prof to some academic council. While that would leave her with a feeling of satisfaction come the end of the semester, the time-sensitive prioritization is for her to focus on learning the material first and organizing a picket line later.

EXTERNAL STRESSORS

We know we mentioned this earlier in chapter 6, but it bears repeating: academic challenges can be exacerbated by personal challenges. If you have a personal emergency on your hands that will most likely last the semester and cause significant distraction, the time to tell the prof about it is now when she can help—not two days before the exam (unless, of course, the emergency occurs two days before the exam).

It's true that profs can sometimes seem jaded about personal emergencies, so be prepared to overlook some rolling of the eyes or a huffed sigh or two if you begin the conversation with "I can't turn in my paper because . . ." It's a standard but true joke among profs that there is a rash of plagues that seem to strike students right around exam time. We knew one professor who had a student tell him that he was in the midst of a crisis and couldn't focus on his work because his high school girlfriend had just dumped him. Fortunately for him, the prof felt empathy for the poor guy since at one point ages earlier he too had been dumped by a girlfriend and remembered it feeling like a cataclysmic disaster. Still, there were real limits to what the prof was going to do for him given the nature of the situation. The professor was able to work with him and his group-project colleagues (this was the real problem—it turned out the student was totally leeching off his group) to develop a solution to their group sharing problem, so this remained only a romantic disaster and not a romantic *and* an academic disaster. So don't waive the possibility of getting help just because you think the prof won't understand. He was young once, too.

It is an increasing phenomenon that students enroll with medical problems that warrant some special treatment within the classroom. It is so common, in fact, that there is an official procedure for getting a letter from the dean to the professors explaining the need and parameters for getting help. If you think your illness qualifies, be sure to get the letter at the *start* of the semester so your professors can alter assignments or exams; it doesn't work so well as a "get out of jail free" card if you dawdle until finals week.

Most profs will honor this sort of alteration, but there will be a range of opinions on the matter. In the last few decades, many more students have been diagnosed with learning disabilities of all forms, and while there is debate about how much help students should receive, most professors tend to agree that some help is warranted.

It is critical to have this understanding settled as early in the semester as possible. If the prof is not amenable to assisting you and you don't think you can make the class work without her help, take another class. Also, you should not use the letter to enroll in a class where your point of weakness is one that most students will be required to employ as their greatest strength. For example, if you are dyslexic, you may want to avoid taking Shakespeare: Every Play He Ever Wrote—in One Semester, since the prof will be less likely to cut you a break after being up front about the unique requirements of the course.

Too frequently students either obsess about their progress (or lack thereof) or ignore it; finding a balance is an art form. If you tend toward the panicky side of things, limit the frequency with which you dwell on the topic; of course, if you lean toward denial, you may need to devise a regular kick in the rear.

Either way, a good yardstick is to track your progress closely up until the second or third week of the course and then to speak with the professor if all is not well. Most minor kinks will have worked themselves out by that time, and if they haven't, then there is good reason to look into it.

It's Hard to Find Good Help These Days
Knowing Where and How to Look

No man is an island, but some people sure try to fake it. Don't be one of them. Admitting your shortcomings and seeking a solution are some of the surest signs of maturity out there. There is someone sitting at her desk right now waiting to help you, and you couldn't give yourself (or her) a greater gift than to knock on her door.

The question is how to find that door. It may seem a little like hunting for the White Rabbit, so here are a few guides you can query for suggestions (no, one of them isn't the Eat-Me box of doughnuts—sorry).

YOU KNOW YOU'RE IN TOO DEEP WHEN . . .

- You've stopped attending class because you "don't get it anyway."
- You treat every decision on campus as your most important decision.
- You believe every prof who tells you that his class is the most important one.
- You notice that you're failing, but you keep doing what you were already doing (with a bit more intensity, perhaps) and actually expect a different result. This is a pretty good definition of insanity.
- You insist you don't need help, even though it's clear to those around you that you do.
- Whenever you are blue or stressed, you go home for the weekend to see Mom and Dad (as opposed to going home for the fun of it).
- You drink large quantities of alcohol on a regular basis, but believe you can quit anytime because you have quit lots of times.

PROFESSORS

It might seem that professors would have their fingers on the pulse of campus resources, but unless the problem is an academic one (and even then . . .), don't be surprised if they don't know where to send you. By all means, ask your professor for help if you think he might be able to point you in the right direction; just don't give up if he grins goofily and tells you he's never heard of that service being offered on campus. A good professor may turn out to have great life advice, but he was hired to be an expert in his subject matter first and foremost, and likely was given very little formal training on being a campus guide.

RESIDENTIAL STAFF

A better guide is your Residential Advisor (RA) or even your Resident Faculty (RF). RAs and RFs are specifically trained to make referrals, whether for personal issues or academic ones. If your need is most definitely an academic one, your Academic Advisor may be able to give some guidance as well.

COUNSELING CENTER

Virtually every college has some level of counseling available to students, whether it be for something serious like having hallucinations and suicidal thoughts, or something less serious but still critical like managing stress or the blues. The most important thing for you to know—next to the point that this counseling is almost always free—is that anything you say during professional counseling is confidential. It's so hush-hush that not even the faculty or the dean can find anything out. Unless you sign a waiver that you are willing to release your records, the counseling center can neither confirm nor deny whether you are *even being seen* by them. So please don't let pride keep you from getting help.

It is extremely important to remember that even though you are on an academic campus, the resources available to you are not purely academic. When I came to college, I had a boyfriend. We tried the long-distance relationship but broke up after a couple months. It was a rough time for me and the effects could be seen in my schoolwork. Being away from my high school friends and family didn't make it any easier. I wish I had known then that the counseling center could have helped me with this kind of personal issue.

Helen—sophomore, U of Chicago

ADMINISTRATION

If your challenge is big enough that it requires help across two or three offices on campus (such as mediation with your professor plus counseling), the dean of students will be the person to coordinate that. In most cases, you can even speak with an administrator and invoke this level of confidentiality, though be forewarned that if you speak with an administrator about issues involving harassment by anyone on the faculty or about incidents of sexual misconduct involving you or any other student, he is required to act upon that information. You are welcome to discuss as many hypothetical situations as you like, but he is legally bound to involve the appropriate people should he learn of any alleged misbehavior going on in the faculty or the administration. So should you or someone you know need to discuss this sort of situation without automatically launching it into a legal issue, you may want to set up an appointment at the counseling center since your counselor will still be able to fall back on client-counselor privilege.

While it's better to use the confidentiality as a crutch if you aren't willing to seek help otherwise, the best scenario is to find help and to free those professionals to talk with other key people in your life. Confidentiality, though well intended, can sometimes keep information from the people who are best positioned to help—like professors—or those who could at least keep the situation from being exacerbated.

A CASE IN POINT

Shock of all shocks, one newly minted freshman began the fall of her college career by learning she had a heart condition that required surgery. Becky had otherwise been a healthy, active individual, so this came as quite the surprise. Not knowing there were campus services available to help, she spent the remainder of the semester in a pharmaceutically induced fog (required to keep her heart rate down) that made walking across campus, not to mention late nights of studying, difficult. What she *should* have done was talk to her AA, RA, professors, or dean about her health situation, but she was one of those independent sorts who figured she could just take care of it herself. At least she had the common sense to notify her professors in January that she would be undergoing heart surgery and would be missing a few days of class.

What came as an almost greater shock to Becky than her diagnosis was when one of her professors claimed that her surgery was an inappropriate reason to falter in class and that it was in her best interest to return to class within the next week. Out came the tears. Becky was appalled, exhausted, and frustrated, so she went to her RA to explain the situation, more out of need for a listening ear than looking for a solution. (She still didn't see the need to ask for help.) He connected the dots for her, and in less than a day Becky met with a dean who provided support for the remainder of her recuperation, handling whatever communications with professors were necessary to keep them abreast of her recovery and to ease her back into her course work.

Admittedly, it would have been a whole lot simpler if she had gone to the RA in the first place—back when she noticed she was falling behind in class. This is not to condemn Becky—she's a good friend of ours and this is nothing she wouldn't say herself. In fact, she's kicking herself right now that her self-reliance cost her as much as it did in her GPA since she didn't ask for any extensions or leeway that first semester. You don't need to be diagnosed with a congenital heart condition to ask for help; any genuine challenge that may affect your college career is worth asking about. Take Becky's word for it.

CAREER CENTER

Since it bears repeating, let us say it again: you don't need to be ill to get help. The writing center might have a Saturday session that takes you to the next level in your essay-writing abilities. The career center offers various tests (Myers-Briggs, for example) that may help you understand yourself and your strengths and interests better. Then there's a whole range of help available for goal setting. Thinking of a career as a lawyer? Talk to a law school dean. It is a sign of mental fortitude and an indication that you are working through the system appropriately to ask for this kind of help. Anne was startled to discover one of the smartest students in her class at Stanford was actually taking a speed-reading course so he could work through literature faster than he already did. His forethought was a sign of just how smart he was.

On this note, one graduate bemoans, "I didn't know there were courses on writing research papers or study skills at my university until the end of my freshman year. I'm sure it had been advertised on one of the DOZENS of colored flyers I received during orientation—it was just too much to process in the beginning and I forgot about it. Woulda, coulda, shoulda. I wish I had sat down with my RA as well as my advisor during the first couple of weeks of college life and asked for the lowdown on all the extras so I could have taken advantage of them." Us too.

> I never needed much help academically in high school or in college, so I lacked familiarity with campus resources; consequently, when it came to finding and applying for an internship I found myself in uncharted territory. The feeling that I was not in control stressed me out until a close friend turned me on to the career center. The staff there were amazing! They helped me with my resume and cover letter and even walked me through a mock interview. I felt so much more prepared because of their help, and learned invaluable tips that were essential in procuring the best internship possible.
>
> **Lauren—sophomore, Northeastern U**

PEERS

The final word on getting help is that if you are going to rely on your informal network of friends (as most students do), be sure you get help from people you trust. The most challenging of trials can cause a person to lack judgment or behave desperately, so choose your loyal listener carefully and with discretion.

Early on, students look solely to their peers for help—and some of the best support does come from them—but it's often difficult for peers to handle delicate information properly. It's not that their judgment won't be sound, though that should also be a consideration, but that they may not know how to handle the information confidentially. It only takes one sentence and your secret is out.

If the stressor is one you'd like to keep secret, be discreet until you know a person well (say, at least a year) and you've had a chance to hear how well he handles *other* people's private information.

"Won't It Hurt My Chances for a Good Rec If I Tell My Prof I Got Help?"

We mentioned earlier that profs aren't professional counselors, but that's not to say that you shouldn't tell a prof *generally* about what's going on behind the scenes. Admittedly it does change the way she thinks about the student, but that is a welcome improvement over her perception of a student who clearly needs help but seems too proud or lazy to seek it out. Of course, this is also much better than believing a student is simply an academic slacker when there really is an underlying problem. You sacrifice something when you acknowledge a problem, but you sacrifice far more if you try to hide it and hide it poorly.

A possible way to salvage your pride is to include a success plan in the conversation. When sitting down privately with your professor to discuss your entanglements, show him you are doing your best to work free of the issue by mentioning some personal boundaries or deadlines or goals you are working toward. There's no need to go into great detail about your troubles, but you will want to outline the solution as a way of earning your prof's trust.

To be more specific, if you struggle with any and all sorts of organization and feel lucky to have found a pair of matching socks to wear today, tell him that you have an appointment with an academic counselor to design a more efficient work plan so that you will be able to stay on top of your assignments in class. Or if you are burdened by a personal tragedy that is so weighty it makes course work seem irrelevant, explain that you have backed out of a course to ease your load and are seeking counseling to prove you are giving your all to succeed in class despite the chaos. By making your perseverance clear, they will most likely be happy to lend support.

"Okay, So How Do I Prevent Myself from Needing Help?"

Since your best bet is to catch a need when it is still small, here are a few sanity-check questions to ask yourself.

DO YOU HAVE A HISTORY OF TROUBLE WITH _____?

Most problems that show up in college could be anticipated before college. If you had a problem in some area when you were in high school, chances are the stressors of college, and your underdeveloped support network on campus, will only magnify it. As we've shown in this chapter, support of some kind is certainly present on campus; it just requires more initiative on your part to get it.

HAVE YOU HAD AN ANNUAL CHECKUP IN THE LAST YEAR?

On a preventative health note, many student health services across the country include an annual physical exam for men and women as part of their campus health-service fee. It's a pretty great service, and taking advantage of it will be the start of a great habit. You may also want to take advantage of various health education classes offered on campus—don't worry, they will probably be much more practical than the ones you took in high school. These classes show how health today will impact your quality of life down the road with topics on nutrition, sexual lifestyle, exercise, stress reduction, and supporting family members with chronic conditions.

HAVE YOU STARTED YOUR PORTFOLIO?

Another service you should take full advantage of is the opportunity to build a portfolio at the career center or in the prelaw, premed, or pre-business advisor's office. The portfolio is simply a file about you that is kept at the career center and filled with letters of recommendation and other evaluative information that can be sent to prospective employers or graduate schools. Once established, most colleges will keep records of this portfolio until you request otherwise. Copies of relevant test scores, letters of recommendation, and career searches will all be kept on file for you. Whether you plan on being employed immediately after college or not, it's best to beat the rush and get your file started early.

DO YOU HAVE A TUTOR?

As we mentioned in chapter 7, by a certain point in the year it is not uncommon for a college to have completely run out of tutors. That means you're on your own if you wait until it's too late. It's a bit difficult to step over the ego and ask for help, but we've found that once students do, it becomes a habit, and they get their friends to sign up as well.

DO YOU HAVE A MENTOR?

A final (and quite successful) measure of help would be to find a mentor on campus who will help you strategize and anticipate your next few steps. A mentor doesn't need to be a hero, so it's not as though by choosing this person you're saying you want to *become* them. At the same time, try to choose someone you can identify with and respect, someone you click with personality-wise who can provide some support or help. It may be a professor, a coach, an administrator, or staff.

Everyone is busy and not everyone will be willing to be a mentor. The best thing to do is to ask the person up front to mentor you in a specific area, whatever that may be—carving a path through your major, providing some accountability in the party scene, helping guide you in some career or relationship decisions. That way, the person knows what's required of her and whether or not she can accept your offer. Better yet, aim to build a team of mentors, since it is rare that one individual has expertise in all areas, let alone the time.

Even if the sun is shining, life is smooth, and you are happy and confident, the best thing you can do to ensure the happy days will continue is to schedule an appointment in a campus resource center a few times each semester. We get our teeth cleaned, have our tires rotated, and take vitamins all on a regular basis—why not add campus help to that list?

> Having a mentor is really important. It helps to have someone who has your best interests at heart, is looking out for you, and is available when you need to talk things out. I had the good fortune of meeting a fellow Nigerian who was a junior when I was a freshman. Although we were in different majors, I admired how she had her priorities straight and knew where she wanted to be even though she hadn't quite figured out how to get there. I went to her whenever I had troubles with classes, friends, or extracurriculars, and she always had a wise word or two. Now she's in a master's program in Harvard and I am mentoring a freshman who reminds me of myself two years ago.
>
> **Onome—junior, Stanford U**

Cheer Up
Where to Find Your Happy Face if You Lost It

You aren't alone. Just because you don't understand everything on the first day doesn't mean that the admissions office has made a terrible mistake. In case someone hasn't already told you, that's a standard fear of college students. In fact, it's nearly universal, much like the dream about a class presentation in eighth grade on the day you forgot to wear your pants. Just because everything isn't immediately clear on the first day or even in the first week doesn't mean you shouldn't be here.

Admissions boards send out their thrilling acceptance letters based on the assumption that if students take advantage of the help provided on campus, they have the capability to thrive.

But college life isn't all about academics, now, is it? If you're feeling lonely or homesick, give yourself a break. Anyone who says they haven't been homesick is lying. Not all students leave a home that is supportive or nurturing, and most students actually come to college looking forward to leaving something behind. Even *those* students are homesick for something. The longing tends to wear off after the first semester once you've got some routines in place and feel more settled. If not, you know what to do.

No matter how much wisdom we may chuck your way, and no matter how much of it you actually swallow, some days in college are just bad days. It's pouring rain, you have no umbrella, you miss the bus, your computer crashes, you run out of money and can't buy lunch, and the girl said no. DON'T FREAK OUT. Just because you hit a rough patch of a few hours, days, or even a few weeks doesn't mean it will continue for the rest of your (what seems to be miserable) existence. Since your dad isn't here to say it, let us be the ones to hand you a mug of steaming sunshine and remind you to take one day at a time.

It seems that my university hosts just as many "resume-help fairs" as the cafeteria hosts lunches. For years all of the tents and tables set up on the student walkways seemed less of an attraction than an obstacle to me. At least that was the case until I graduated and applied for my first big-girl job and needed— wouldn't you know it—a polished resume. As I stared blankly at the screen, I wondered what I really needed to include on that list of personal accolades, I wondered what potential employers were looking for, and, mostly, I wondered why I did not attend one of those "resume-help fairs." Oops.

Rebecca—recent grad, Point Loma Nazarene U

CHAPTER 10

This Just Isn't Working

Delaying, Transferring, Studying Abroad, or Dropping Out

After writing the first edition of the book, we got a smattering of questions from students and parents about circumstances that rearrange the typical undergrad experience. Most of their what-if scenarios could be grouped under "Plan A isn't working; is it time for Plan B?" We have collected those questions here and added, for lack of a better spot, another very different departure from college—study abroad. Collectively they add up to a single idea: sometimes the way to get the best out of your college is simply to get out of college, at least for a while.

Delayed Entry

WHEN IS IT APPROPRIATE OR EVEN BENEFICIAL FOR HIGH SCHOOL STUDENTS TO DELAY ENTRY INTO COLLEGE?

More often than you think. Some eighteen-year-olds are ready to take full responsibility for their every action and decision, but there are many others who are not ready intellectually, emotionally, or financially. If we had to make an educated guess, we would suspect there are more students erring on the side of going to college too early than going to college too late.

Increasingly, students are delaying entry into college by a year or two; we see this as a positive trend. In England, this is called a "gap year," and it is a well-established custom.

The stress of getting good grades, padding the resume with interesting activities, drafting clever admission essays, filling out onerous financial aid statements, and visiting countless campuses to hear the same overly cheerful tour guides brag about their lives—all of this can leave a student drained. Sure, you are excited to get the big, fat envelope, but you are also likely emotionally exhausted and need a break.

Another contributor to many students' decision to leave school is the upward-spiraling costs of college and the downward-spiraling economy. Many families are discovering that they simply are not yet prepared for the financial burden of tuition.

Finally, some students are just not sure what they want out of college. They reason that it might be better to at least have a general aim before signing on for four years. Even if you are *very* ready to leave home (and Mom and Dad aren't too sad about the idea either), that doesn't necessarily mean you are ready to go to *college*.

Whatever the impetus, we tend to agree. College is a costly proposition and shouldn't be what high school seniors do next simply because high school is over. The gap year is not a negative; it's an alternative. And in many cases, it's a positive.

As a rule of thumb, we recommend that all students give serious thought to taking a gap year and that some students actually do, but here are a few of what we would consider to be good reasons:

> College is a costly proposition and shouldn't be what high school seniors do next simply because high school is over. The gap year is not a negative; it's an alternative. And in many cases, it's a positive.

You can't afford college. If you have exhausted all possibilities by speaking with financial aid officers at various universities and you still can't make the numbers balance, take a year off to work one to two jobs and live a very meager lifestyle in order to save enough money to enroll next fall. Delaying college for that purpose will make for a very rich experience, will help you value your education even more than the average freshman, and will enhance your educational narrative when you interview for your first job post-college and speak on the subject of dedication and being self-motivated.

You are burned out emotionally and intellectually. Yes, college can refire students who got listless by the end of high school. But we have seen the opposite happen too: a student arrives with little gas in his intellectual engine and quickly stalls under the academic and social pressures of college. Many of the crutches that propped up students and helped them hobble to the finish line in high school are absent in college (or are harder to access because they require student initiative). If you are already limping, take a year off to restore yourself.

You are immature. This is a hard one to assess on your own, as most people who are too immature for college are not mature enough to realize that fact. All we can say is if there is any doubt in your mind (or your parents' minds), take a gap year. The freedoms of college are heady stuff even for mature adolescents, but they have laid low many a first-year student who simply needed more time to grow up before jumping into the fray.

You have a very focused and narrow interest, and it is not well-suited to the schools you got into. One of us has a goddaughter, Tracy, who faced that very situation. She applied to Carnegie Mellon because of its unique program for directing plays that, in her estimation, is unrivaled nationwide. She didn't get in, though she did get into other schools with programs that were not as attractive. We advised her to take a year off and work; she was heavily involved in directing local community theater during that year and when Tracy applied a second time, she got in. That extra year made her a better actress and director and a more attractive candidate.

However, having played up the gap year, let us provide some perspective and balance. We are not saying that you shouldn't go to college until you know exactly what you want to do and have a detailed road map for every class, major, and extracurricular decision you need to make. That's hugely unrealistic. Some degree of uncertainty and apprehension is healthy, not to mention unavoidable. It is the incredibly rare student who accurately perceives the end point from the start of his undergraduate career. What we're suggesting is that you go to college in pursuit of something.

Your grand entrance into the college scene should not be determined by traditional age of entry (because your dad went to college when he was eighteen), by smarts (because academic intelligence doesn't equal social intelligence), or by your peers (because everyone else is leaving for college and you don't want to look like a flunky). It should be based on your individual ability to embrace the learning for what it is and encounter the challenges and opportunities of college with as much maturity and wisdom as can be hoped for in a freshman.

There is almost no stigma in taking a gap year. Once you are finished with college, no one cares when you started. If you have a good story for why you took a break—such as to save money or experience a 9-to-5 job without the benefit of a college degree—it can only help you. Just don't waste that year.

WHAT SHOULD I DO DURING THE GAP YEAR INSTEAD OF GOING TO COLLEGE?

If you are going to waste your year, you might as well waste it out of college, without paying the tuition or racking up Fs on your transcript. So in that sense, if you are going to blow it, blow it on a gap year.

That massive disclaimer aside, our vision for the gap year is something far more intentional than sitting on the couch mastering a fine array of consoles from Sony, Apple, and Nintendo.

The optimum plan depends on the reason for delaying entry. Tracy, who applied to CMU, used the time to beef up her acting and directing portfolio. What could you do with the time?

If finances are holding you back, the optimum plan is clearly to save as much money as you can. If you are in this situation, it really doesn't matter how prestigious your job is. This is not the career-marking internship we describe elsewhere in the book. Whatever piles up the tuition money the fastest—whether waiting tables, catching crab in Alaska, or nannying—is the job you should take. In fact, this kind of experience will likely yield a double benefit. It will improve your prospects for getting into a more prestigious college because you show the initiative and responsibility of managing your finances. And it will help you appreciate college more because you will get a taste of what jobs you would be eligible for without a college degree.

If you are burned out intellectually, a year of menial labor or, if you can afford it, stimulating international travel may be just what the doctor ordered to reenergize your fried neurons. We recommend that you assign yourself some quality reading during the interval so as not to get out of the academic groove altogether. We realize that *Catcher in the Rye* can be a drag if it is forced on you by your high school English teacher, but you might discover that a year spent reading the classics is fun when you are doing it just because you can.

If you are immature, the gap year can help you grow up. Heck, even if you are mature, a year in the "real world" can add some valuable wrinkles to your brow. The gap year enables students to take on some of the responsibilities and life skills a freshman would face—such as setting your own curfew and choosing how to eat and when to exercise—without the added pressure of academics.

For this to work, we recommend that gap-year students negotiate an arrangement with their parents that is different from high school. Tracy and her parents worked out a deal where they charged her partial rent during her year off in order to incentivize her to stay focused on the goal (and to keep her from staying home longer than she needed). While it may have been frustrating at the time, even that little bit of "tough love" gave her the extra push she needed.

We know of some students who have taken a gap year to work on a political campaign because they feel so strongly about a candidate or issue that they want to devote themselves to it completely. Others have taken the year to volunteer for some significant community service, such as Clark, who went to South America with his church during the fall semester to help take medical support and basic education to a village there. He wisely chose to delay for the entire year rather than enroll in the spring so that he could enter the university in the fall with an entire class of new faces.

Khalita's is another unique situation—she had an opportunity to dance with a professional dance company out of high school, so she delayed entry for that year and joined as a freshman with an incredible experience bolstering her confidence. The bottom line is that if there is something you want to explore—a profession or a culture or a way to give back—and it is within your means to do so and seems a wise use of time, go for it. College can wait.

It's important to note that while universities support students taking a gap year, there is no guarantee that if you have already been accepted by a particular college that they will let you defer without a significant reason, such as a unique learning opportunity, life experience, or health issue. If you ask to delay simply because you don't feel ready, they may ask you to reapply once you *are* ready. It's not that your future university is trying to punish you; it's that they want to be sure you will return to campus the following year as the best you can possibly be, and sometimes the best way for them to know that is to reevaluate you a year later . . . which leads us to our next question.

IF I DECIDE TO DELAY ENTRY, WHAT SHOULD I ARRANGE AHEAD OF TIME?

There are two schools of thought on when you should apply if you anticipate you may want to delay entry. (And this rests squarely on our first point that timing is really critical to the whole discussion of taking a gap year.) The first school of thought suggests that you go ahead and apply at the same time as your peers even if you expect to delay. The reasoning behind this suggestion is that your mind will be thoroughly entrenched in academics and you will have a support system of teachers and school counselors ready to help look over your application essays or SAT scores and give you advice. The challenge with applying before the delay, of course, is where the other school of thought comes in—that you're already burned-out and busy. It may be overwhelming to ask that you have your credentials perfect by fall of your senior year when your sophomore SAT scores may be horrendous and you're already challenged with staying on top of academics and extracurriculars without adding college tours and applications to the mix. Included in that is the possibility that, once accepted, the university may not approve your gap year request. Assuming you know going into your senior year that you'd like to delay entry into college for a year, consider skipping the application process entirely. Since the college that accepts you now may or may not be willing to allow you to delay, save yourself the headache and the double application fees!

If you decide to go the second route, be sure to get all of your letters of recommendation ahead of time (your high school counseling center should be willing to store them confidentially for an extended period of time once they understand you plan to delay). As for SATs and other tests, you will do better to take them while your mind is at its sharpest, so take them on a normal schedule, if possible, during your senior year. The scores tend to have a shelf life of a year or two, so do your research. Polish your senior year transcript so that once you do apply it will be clear that you finished high school at the top of your game. Even if your gap is spent burger flipping by day and babysitting by night to save money for books, that's a very respectable use of a year and one that will prove to colleges that you are serious about getting an education.

WHEN IS ENLISTING IN THE MILITARY A GOOD CHOICE, AND HOW DOES THAT RELATE TO THE COLLEGE EXPERIENCE?

The military has a sharp dividing line between the enlisted ranks and the officer ranks. Enlisted is roughly equivalent to blue collar and officer is roughly equivalent to white collar. The officers are in command of the enlisted, but there is a rigid hierarchy of senior versus junior within both. Historically, few in the enlisted ranks had a college degree (though that is changing), whereas almost everyone in the officer ranks had a college degree. There are a few exceptions, but generally you cannot start out as an officer unless you have a college degree.

The great strength of the US military is the quality of its personnel, especially the enlisted ranks. And the US government has found ways to try to repay those soldiers for their service. One important way is through the GI Bill, which provides funds for college and other post–high school educational opportunities to veterans who have served in the military. Another important program is the Reserve Officer Training Corps (ROTC) program, which recruits new officers by giving them partial college scholarships in exchange for their commitment to serve in the military for a given period of time.

Both of these pathways are time-honored ways to meet the costs of college tuition and to serve one's country. But there is a substantial difference between the enlisted and the officer experience. As valuable as the enlisted soldiers are, it's worth pointing out that officers enjoy higher rank, more perks, and, on average, significantly higher paychecks. Should you decide to join the military first in lieu of college, there is an opportunity to transfer from enlisted to officer once you have earned your college degree, but it isn't automatic and requires an extra measure of planning.

Beyond the financial incentives, the military is also an exceptional way to gain life skills. Indeed, it may be the absolutely fastest way to grow up. But it is not for everyone, and you should weigh the decision carefully. Nowadays joining the military means you will face life-and-death decisions not only in theory but also in practice. If you join, you should expect to be deployed to a war zone, no matter what your recruiting officer tells you. Joining the military is not even close to taking a job stocking shelves at Big Mart for a gap year; expect it to be the greatest physical and mental challenge of your life. We have a great deal of respect for those in the military and for the sacrifices they, and their families, must make on a daily basis: Anne worked as a contractor with the US Army in Seoul for two years and Peter served in the Naval Reserve for nine years. Because of our respect for those sacrifices, we believe you should understand the full picture of possibilities and choices before making a decision.

Transferring

IS ATTENDING A COMMUNITY COLLEGE A GOOD PLAN?

Many students decide to attend a community college (CC) for two years to save money and get grad reqs out of the way, and then transfer to a larger university for the last two years of college. The upside of this plan is that it is cheaper than doing the normal four years at a regular university. The CC experience can also be a valuable stepping-stone for students who don't feel academically prepared for a university experience and want to start a little slower.

The pattern of transferring from a community college to a university is more prevalent at large state schools, since they compete well for students whose financial situation requires a high degree of price sensitivity. A CC transfer can function quite well in a large school, as there are often many others in the same situation. Students find it more difficult to transfer into a small college because freshman year is a crucial time for forging bonds of friendship, and it becomes increasingly difficult to penetrate the culture off schedule.

Another critical difference in where you transfer is the exchange of classes. Transfer from a CC to a typical regional public university and you will find that the class size and quantity of prof interaction will not be that different; however, transfer from a CC to a typical liberal arts college and you will find yourself in a totally different world. The best fit depends on the individual. While one may be easier than the other, the harder option sometimes has a higher payoff.

WHAT ABOUT TRANSFERRING TO GET INTO A BETTER OR CHEAPER SCHOOL?

Bluntly put, we believe a move of less than ten or twenty spots on the ladder simply is not worth it. The measurements are not that precise and there is not enough difference between the fifteenth-best school in the US and the tenth-best school to warrant the costs associated with transferring. However, if you're in a school ranked seventy-five or lower and you get the chance to transfer to a top twenty school, that could make enough of a difference in your postcollege options to justify all of the disruption of moving.

Transferring to make college more affordable may make more sense. But first talk with a financial aid counselor on campus to be sure you have fully exhausted your resources, especially if you feel that your current school is a great personal fit for you. There are a lot of different possibilities with loans and, too frequently, students make assumptions about loans without first checking with the financial aid office.

We are more sympathetic to transfers driven by economic necessity than by transfers driven by personal unhappiness. The key to college happiness largely revolves around the decisions you make within your setting and the attitude you bring to campus, and is determined less by the setting itself. There is an old joke: the common denominator in all your problems is you. A lot of the problems that made you unhappy in school A will likely follow you to school B. Over the years, we've come to realize that students' "happy meters" are not determined by campus climate, eateries, or architecture. Students will notice them and campus guides will wax eloquent about them, but the primary influencers on students' well-being are relationships with their peers and professors, which you can more easily influence by changing your approach than by changing your address.

We know many successful transfer students (including Anne Crossman), but our general advice is to avoid transferring if possible. A lot of what you pay for with your college degree takes a solid four years to accrue; that experience is amputated when you divide your time between two institutions.

TRANSFERRING SEEMS LIKE A BIT OF A JUMP—WHAT RISKS DO I NEED TO BE AWARE OF BEFORE MAKING THE LEAP?

Above all, recognize that a college course is not a college course is not a college course. Every college jealously guards its curriculum, and every college has its own unique curriculum requirements. While a beginner French course will likely be viewed as interchangeable, an intermediate course in psychology may not. Swapping those credits will be difficult, and even if you earned distribution or grad req credit for the course at your original university, most likely you will not be able to use that course to meet those requirements at your new school. As a rule, colleges prefer *their* own courses and as a result will apply *only* their courses to their grad requirements, even if your courses were taken at a well-respected university.

We know of one student who transferred from one top ten university to another halfway through his undergrad career, not for academic but for personal reasons. Even though Jed had performed strongly in his sociology courses at University A, only a third of them were accepted for credit at University B. The great number of courses (and graduation requirements) that were not fully accepted had such a crippling effect on his transcript, in fact, that he was faced with the choice of starting over with his sociology degree or selecting a new major entirely. His list of accepted sociology courses was so puny that he couldn't even use them to earn a minor (and he was unable to take further courses to meet the minor requirements until he had first retaken all the introductory courses that he had taken at his previous school). It was devastating. All that money invested into courses that, in the end, didn't add up to a degree. Strangely enough, a few history courses he had taken on a whim transferred unscathed, so he decided to become a history major. As he puts it, he worked his butt off with course overloads for the next four semesters to graduate on time, taking whatever classes met grad requirements whether the professor was good or not; transferring came at a great cost to the quality of his academic and social life, but he pulled it off.

As in Jed's case, should you transfer halfway through your undergrad career, you will have only two years to complete your new university's graduation requirements instead of the usual four. As a result, you won't have the luxury of shopping for professors as much as you would have had if you had been at that institution for all four years—you will have to take what you can get, and do it fast.

So check with your destination school FIRST to make sure they accept the credits you are about to earn. They may not be able to give you a solid (that is, written) answer prior to transferring, but it's worth looking into. On the other hand, some large universities may be used to working with transfers from your school, in which case it may be easier to transfer credits.

Our final key point is to be aware that once you have transferred, your relationship with your first school will be substantially weaker than most alums. In some ways, you are a black mark on the roster, so if you need letters of recommendation for future interviews, you will want to secure them *before you tell your profs* you are going to leave, lest you plummet to the bottom of their priority list. It sounds harsh but in their eyes, if you aren't a graduate, you're a disgruntled customer.

WHEN IS TRANSFERRING THE RIGHT DECISION?

For some students, transferring is the best option. A good reason to transfer is if you have a focused academic interest you have discovered since exploring courses your freshman year, and you realize that it requires a specialized degree or training you have to pursue elsewhere. At this point, your interest in this program is not the wishful speculation of high school but is based on genuine college performance, which will help guide the authenticity of your decision. This was the case with McKenzie. She transferred from her state university to Duke during her sophomore year once she realized her engineering passions were leaning heavily toward biomedical engineering, a specialty offered at the undergraduate level at very few universities. For her, transferring was a sound academic decision and worth the social costs.

We see another benefit of transferring in the case of Dean, who made a hash of his life as a freshman by getting into all manner of academic and relational disciplinary trouble. Dean had earned himself an unshakable bad-boy reputation and needed to reboot; he took some time off to do some minimum-wage soul searching, then transferred to a new school, where he would no longer be associated with his mistakes from freshman year. Certainly his transcript and disciplinary history shadowed him and limited what universities were willing to take him, but that was something his peers never needed to know; for him, that social break made all the difference.

Leave of Absence

WHEN SHOULD A STUDENT TAKE A SEMESTER OR MORE OF LEAVE?

The textbook case is the student who comes in totally immature and academically unprepared. He spends too much time at the frat parties hugging the keg and doesn't realize how tough a final exam is, and at the end of his freshman year has less than a 1.0 average and the beginnings of an alcoholic dependency. A student of this ilk would benefit from taking his spring semester off in order to start fresh next year.

Another equally common reason is the student who, through no fault of her own, develops mono or some other illness in late September and misses a third of her classes. That student is probably better off taking a medical leave immediately and starting over in the spring or, better yet, the next fall with a batch of fresh classmates. A semester off for a major medical procedure is a no-brainer, and universities are very good at easing the transition so students can take as much time as they need. It is in everyone's best interest to have that student take time off and restart at full capacity.

In the case of an ill family member or divorce, it depends. We covered this in an earlier chapter a bit more extensively. Ultimately, if you are unable to focus adequately on your studies, it may be best for you to take a leave. The key here is that you not reason it out alone. All universities have very elaborate counseling programs to help students figure out the right answer for them to precisely these questions, so make an appointment with the dean of students at the first sign of diagnosis or separation.

Other reasons to take a leave are similar opportunities we cited earlier for students who decide to take a gap year. It's a fairly automatic right of return, but students will likely need to tell the school what they have been doing while they have been away.

Of course, there is one other big reason students withdraw. David took a leave from Stanford after his sophomore year to try his hand at a dream. He told us, "I took two years off during the initial dot-com flare to learn about start-ups—and to try to make my millions! It was one of the best things I've ever done. At one point, I lost direction at school because I was so enamored with the wider world. At the time, I was studying computer science, so when I left I used my education to see how programming is executed in the real world. By the time I got back to college, I had written hundreds of thousands of lines of code, had administered serious chunks of infrastructure, and knew that I loved everything about technology companies. As a result, when I returned I was intensely focused on the classes that mattered to me, and frankly I had a huge leg up on my classmates because I had *already* learned what they were *just now* learning in class." Were there any downsides to David's leave? Keep reading for part two of his story in the next section.

Should you decide to take a leave, discuss your options with your academic advisor or dean early on, as timing is key. With something unplannable, such as a medical leave of absence or personal trauma from the death of a close family member, the university is much more flexible in cutting through the restrictions.

WHAT ARE THE RISKS OF TAKING A SEMESTER OR MORE OFF, AND WHAT ARE THE BENEFITS?

Friendships, particularly in college, are a bit like sharks: they need to keep moving or they die. Among many opportunities in college, one is to develop intense friendships, but should you take a semester or more off, you will find those friendships are almost impossible to sustain if they are at college and you are not. Thus, one of the risks of taking leave is losing that close connection.

At the academic level, if you are pursuing a program that is heavily cumulative you risk losing momentum in your track. While you may be technically qualified to take third level Mandarin when you return, if you've been out for a semester, what you learned in second level Mandarin nine months ago will be fuzzy, at best.

One of the greatest risks, even with these two risks in mind, is that once students leave some don't return. David, the Stanford alum who eventually took seven years to complete his undergrad degree, agrees: "The risks are pretty clear. I met many, many people in the dot-com world who advised me, 'Whatever you do, GO BACK,' because they had dropped out and never returned. It's very hard to find a *convenient* time to return to college. You get hooked on making an awesome salary, and returning to paying and taking loans and making no money is pretty tough. There are lots of ways to get trapped in the real world, and it's easy to come up with excuses to never return. If you take a leave, don't make excuses. When you decide to return, do it no matter what the consequences."

WHAT CAN I DO TO EASE THE TRANSITION BACK INTO COLLEGE ONCE I'VE BEEN AWAY?

Whether you are leaving as the result of study abroad or a personal leave of absence, its best to anticipate a challenge in transitioning back to campus life. The challenge comes because both you and your friends have changed. If you used the time away wisely, you may have grown faster than your friends. Don't be surprised if, upon returning, you discover you have lost interest in some of the campus activities you previously enjoyed and are more engaged with the world beyond your dorm.

This transitional culture is significant enough that many universities have developed a debriefing program so that students returning from abroad can talk with other students about their time away and develop a new community with the shared interest of travel. Some study-abroad students have told us they actually feel more like a foreigner returning to their home campus than they did as an actual foreigner studying internationally, and many are not prepared for that reverse culture shock.

In the event that your leave had nothing to do with study abroad, be aware that the university may not have an elaborate system in place to help you transition back to campus life. As opposed to study abroad, taking a leave of absence is not something the university promotes widely. However, should you return and feel at a loss, there is always someone at the counseling center to help you reconnect.

> Some study-abroad students actually feel more like a foreigner returning to their home campus than they did as an actual foreigner studying internationally.

When we asked David about challenges he faced upon returning to Stanford, he agreed that his return was difficult: "That was really, really hard for me. When I came back, all of my friends had graduated. I had to start over, and the best way to do that seemed to be that I join a co-op where we cooked and lived together. It felt *really* weird to be a part of this at twenty-five when everyone else was nineteen or twenty. By the end of the first semester, I knew everyone in our co-op and they elected me to an officer position, so I felt like I was able to make a home for myself there."

The best advice we can give you upon returning is to be realistic. The university has changed—as have you. Try not to panic if campus doesn't feel like home for a little while, and stick with it.

Study Abroad

WHEN IS STUDY ABROAD WORTH THE TIME AND THE DIME?

Study abroad is very much a luxury item. It's like traveling internationally in business class—you all reach the same destination, but it can significantly improve your journey. Study abroad is particularly great for American students who, as a general rule, have less of a global perspective and yet are forced to operate in a world that is very globalized. If you've never been out of your suburb in the Midwest and you are going to school in a suburb in the South, you might really benefit from studying overseas for a semester, assuming you can afford it. However, if you are on a tight budget, study abroad is by no means a necessary thing. The world is filled with great leaders who are changing the world but didn't study abroad.

As you debate with yourself (and maybe your parents) the value of study abroad, our advice is to only do it if you can afford it comfortably. We find that the quality of the classroom and professor-interaction experience is actually weaker abroad, and you may experience the loss of other opportunities, such as losing touch with those professor relationships you were working so hard to forge back home, or a weakened involvement in clubs where you may have been seeking leadership positions. These are harder to pursue if you disappear for a semester (or two, once you add in summer as well).

If the decision is a close call financially, you can gain a lot of the study-abroad experience by doing internships in the summer at the State Department or a business internship in another country. If you can't afford *study* abroad, you might be able to afford *travel* or *living* abroad. You will learn a lot living on noodles while you backpack all over Asia, and it is significantly cheaper because you are only paying living expenses, not tuition. If you go the backpacking route, another perk is that you don't have to spend your free time in the library writing papers about Thailand—you can study the rock formations of Koh Phi Phi while you snorkel instead.

So when is it worth the cost and time? If your career goals require fluency in Vietnamese, that will be hard for you to get taking classes four years stateside. There is no better way to learn than immersion, and a semester in Vietnam will help you enormously. The feedback we get from students and their parents is generally that the study-abroad experience is priceless if international travel is a new opportunity, and it tends to be worth a little less when a student has traveled abroad a lot already. That being said, we've yet to meet a student who says their study-abroad program wasn't worth it.

We have, however, met many who said their study-abroad *courses* weren't worth much. Many programs out there are not academically rigorous, nor are they the luxury dining and lodging experience you might be expecting. (Yes, clean sheets are considered a luxury in many places.) Some students are surprised when they experience that; others are delighted, particularly about the lighter academics. It goes without saying (but we'll say it anyway) that if you are about to hand over a significant chunk of change, you must research the program well. If the program is offered by your university, it is probably acceptable and will likely earn you credit, but even then the academic value is uncertain. Just like we advised you in chapter 3 about course selection, you will want to ask peers for pointed feedback about their programs, and make a special note of when they took them since programs (not to mention countries) change rapidly.

WHAT QUESTIONS SHOULD I ASK IN ORDER TO FIND A QUALIFIED PROGRAM?

Start your research with a program within the university. It is likely that if your university recommends it, it is prepared to give you full academic credit for the courses you take overseas. Note that we said "likely." You'll want to double check that with your academic counseling center beforehand, of course. The beauty of using a program endorsed by your university is that it is already prepackaged for you, and will require significantly less planning and legwork on your part.

Once you've pared down your course load, be sure to select courses with significant amounts of history, art, and religion that will enable you to get a slightly different perspective of the material as you travel through the country than you might if you were studying it in the US. There is nothing quite like having an art class in the Louvre and getting to see *Mona Lisa*'s sfumato up close.

Nick—recent grad, Point Loma Nazarene U

Perhaps your university doesn't offer study-abroad programs, or, at least, none that are of interest to you. If that is the case, look at programs that other schools similar to yours have approved, even though your school may not yet fully embrace it. Be aware that there are all kinds of transaction costs with using a program your university hasn't officially preapproved; it's also possible that courses from another university may not transfer to yours.

A less common but still plausible scenario is that, for whatever reason, you are unable to find any program for study overseas that offers what you're looking for. If that is the case, approach this warily (and be prepared to invest a considerable amount of time in the research of something that may possibly prove futile).

There are significant transaction costs associated with blazing your own academic trail overseas, especially if you expect your home university to give you full academic credit. For most students, it isn't worth the time. However, if your career goals require you to learn Urdu and no programs offer classes in Pakistan, you will need to create a program on your own. Perhaps you want to study there because you have a strong cultural connection, such as family there who can provide housing for you and perhaps lighten your logistical load. Sure. For the sake of your own identity formation, it may be worth the extra effort at this stage in your academic career and developmental trajectory to dive head first into your heritage. Recognize, though, that your university may be less willing to endorse study overseas from institutions that are unfamiliar, especially if they believe your presence in that country may expose you to unnecessary risk of harm.

A weighty alternative to study abroad is a domestic study-away program. Many universities now offer programs domestically where students can study on Wall Street for a semester, study in New York in the arts for theater production, pursue film and video in Los Angeles, study politics in Washington DC, and, essentially, find a way to respond to a particular interest of study in a format that is more academic than a typical internship. (Although, now instead of working for free as with an internship, you will be paying to work; but a lot of learning takes place and many students have told us that the time spent studying away from campus breathed life into their studies once they returned.) Depending on the program, it might also be open to students from other schools, which broadens your education further.

> As a general rule study abroad should NOT be used to discover your path; it should be part of the path you've already chosen.

Whatever you do, we generally recommend avoiding programs that don't give you college credit. If you are going to travel, travel. If you are going to study, study. But don't study-travel and have nothing to show for it on your transcripts.

Traveling abroad is expensive. Make sure you have *more than enough* money in your bank account when you leave so that you can live comfortably, and approach a few financially savvy folks on campus and in your study-abroad program ahead of time to ask what a moderate budget might look like. Keep in mind that eating can be a cultural experience too, and only having money for a baguette and a block of cheese every day will really limit your experience.

Nick—recent grad, Point Loma Nazarene

ARE THERE CERTAIN MAJORS THAT DON'T MIX WELL WITH STUDY-ABROAD PROGRAMS?

Yes. It probably doesn't come as a surprise that science and engineering majors, where the precise content and sequence of the course matters significantly, don't complement study-abroad programs. Premed is slightly easier than engineering, but it's still a challenge. Your best bet might be to go during the summer when it won't interrupt the normal course sequence.

WHEN IS THE BEST TIME IN MY CAREER TO DO STUDY ABROAD?

The best time for study abroad is spring of your sophomore year. Second to that, and slightly more debatable, is fall of your junior year.

The reasons are these: Freshman year should be devoted to navigating your home institution, developing healthy habits of independence as a fledgling undergrad, and getting a solid lock on your social network for your graduating class. Interrupting this season of development could be socially catastrophic later on, leaving you feeling very un-at-home on your home campus.

Junior and senior year you will likely be taking your most challenging courses for your major, and you'll want to take those at home where professors can write letters of recommendation. Spring of your junior year (and anytime thereafter) is not ideal timing, given that your job search begins in the fall of your senior year and so is parlaying your junior year transcript. The more advanced courses graded at your home institution the better, since most employers will know that study abroad, academically speaking, is second tier and won't be impressed by study-abroad grades. And that's assuming you get good grades. Should you get caught up in the grandeur of travel and lose sight of your GPA, it would be incredibly difficult to explain the poor quality of your most recent grades to the professional interviewing you.

It makes the most sense to go abroad once you've figured out your major and a general plan of how that moves you toward your future career. Put differently, as a general rule study abroad should NOT be used to discover your path; it should be part of the path you've already chosen.

The good news in all this stringency is that grad reqs do not need to be out of the way before going—you can still leave some of those for your senior year as we advised in an earlier chapter. Be wary, however, about study abroad if you are significantly behind pace, because study abroad will oftentimes slow your momentum.

> I recommend cutting your course load in half and certainly taking no more than three-quarters of a typical load while studying abroad. There is so much culture to soak in and so many other opportunities for learning outside the classroom that it is a shame to waste that time on your hostel bunk, studying. This is true particularly if you decide to go the route of a sampler tour across a series of countries, where you are constantly relocating and need to exchange your money, clean your laundry, and buy an inexpensive meal in every new city you reach. Traveling becomes a full-time job in that instance, and the last thing you want to have to do when you arrive in Rome is post up in a dingy Laundromat and study for a midterm.
>
> **Nick—recent grad, Point Loma Nazarene U**

ANY CAUTIONS ABOUT STUDY ABROAD?

Courses. It's a mistake to take courses that are vastly better taught at your home institution, where the star prof in the subject may be teaching. Save the course for when you return home rather than studying with Dr. Vatsisname, who is a visiting lecturer in Barcelona. It's better to take courses while abroad that are not offered at your school; you will be able to take advantage of the cross-cultural dimension. Medieval Spanish poetry might be much better taught and far more fascinating on its home turf than at your home institution.

$$$$. Three thousand dollars may sound like a lot of money, but once you begin your travels you'll come to realize just how little that will buy. Too frequently we hear of students who miscalculated the cost of living and ended up eating a lot of white rice for a semester because they didn't budget enough for—and all the incidentals that come with—travel.

Dating. Ah, the allure of the Latin lover. Enticing as those stories may be, use caution in pursuing any kind of relationship while studying abroad. We find that students are frequently naive or far too trusting about the intent of romantic flings in other countries. Too many wind up heartbroken, conned out of their money, or worse. Tourists are common prey, and you will be living as such 24/7 for a semester; a healthy dose of suspicion will serve you well at this juncture.

Laws. Know the laws. Just because it's legal in the States does not make it legal overseas. You really don't want to get involved in a drug arrest in certain countries; trust us on that one. Unfortunately it happens frequently enough for us to mention it. There are other legal questions to know ahead of time around driver's licenses and such, so query the host of your program ahead of time.

Conduct. Most study-abroad programs are not tolerant of misbehavior. They consider their program a privilege and are more inclined to discipline harshly and send you home on a first offense than if you exhibited that same behavior at your home school.

Safety. Students tend to be optimistic and hopeful about their safety in other countries—too optimistic. We have known students who have been robbed, beaten, and sexually assaulted while overseas. So please . . . keep your street smarts on you at all times.

It's worth ending on a positive note with this section. We've given study abroad a bit of a sandpaper treatment in this chapter, but that's only because we've seen so many students enter into the opportunity expecting a vacation and giving less than their best. We've also heard countless stories from students about how study abroad had a major impact on their perspective of the world and their place in it, so we know it can be a valuable experience. In fact, some universities are beginning to augment their programs to include a service-learning component to give a full flavor of a country beyond the typical tourist icons. Universities overseas are investing heavily in their programming to attract students such as you, and there are many exciting, interesting, attractive, worthwhile programs worth looking into. (Do all those adjectives make us seem jealous? Well, maybe we are a bit.) Even with all the fantastic course titles the programs offer, it is less about the academics and more about the experience; if the experience is worth the payoff, go.

> Invest the time to write in your journal every night before bed— what you saw, what you imagined, what you think you'll always remember—because you likely won't remember. It will all be a blur before the decade is out and having journals to complement those piles of jpgs will be incredibly valuable to you later on. Oh, and be sure to buy a waterproof pen: you'd just hate to put in all that time writing and then have someone spill his Nalgene water over your tireless work.
>
> **Nick—recent grad, Point Loma Nazarene**

Drop Out

WHEN IS IT A GOOD IDEA TO DROP OUT OF COLLEGE ENTIRELY, AND HAS IT EVER WORKED IN SOMEONE'S FAVOR?

Bill Gates. Next question? No, we're kidding. There's a lot more to it than that (though you'd be surprised how many students cite him as some sort of guarantee that dropping out equals making billions). Gates proves dropping out isn't a fatal wound in every case, but not everyone is Bill Gates.

If you're going to drop out, it is better to do so sooner rather than later, because you'll have less college debt; in other words, spend less on a degree you don't plan on earning, because a partial college degree is worth less than you think. There is a real benefit to discovering college is not for you before you get too far into it, and that is part of the reason we recommend a gap year—to take that pause and gain some perspective. Should you take a gap year or a semester's leave, you may discover you have a passion for a trade that doesn't require a college degree. Without electricians or plumbers, we'd all be sitting in the dark or perhaps something much worse. It's better for you to discover that you are a tradesperson at heart before you sink a lot of money into a degree you won't need.

That being said, because the value of an unfinished education is low, if you are at the three-year mark, it is better to just finish. You will reach a point where even limping across the finish line is better than not finishing at all. The economist may argue against seeking to recoup sunk costs, but in this case we think it makes more sense. Once you're through the tunnel far enough, it's best to keep going.

Should you decide you want to withdraw, try to do so while you are still in good standing with the university. Whether you withdraw and never come back, try to return to the school later, or transfer, you are always best leaving while your grades are somewhat decent. And honestly, that's the hardest thing to do because optimistic undergrads want to believe they can turn it around. Your dean of students is the best resource for this conversation.

WHAT ARE EXAMPLES OF BAD REASONS TO DROP OUT OF COLLEGE?

A bad reason to drop out would be to get married. Seriously, it happens. Certainly being married as an undergraduate changes the college experience, but it doesn't require dropping out. On the downside, married undergrads find it to be socially ostracizing: they miss out on dorm life and campus interactions, they don't attend events like they thought they would, and, all said, it cuts their student experience short. That's not to say getting married while an undergrad is a mistake—marriage is its own classroom on life. The upside of getting married while you are in school is that you grow up together, travel together, and experience more of life together. That slice of life is simply bigger because it starts earlier; it doesn't mean the end of life and freedom as you know it. One of us has been married for twelve years and got married in college; another of us has been married for twenty years and got married after college—we're big proponents of marriage. You can make the timing of getting married work either way—just don't drop the college part.

Should you be thinking of dropping out so you can pursue your lifelong ambition of becoming the next Shawn White, think again. We know of one such character, CJ, who is a professional racer of sorts. He could have easily dropped out along the way and used his racing career as a reasonable excuse, but instead he has been flexible and smart about his academic choices and his racing schedule, and he has been diligent in his conversations with his professors so that they've all been able to make it work. Shiny gold medal to CJ.

Speaking of gold medals (seamless transition, right?), what if you want to become an Olympic-quality skier? We know of a young woman named Amber who has that as her ambition. Her big training will take place spring semester, so she scheduled a heavier load fall semester and a lighter load spring semester, with classes Tuesday through Thursday in the spring so she can travel on the weekends. We include these real-life anecdotes if only to say that pursuing your dreams qualifies as an unnecessary (aka, bad) reason to drop out of college.

If you are doing well in school and enjoying it, there are ways to make the system work with you, even if you are trying to pursue a fairly extensive activity on the side. Put forth the effort to see how your university can work with you before simply dropping out. Your university will likely be eager and honored to find a way for you to remain their student while achieving your goals.

Of course, if dropping out of college is your way of avoiding growing up, that would also qualify as a bad reason. If you don't like the idea of waking up before 10 a.m. to go to class, don't like being held accountable for your performance, or have a penchant for laziness, dropping out of college will only magnify your problems. Maybe you are a hard worker but you have low self-esteem, thinking you are a loser and will fail anyway; rather than work on that with a counselor on campus, you take the path of least resistance and prove yourself right. Yup, that would be another bad reason. If dropping out is a way to avoid dealing with a deeper, underlying character issue, it will only make your life more difficult than if you face that character flaw head-on and use the support systems your university offers in mass quantities to help refine your perspective of yourself and your place in the world.

Our society increasingly privileges college degrees, and the economic opportunities for those without them are significantly less today than they were fifty years ago, especially with jobs being farmed out overseas. Should you decide to drop out, you could fall through the cracks of society in a hurry. The mistake in all this, of course, is not having problems—we all have them—but rather not addressing those problems. Staying enrolled will give you access to resources tailor-made for people your age with the challenges you face.

IN THIS AGE OF START-UPS AND INTERNET MILLIONAIRES, IS A COLLEGE DEGREE REALLY WORTH THE INVESTMENT?

Again, we find that popular culture likes to cite Bill Gates—his story is the dream of every Tevye ("If I were a rich man . . ."). The truth of the matter is that someone with Gates's drive and ability would have excelled even if he had finished college and exited via the time-honored door instead of the window. The key to his success was not dropping out; it was developing an idea so powerful that it didn't require a college degree. There are reasons why there are a lot of dropouts but only one Bill Gates.

Okay, but doesn't it seem like a lot of Internet billionaires dropped out of college to start companies like Microsoft and Google and Yahoo and yadda yadda? Yes, but what was the common denominator in their stories? They met people at college, and it was those partnerships and collaborations that took them to success. Very few dot-com successes are solo acts. Part of what you're buying at your university is valuable interactions and networks. Facebook. Pandora. These are all the products of interactions and brainstorming with other bright people, which is a pretty good working definition of what college is or should be about.

CHAPTER 11

So What Do You Want to Be When You Grow Up?

Choosing Your Major vs. Choosing Your Career

There is a great misconception among students (and especially their parents) that a student's major determines her career. Rarely is this true.

What determines your career—and what employers look to see in college graduates—are the qualities that a college education hones: the capacity to think critically, the ability and desire to problem solve by learning new things, excellent communications skills (both oral and written), and a commitment to success. Did you see economics major listed anywhere in there?

Of course, there are some jobs where a specific major is all but required: it is hard to be a civil engineer if you didn't major in civil engineering. But increasingly in the information age, the line from major to career is a dotted one, with lots of curves thrown in for good measure. Even graduate schools will accept promising students from outside the "traditional field." So the title of this chapter may be catchy (it caught your attention, right?), but it is deliberately misleading. Repeat this mantra: a major rarely makes a career.

In selecting a major, the best approach is for a student to pursue her passion and then to perform passionately well, thus demonstrating her desire and ability to succeed. If that is clear enough for you, skip to the next chapter. Chances are, however, you might still have a question or two—we are certain your parents will—so keep reading.

Why Do They Call It a BS?
How a Liberal Arts Degree Prepares You for the Work World

The theory behind a liberal arts education is that exposing a young-adult mind to a variety of fields and asking it to synthesize and analyze that information helps develop the character and intellect of that person. If a liberal education were about getting a degree that would immediately, directly, and narrowly translate into a career, you'd be attending a vocational college. Please don't misunderstand: vocational schools are a great thing; in fact, the modern world depends on them. But their goal is different from a more traditional university, and it's critical you recognize the difference going in.

The rapid pace of change in the information age puts a premium on learning, relearning, and retooling. Think of how many variations of computers or cell phones you have used in the last decade, and how they continue to get smaller, thinner, lighter, and more complex. You had to learn anew each time you upgraded. Properly done, a college degree is supposed to certify that you know how to "learn anew." The certification of survival skills for the twenty-first century has an exotic name: bachelor of science or bachelor of arts. You may think the premise is nutty, but it has helped make US higher education the envy of the world.

> A student should major in a topic that excites him rather than the topic that looks like it might lead to the highest starting salary.

You will need these skills because it's very likely that you will engage in multiple (maybe more than a dozen) career shifts in a lifetime. You would either need more than a dozen separate qualifying degrees, or you need one (with maybe a graduate degree thrown on top) that demonstrates you can learn, relearn, and retool.

If you are still skeptical, don't take our word for it. If you have a particular career path in mind, it's wise to do some research and see if it requires any specific undergraduate major. The betting money—and given tuition rates, you are betting a lot of money—says there are many majors that might end up on that same career path.

Hopefully this will come as a breath of fresh, minty-clean air. Bluntly, what we are saying is that students are freer to pursue fields of interest than they (and their parents) may have realized. True, it may require a bit more from the art major than the econ major to get an interview at the bank. However, once he has that degree and if that art major has a stellar narrative (that is, a transcript of well-chosen courses plus complementary extracurricular activities), his profile could stand out in a uniquely positive way. It might even garner more attractive job offers than a more pedestrian profile would.

A student should major in a topic that excites him rather than the topic that looks like it might lead to the highest starting salary. A student who picks a major merely because it implies a job will be less motivated and may end up doing poorly—ironically making himself less employable than if he had picked a different major in which he would have excelled.

> The value of a liberal arts education can be hard to fully appreciate up front when you're eighteen and you're looking at a complicated matrix of distribution requirements (or if you're a parent and all you can imagine when you hear "cultural anthropology" are dollar signs and a giant sucking sound), but in the fullness of time all of the seemingly disparate pieces of the puzzle somehow fit together. The result is a broadly educated human being capable of responding to the complexity of the modern world and to ever-changing circumstances.
>
> **Hans—recent grad, Duke U**

"I've Always Wanted to Be a _____, so I Shouldn't Major in _____"

Most of the advice in this book is premised on the idea that students are by nature inclined to be too casual about their college experience. This chapter assumes the opposite. For some reason, choosing a major is the one activity that arouses undue anxiety—even for slackers.

One metatheme of this book is that students should spend less time worrying about what college they get into and more time working to get the best out of the college they have picked. It also applies to majors: spend less time worrying about the job at the end of your major or the major you need to get that job, and more time enjoying and creatively developing the major you have picked.

The bottom line is to pursue your passion studiously even if it cuts against the well-trod career path. We tend to be most successful in areas that intrigue or fascinate us; if not, human beings would reduce to human "doings." So choose a major that makes you look forward—for at least three years—to going to class, reading your texts, and, dare we suggest, even writing your papers.

What this means practically is that if Kelly is interested in a career in international economics but is fascinated by psychology, she should major in psychology. However, being a psych major doesn't prevent Kelly from taking classes in other fields. The wise student who is willing to take a risk in her major for the sake of pursing a passion will hedge her bets with a well-chosen minor or a well-crafted set of auxiliary courses that weave a narrative of breadth and potential. In Kelly's case, a few courses in economics and international affairs are a prudent complement to her psych major.

As long as you excel in whatever major you pursue, and as long as the major is respected as one in which you truly worked for your grades as opposed to one in which you merely warmed a seat each week, you should be in good shape. In fact, it's almost better to stand out with the odd major as long as when you stand out, your academic record truly shines.

I have no idea what kind of job I want or what I should major in. Guess what question my relatives ask when I see them? You've got it. In my case, rather than just saying I'm undeclared or undecided or that I just don't know, I've started asking them what *their* major was and started talking about *their* career path. I asked that question at my family's Christmas parties and learned about all sorts of majors that I didn't want to pursue, and also a few that sounded interesting. Take advantage of the knowledge and experience of those who surround you.

Brian—freshman, U of Oregon

Of course, if you *haven't* done well in the major, and by lacking excellence your major is merely odd, that could significantly slow or deter your progress in winning the career of your dreams. We won't lie to you: a so-so economics major has more options than a so-so art history major. Whether or not that is as it should be, it is what it is. However, a stellar art history major probably has at least as many options as a so-so economics major. Okay, we admit it. The stellar economics major may have even a few more options. But how many people do you know who can actually stay awake through four years of economics courses well enough to succeed in them if their principal motivation is simply to get a better job? Plus, whom would you rather take to Italy?

Please don't misunderstand. We are not suggesting you major in scuba art just because you know you can get an easy A. There are some fields that are more respected than others—and we'd be flogged if we listed them here, so do your own research. Don't be fooled—grad schools and employers *do* consider your GPA, but they couple it with the rigor of the major in sifting through applications. While we wouldn't dare hint that you should choose a major just to build your resume, you don't want to be naive about the fact that there are a few majors out there that have not yet garnered the respect of the professional world. If you really must take classes in scuba art and your life will forever be marred by regret if you don't, then consider it as a minor (at most) or immerse yourself in as many supplemental courses as your schedule will allow.

If you have always wanted to be a consultant or a politician or a _____ (fill in the blank), how do you know which major is "the one"? Here are a few questions to help guide your thinking:

- What section do you turn to first in the newspaper? (Okay, *after* the sports section, what section? If it is sports and more sports, there are good careers there: sports writing is a noble profession, not to mention sports medicine, coaching, or teaching adaptive physical education.)

- Where do you go first when you have twenty minutes to kill in a bookstore? (If you spend the whole twenty minutes deciding which scone to buy, you've got bigger worries than your major and we probably can't help you.)

- What subjects excite you most frequently into discussion or even debate?

- Other than fantasy football, what gets you reading articles online or talking around midnight pizza in your dorm?

- What makes you eager and willing to attend class multiple times a week for multiple weeks a year for multiple years?

If you get stuck answering these on your own, don't hesitate to get professional help. Most colleges offer two resources to help you find a major. The first is the formal premajor advisory system. It is called by many different names, but it functions basically the same: it assigns students to an advisor who—in theory—is knowledgeable about the array of majors and so can help students plot their way. (Once students pick a major, they get another advisor who—in theory—is knowledgeable about the array of opportunities *within* that major and can advise accordingly.) In practice, it is a mixed bag. No one can truly understand all a modern college curriculum has to offer, and so advisors tend to specialize. If you know the area in which you are interested, you can get an advisor who knows that area and how the system works. If not, it is hit-or-miss.

Which brings us to the second resource (da-da-da-dum!)—the career center. Appearing this evening in resplendent sequined bulletin boards, the career center offers testing to help students narrow down skill sets and fields of interest; with abundant staff who are eager to help and sure to impress your next dinner party, this picture says, "I can do it" (if only selecting a major were as glamorous as *The Price Is Right*). At the very least, the career center might help you knock a few options off the list based on your personality type and whether or not you see yourself plugging away in the dungeons of the library for the next eight years (which is what some majors require if you intend to pursue the degree to its intended end in a PhD). So you might consider starting your journey there.

Once you've narrowed it down to a couple of options as a starting point, research carefully to take the "best" course each major has to offer. (And now that you've read chapter 3, you know how to do that.) If you like it, take a second course with a *different* prof the following term to test your interest as the subject expands. Don't dismiss the course as not being "real learning" just because it comes to you easily.

In fact, Jasmine did just that. She thought she was a psych major who was taking some English classes for fun. Each semester she found herself battling it out, barely making Bs and Cs in her psych courses while the English As and Bs came easily. Why did it take her until her junior year to realize that she should be majoring in English instead of psychology? She admits that she doesn't have a good answer. She just thought that since studying English seemed enjoyable, it must not be valuable; she didn't realize it was easy because she was naturally skilled in that field.

> If you are in a preprofessional program, don't feel the pressure to major in something similar to that subject. No one will think less of you later on. If anything, it will be an asset in that a different major will set you apart. One of my friends is planning on going to veterinary school and he is majoring in religious studies.
>
> **Helen—sophomore, U of Chicago**

Oh So Many Majors
Factors to Consider in Narrowing Down Your Options

In our experience, most students do not know from birth what is the "right" major for them. In fact, for most there may not be a single right answer. As you narrow your search, here are a few questions to consider.

WHAT IS THE STRENGTH OF THE DEPARTMENT?

You could be one of the lucky few who has already narrowed your major options to two or three possibilities. If that is the case, and one department is stronger than the rest, go with that one. You'll get a better education. After all, that is what you're paying for. The best professors can make a field come alive, even if the subject didn't get a second glance from you in high school. College is about expanding horizons. And should you have time in your academic schedule, you can continue to take classes in the other major for the sake of personal interest. (As a general rule, we would shy away from majoring in both, as attractive as that may seem. We'll explain why later.)

Departmental strengths (and thus the desirability of certain majors) differ from school to school. Find the best departments at your school and consider majoring in them. Sample at least a course or two before you commit to a specific major, because even within departments, the quality of the experience can vary widely depending on the professors you choose.

DO YOU NEED TO GO TO GRAD SCHOOL?

Are you looking to take your major further, or are you content to get your undergraduate degree and call it quits? If you want to go further, there are two tracks of grad programs: professional and academic. Professional graduate programs (such as law, medicine, and business) rarely require an exact major for entry. A lot of great majors provide an entry into law school (especially if you perform well on the LSAT), and virtually any major can work in applying to business school if a student can prove some knowledge of economics. Most business schools, in fact, care more about your work experience than your major. Medicine is fairly flexible as well, though there are many more course requirements in math, biology, chemistry, and physics. Medical schools love students who have majored in nonscience areas. A career counselor or perhaps even your academic advisor can advise you more specifically.

The academic grad schools, on the other hand, are a bit more demanding in that they expect students to have a strong background in the field (or a close cognate of that field) as their major. While it isn't entirely unheard of to see students jump majors into grad school (such as having a BA in history and applying to a graduate sociology program), they would need a compelling narrative—such as having taken courses in that area beyond their major track, having worked closely with a professor in research, or having participated in multiple internships— to explain why they are still a good match for this particular program given their major. It can be a bit difficult to choose a grad program before even having declared a major, but if you find your interest piqued by architecture and are curious what a grad program would look like, take a look at the requirements. There is a lot more flexibility in transitioning to grad programs than most students realize.

One final caveat: don't attend grad school in a subject that doesn't interest you just because you might pursue a career in that field later. Grad courses are difficult enough, and having a lagging interest will only make the work distasteful.

HAVE YOU SAMPLED A DIVERSE SET OF CLASSES WITHIN THE DEPARTMENT?

You never know what classes you'll find absolutely wonderful until you try them out. However, in testing out a department, try to hold off on declaring your major until you've taken courses from at least two or maybe even three different professors within that department. A single professor is not a good representation of what to expect. You may have accidentally discovered the most fascinating professor and topic in the entire department. Or the opposite may be true. Not only will this give you a good idea of the strength of the faculty, it will also give you a flavor of the work and classes available in that major before you declare.

It may not be realistic to take multiple courses yourself, so at a minimum take them "virtually." Talk with upperclassmen who have had the professors you have had and who have had others in the department, and ask them to compare. But ask several and, if possible, ask a diverse range of students, since individual opinions will vary widely.

Don't dismay if you take some courses you dislike. Part of the selection process is weeding things out, and it may be that by taking a course that combines statistics, engineering, and science you realize that all three stop your brain waves cold. Consider it a valuable part of the narrowing process, not a mistake. It fits well into your narrative, too, in showing not only your willingness to embark upon new fields but also showing the weight of your certainty.

DOES YOUR PERFECT MAJOR EVEN EXIST?

If not, designing your own major is another option to consider. However, it is not done frequently, and for good reason. Designing a major is not as easy as it may sound. Not only does it require heightened scrutiny by the faculty (because there is the presumption that students designing their own majors are trying to avoid something already being offered that they very well might need), it also requires an unusual degree of clarity from the student in purpose, imagination, and explanation of how courses might fit together. Coupled with this is the significant time investment needed to plot a course and alter it (with permission from the school administrators) as professors or classes come and go. Tack onto those reasons the possibility that you'll spend the rest of your employment interviews explaining exactly what majoring in Symbolic Structures (or whatever you decide to name your course of study) means, and you'll see why few students choose to go this route. Still, for some it is the right way to go.

A thumbnail sketch of the process begins with a student who proposes a major as well as its specific course work. A faculty committee reviews that proposal and provides feedback and suggestions or criticism. The student then makes adjustments to the proposal and resubmits it. Some schools may limit the number of times a proposal can be reviewed, but even if not, such reviews can take weeks or months, and most students are restricted by deadlines to declare. What students often find is that, by the end of the process, the major has morphed into an unattractive structure because it no longer reflects their original intent. Don't be discouraged. You have an entire lifetime to study random topics of interest to you; you don't need to be registered in college to visit your local library or purchase copies of lectures online.

Of course, there are students who have designed their own majors and gone on to be incredibly successful in them. We know of one student named Lauren who was bored by the usual premed major of biochemistry. She designed a special major in medical ethics and health policy that blended political science, philosophy, and public policy, as well as the more traditional science courses. She went on to do postgraduate study at Oxford and then entered medical school. Designing your course work can be a way to turbocharge your college career (it was for Lauren), but it's tough to pull off and, except in rare circumstances, probably not worth the effort. A similar effort invested instead into a more traditional major tends to yield a higher dividend.

"Just Because They Used to Change My Diapers . . ."
Your Parents' Role in Choosing Your Major

In *most* cases, any parental pressure you may receive in declaring your major is well intended. We are fairly confident in saying your parents do love you and have probably sacrificed greatly just to get you to this point. Money gets to talk too.

However, just because your parents think you should major in what *they* want doesn't mean you should. After all, you are the one who will be studying the topic for the next four years, not to mention answering questions on the topic at interviews and cocktail parties.

We aren't suggesting you ignore their advice entirely. After all, they probably know you better than many others you will consult. But we suggest treating their insight as counsel, not gospel. This is an issue on which there are ample opportunities to compromise by altering how you design a schedule with extra courses, including a supplemental minor, or even registering for well-chosen summer internships.

The conversation could look something like this: "No, Dad, I'm not going to be an econ major, but I *am* going to hold an office in the Young Entrepreneurs' Club on campus as well as do an internship this summer at a corporation so I can give the field a fair try; I still think I really want to be a philosophy major." Of course, be prepared for your dad's counterproposal: "Why don't you hold an office in the Philosophers' Club and major in economics?" Look for creative compromises; your folks probably have enough gray hair already.

Arguably the top two majors that give parents cause for concern are music and art history. Parents who hear the dreaded news that their son wants to be a music major (why did they spend all that money sending him to math camps?) picture their little drummer boy being forever consigned to a garage band—and worse, it might be *their* garage. It's not that their concerns are irrational. As we mentioned earlier, the more exotic the major, the more will be required of you to make it work in the professional arena once you graduate.

In holding up your end of the conversation, be sure to communicate to your folks that a major that enables you to thrive while challenged (even if it *is* religious studies) will serve you better in the long run than scraping by in a major traditionally thought of as sound (which really means "diploma comes with a high-paying job"). You may also want to add that college offers you a fleeting opportunity to study a subject you most likely won't have the opportunity to revisit so intensely at any other point in your life—and you may even be learning from some of the leading minds in the field.

We recognize that the following tip may only work at small colleges, but it's worth a try: encourage your folks to speak with a professor in your proposed department. Regardless of school size, your parents can probably connect with a few alums who chose a risky major and then succeeded professionally years later.

In all of this back-and-forth about your future, *do* talk with a few other adults from your parents' generation about what they majored in and how it mattered to their careers. We're guessing you'll be a little surprised to see how loose the connection is. But even if you see an airtight connection, be sure to interview people between your parents' generation and your own—people who have entered the marketplace in the last fifteen years. The economy is changing its opinion of what criteria are used to hire and fire, so for the immediate future, the major might actually matter. What you'll most likely find is that the longer folks have been out of school, the less significant their major will have been to their career.

It's rare, but not unheard of, for parents to insist on a particular major. If you *do* find yourself in that unfortunate position, it is time for a gut check: how badly do you want to major in art history versus fulfilling your parents' hope for biology? Enough to foot the bill? Should your parents prove to be more unmovable than Rushmore on the topic (even after you have had the reasonable conversations prescribed above), our inclination is to give in to their demands. If you are strategic in how you organize your schedule and major requirements, you may be able to satisfy your art itch by taking as many courses outside the premed track as you can. Then, once you've graduated and are footing the bills, apply to the best art history grad programs you can find. It's not exactly having your cake and eating it too, but at least you won't go hungry.

To Those Who Know Exactly What They Want to Major In, and Have Known It Since They Were Five . . .

Lucky you. While a rare breed, this will be the case for some. Political science may have fascinated you since your prepubescent years. The fact that a prof in this field may have been a close friend of the family didn't hurt matters much either, and you can't imagine doing anything else. Great! You've found your major. But don't stop there. While starting your major early opens the possibility for you to delve deep into this field (and we encourage you to take a few grad courses by the end of your undergraduate term), take as broad a range of courses *outside* your major as you can. Don't be ashamed if poli sci is your dream world, but test it regularly with a broad range of other courses that will make you appear less narrow than if you are only versed in one subject.

Be careful of being overconfident that your major is encoded in your DNA. We know of one successful professional who thought she was meant to be a doctor. Frances did well in all her classes and fulfilled her requirements for premed in record time. What she couldn't figure out was why so many medical schools kept rejecting her applications. Then she spent some time interning in a hospital. It quickly became clear that she had no idea what the profession of a doctor was like, and she was both ill-prepared and ill-suited for medical work. Somehow the med schools had seen through her interests better than she had, and she now looks back and admits that she is grateful she got turned down cold. It's good to have an interest in a field, but be looking for yellow flags that say perhaps this is more an avocation than a vocation. Oh, and Frances is now running a college campus somewhere and doing marvelously, so don't feel too badly for her.

I love to watch adults squirm when I answer their question about what I am studying in college: theater and music. "Ohh," they reply as they unsuccessfully try to keep their concern from flashing across their eyes, "do you have a backup plan?" No, I do not have a backup plan because I am passionate about my work and well suited to my chosen career path. However, this chapter brought the very comforting news that though I chose a major that leads into a very competitive field that is probably not going to make me a lot of money, if necessary I could still get a financially supplemental job in an unrelated field that pays more than waiting tables.

Rebecca—recent grad, Point Loma Nazarene U

Common Worries before Choosing a Major

What will I do when I leave college with this major? It matters very little what department you choose as long as you do well.

What painful course requirements must I endure to complete this major? It is worth both doing well in your passion and pursing a passion where you will do well. Please note, however, that it is also worth being stretched by ideas that you might not find easy to master. Fulfilling your passion doesn't mean simply taking courses you find simple. That your major takes you beyond your comfort zone is a good thing. Employers want to see you perform well, but they also want to see how you've succeeded in the face of obstacles and opposition.

I'm halfway through my freshman year and don't know what I'm doing with the rest of my life! Relax. Most adults are halfway through their lives and say the same thing. Not knowing your major even after the first year is okay, provided you have been strategically choosing courses and getting exposure to a range of possible majors in a reasonable fashion. Students who are not at this point by the end of their second year are in trouble, and most colleges will provide pressure from administrative watchdogs.

I aced biology in high school and loved it, but it seems so much harder in college. I thought I'd be a bio major, but now I'm having second thoughts! Virtually every subject on the college campus is approached differently from the way it was handled in high school. There are lots of students who like high school _____ but not college _____. Rather than memorizing equations or anatomical structures, you will be asked to analyze them and produce new ideas or conclusions based on your analysis. Subjects that you excelled in or enjoyed during high school are a good place to start, but don't despair if you find that the college version is not for you.

Before You Sign on the Dotted Line
Knowing Your Major's Requirements

One mistake we see too often is students who've taken a course from a single fabulous professor in a department and, because of his class, decide to major in that field without researching what else is involved. A year into her major, one student discovered that she had to take advanced Arabic in order to complete her degree, which she wasn't willing to do. Due diligence is critical.

Entire departments thrive on students who arrive premed and then meet (and fail) organic chemistry. They also attract students who remain too long in a major they chose in error, either because the end-result career looked sexy on TV or because it was what their parents wanted them to choose. After a rickety semester, they disregard the signs (that is, failing grades, panic attacks, dread of attending class, unalterable confusion) and pursue the major for two or even three more semesters and then find themselves with a transcript full of classes they wish they could hide. They may try to apply it to a major that is a distant cousin just to graduate on time, or they may have to extend their stay at the university another year to earn a degree in a major they truly love. To the tune of thousands of dollars, those are some expensive little yellow flags to ignore. The bottom line is pay attention to any and all flag waving that signals this may not be the right major for you. While you shouldn't jump ship at the first sign of a bad grade, continued poor performance deserves at least some reevaluation.

Finally, we land upon this oh-so-worthy point. There is an overwhelming notion in the student body that two majors are better than one. Sometimes yes, but often no. The primary reason we resist so strenuously the suggestion to double major is that the time required to fulfill both majors will cost both depth and potentially unique study opportunities—there are only so many hours in the semester. It sounds impressive to brag about holding your own in two majors to your peers, but unless it is something you absolutely must do for your career path (like economics and Russian so you can work overseas as an advisor neck deep in snow) or because you are trying to indulge an exotic passion (your parents insist that you graduate with a sociology degree, but you really want to major in engineering), you may find it just as rewarding to focus on developing one major with a host of skill sets and unique course work surrounding it. Plus, a year or two after you graduate no one but your interviewer will ask what you majored in, and should you try to insert said boast into friendly conversation, be prepared to be verbally backstabbed after the party.

Two majors are not always better than one. You want your transcript to show depth in at least one topic (meaning you have gone well beyond the introductory level and are engaging the material at a sophisticated level) and breadth beyond that topic (meaning you are not limited to baby-step intellectual excursions out of your comfort zone). And, sure, sometimes a double major will do just that. But what is more likely is that the double major will force your schedule into little more than checking off requirements instead of choosing courses.

At the End of the Day

Just as it matters less what college you attended when compared to how you performed in college, it matters less what major you chose when contrasted with how you conducted yourself within that major. If financial considerations have forced you into a college that isn't your first pick, you can still excel. And if a parent ultimatum has forced you into a major that you wouldn't have chosen for yourself, you can still build a narrative in your transcript that will enable you to be successful in your chosen career later on. Take heart. College will be over someday soon and no one but the freshman from the alumni office hitting you up for donations will ever ask about your major.

> Don't get too caught up in the social stereotypes of majors or future plans. Just because someone can do insane physics problems does not make her smarter than the art history major student.
>
> **Helen—sophomore, U of Chicago**

It'll Be Over Before You Know It

Preparing for Life After College

Alas, even something as wonderful as college cannot last forever. Before you know it, you will join the ranks of alumni dodging solicitations from your alma mater. It is a mistake to be so completely preoccupied with life after college that you miss opportunities you'll only have as a student. But it is also a mistake to ignore planning for the future (or to put it off until after spring break of your senior year).

Students determined to get the best out of college can take steps even as early as their freshman year to position themselves for maximum success as college graduates. The key is to develop a plan that not only flexes with natural growth but that also has planted enough beacons along the way to form a discernible path.

It's the Journey, Not the Destination— and Other Fuzzy Clichés

Planning your life after college while you are still in college is relatively easy since it's all about theory. Theoretically you are willing to live on less than your colleagues to teach in the inner city because it's something you're passionate about. Theoretically you don't mind postponing marriage and kids until you're done with grad school.

These choices work in theory, but not always in practice. We have seen people show uncanny foresight and map out a plan they actually follow. We have seen others get ambushed by surprises—some happy, some not so.

The wise student will find a way to strike a balance between preparing for potential careers early on and recognizing that those careers are not the irrevocable fate of a Greek tragedy. You are not doomed to one and only one future. Our priorities change as we age, and for most there are many job changes and interludes between "passing go" and "game over."

> College offers a brief season to test out new ideas and adventures. It's not that college is four years of risk-free anonymity where consequences are minimal; instead, it is four years of intense focus on building your future.

It's the old cliché from the strategic planning business: it is not the plan, it is the planning. The real value in thinking ahead is not in developing some detailed and rigid blueprint that actually charts your course. Rather, it is that in developing that plan (or plans!) you go through a series of steps—self-inventory, self-discovery, exploration—that stand you in good stead whatever happens.

Check Your Reality for Defects
A Second Look at Past Choices Now that Your Future Is in Sight

College offers a brief season to test out new ideas and adventures. It's not that college is four years of risk-free anonymity where consequences are minimal; instead, it is four years of intense focus on building your future.

In this season of exploration and risk, we encourage you to weigh some reasonable life choices, and once you have landed on a couple, test and countertest them. Are you interested in becoming a lawyer? Sign on to be a paralegal for the summer. Spend the following summer as a construction worker to see if you prefer working outdoors. Over time, the back-and-forth between possibilities should help you file down your choices.

In terms of social choices, be wary of taking on too many risks since they will influence the rest of your diligent plan. Once the consequences start rolling in, some students find that they have experimented too vigorously in sex, drugs, or alcohol, which constrains their options post-college. This four-year interlude doesn't suspend the law of reaping and sowing. Even activities that are totally innocuous in one setting could be problematic for some jobs. For instance, some positions in the intelligence community are supposed to be so apolitical that membership in any politically oriented clubs as an undergrad will raise yellow flags on your application. And yes, joining the Make Weed Legal Club is going to make for a rough interview should you apply to the FBI.

One alum named Brad recently told us about how he had never completely bought into the precept of "your past will find you" until the day he went before a judge to be admitted to the bar in New York. As Brad's name was called, the judge listed off many of his inane escapades during college that had resulted in fairly minor disciplinary action. Brad was at first stunned by the retelling of his glory days, which then turned into horror when the judge asked him to wait outside the courtroom until the other candidates for the bar had been considered. At the end of the review, he was called back into the courtroom, where the judge said, "Don't worry, you passed—I just wanted to scare you a little bit." It worked. Brad told us he reeled with panic while he waited in the foyer, wondering if all his hopes for his career and future would be terminated. He realized then just how stupid his entertainment choices in college had been. If you have erred by experimenting where you should not have, the game isn't over. While you won't be able to shrug off the outcome entirely, now's the time to begin writing the next chapter of the story that shows a *strong response* to those mistakes in your narrative. You are not rewriting the past; you are writing an alternative future, one that puts the past in a more favorable light.

Making mistakes during your freshman year (which is largely preventable, especially if you've read this book) is more "acceptable" than making those same mistakes as a senior. Should you find you have an evil to explain away, your story will hopefully be "I goofed around the first semester of my freshman year and then realized I was ruining my college career so I reformed. During my junior year, I got interested in working for the CIA and that summer interned for a think tank in DC." It's not that you should give yourself carte blanche as an underclassman to do what you will in the hopes you can apologize and reform later. Success may not feel in the mood to be merciful when she calls your number. That said, everyone makes mistakes, and the mark of those who succeed is that they have learned from their mistakes. Where students find poor choices especially hard to disown is when episodes occur during spring break of their senior year, proving to the outside world that in four years at college they haven't grown up at all.

How rigid will your future career be in its demands? That's hard to say. Far better to be narrowing your choices for yourself than to have them narrowed for you *because of* your choices.

Establish a Network

On a personal note, Dean Sue admits that her expectations would have been different had she extended her professional network early on as an undergrad to query a variety of colleagues who had gone before her. Would College Sue have been able to fully understand the costs of her career path, financially and especially personally? Hard to say. Going through the exercise of imagining and planning out various hypothetical scenarios and talking them through with someone five and ten years ahead of her certainly couldn't have hurt.

In Sue's case, one particular mentor played a key role in helping her sort through many of the initial demands and opportunities of her career. To this day, how she prioritizes work or responds to professional relationships has been profoundly influenced by that former mentor, both for good and bad. She credits a lot of her great work tactics (such as time management and organization) to him as well as some of her misconceptions about the balance between professional and personal life. Because her mentor seemed to be at work all the time, Sue thought she needed to do the same thing to be successful. In spite of the fact that Sue loved her work (and still does), it was not healthy to spend as much time at work as she did. She reached a point where she was not able to distinguish between work and play since everything in her life seemed to be related to her work. And, although being passionate about one's work is a good thing, there needs to be some balance.

Unfortunately Sue says that this sense of balance was not something her mentor was able to model for her (and even today, Sue warns her younger colleagues NOT to look to her as a role model for establishing balance between work and play). This is another good reason why it may make more sense to have a "board of mentors" instead of relying on just one. In that respect, Sue (with seconds from coauthors Peter and Anne) encourages you to choose your mentors carefully. While mentors may not mentor you in your personal life, still note how their career has influenced their home life and weigh their words on that topic carefully.

Counselors, colleagues, mentors, and alums from your school are all excellent resources, and you may find yourself surprised at their wealth of wisdom and eagerness to share it. Many successful adults have more advice to give than they have time to give it—but they also have more advice to give than they have people asking for it. Some schools have compensated for this by hosting lunches solely for the purpose of encouraging students to engage with faculty, notable alumni, and administrators. Should you find yourself in a conversation with them—and you should, if you have been following the advice in this book—and if your listener seems agreeable to it, work your way up from a discussion of the weather to questions like "What personal sacrifices are required of a woman who wants to be a professional in your field?" or "How is it possible to be an international leader and yet raise a family?" or "How does one go about rebuilding a department and yet not be engulfed by its demands?" Most people enjoy telling their stories or giving advice, as long as the questions aren't too intimate.

This can be valuable on a number of fronts. First, it makes you an interesting conversationalist—most people like to talk about themselves and may consider you witty just for prompting such soliloquies. Second, the more you engage them in meaningful conversation, the more you will see the wisdom of the "many roads up the mountain" aphorism—that is, that there are many different ways to reach your

Looking Ahead to Potential Careers

When it comes time to consider a career, oddly enough, the career center can be a helpful resource. Here are some questions that counselors generally ask which you might consider even now:

- Do you expect to make a lot of money?
- How important is your standard of living, and what would that look like?
- Where do you expect to live—a large city, on the East or West Coast, another country?
- What level of commitment do you plan to make in terms of having a family?
- What kind of work schedule do you prefer—one with flexibility or dependability?
- Have you thought about working various shifts, and could you be nocturnal if your job required it?
- In what sort of schooling are you willing to invest?
- What does it mean to you to sacrifice one of these priorities for another?

The value of the various tests at the career center is not necessarily in what the computer spits out as the single "correct" answer for your future. (One of us actually took a test that recommended becoming an assembly-line worker. After deleting and inserting commas on a couple hundred pages during the last round of edits of this book, maybe that test was right.) The value of career-center testing lies in what the results teach you about yourself and what they make you consider as you go through the process.

goal. Third, so many of life's lessons are age-and-stage-related, so talking with people at different ages and stages will give you insights that your peers simply don't yet have. It doesn't matter how smart your roommate is, chances are she does not have deep personal insight into the "biological clock versus promotional clock" problem.

Peter remembers how one of the most perceptive and piercing things anyone has ever said to him came from a retired cabinet secretary who talked to him for less than five minutes at a cocktail party. In that brief time, the gentleman sized him up and pointed out some weaknesses that Peter admits he has guarded against ever since. People who are deeply wise may be able to say deeply wise things, even in a brief encounter.

So talk to lots of people, and then winnow down their ideas. It's probably better not to start the conversation with "Will you be my mentor and teach me how to find success?" Jumping in too quickly can be a little embarrassing—for both of you. Simply enjoy the conversation and you never know—a mentor might emerge or, if not, perhaps at least an invaluable insight.

Racing the Clock
Deciding on Life's Trade-Offs
Before They're Decided for You

Shelves of books have been written on the topic of home life versus advancing career, and it is a matter of ongoing, painful debate. No gender has it easy, but the ever-ticking clock seems to hit female graduates harder. Many women want to establish themselves in a career before starting a family, and so they postpone having children until their mid- to late thirties. Seems smart enough.

However, women who adopt that strategy must confront the reality that the risks of complications or birth defects rise significantly once the mother ages past thirty-four. Doctors are frequently surprised at how many highly educated women in their forties walk into their clinics expecting some miracle fertility treatment to work. Miracles can happen and certainly have, but there are many sad cases where they haven't. Medicine has yet to outsmart the clock completely.

This dilemma then transfers to the men, who may expect to marry later in their thirties yet also hope to travel and enjoy the "five-year plan" with the new wife before starting a family. Once the kiddos *do* arrive, today's dad is expected to do far more hands-on parenting than dads of yore, and when he's nearing fifty and driving a car of kids to soccer practice, he wonders if he's too old to have kids this young. There is a proven link between the age of fathers at the time of conception and biological and developmental risks in infants—it seems we have all swallowed a ticking clock.

We aren't trying to scare you. Each of us—Peter, Sue, and Anne—has made our own choices on the matter, and they are all different. Plus, it's not like you can schedule meeting your soul mate. The point is to understand your expectations around career and family and, to what extent you can, plan accordingly.

"What If I'm Not Ready to Go to Grad School?"

Unless you have a beefy trust fund that can only be spent on schooling, it is probably a mistake to view graduate school as "the thing you do when you don't know what to do after college." Graduate school would be better thought of as a strategic investment. Well chosen and well timed, it has huge payoffs. Poorly chosen or poorly timed, it's a waste of money and, even more precious, time.

> There is an almost irresistible undertow that whisks college seniors away to grad school. Try your best to fight the impulse to jump straight into grad school if it feels anything less than totally authentic. Give yourself a couple of years to get out into the real world, to figure out who you are, and to let your ideas about your future percolate.
>
> **Hans—recent grad, Duke U**

Grad school probably warrants a whole other book. Here, all we can say is this: imagine your toughest seminar, then imagine taking only those kinds of seminars for all your courses every semester; think of the smartest peers that left you a bit intimidated in class discussions, then imagine taking a class where most if not all of the students are just like them. Welcome to grad school. Yes, grad school still has the perks of an academic calendar (though summers involve far more work, usually). And yes, grad school does give you access to many of the social amenities of college. But you will have less time—and less willingness to risk time and probably even less money to indulge those risks—in grad school. Another senior year it ain't.

What we are seeing more frequently is that those students who are considering grad school for the right reasons usually plan to do something else before going to grad school. Some students apply in the hopes of deferring enrollment, and in many cases that is permitted. Should you decide to consider this an option, get your test scores in place (while your brain is still toned) and your recommendations written (while your name still summons a face) and then perhaps delay applying as long as your scores will permit. For ideas of what to do with this time off, see our "Delayed Entry" section in chapter 10.

I Know What You Should Have Done Last Summer

The three summers in between your undergraduate years are some of the richest pockets of time you will have as a college student. Spend that time wisely. Too many students fail at this in one of two ways: either they waste the time by treating it as three solid months of recuperation via TV reruns, or they panic and try to secure an internship at The Company I Will Work at for the Rest of My Life. The former is a clear waste of time, but the error in the second is that by trying to start their professional life too soon, they miss the chance to try something they otherwise would not have had time to explore, such as study abroad, an outdoor job with the Forest Service, short-term volunteer work overseas, or an internship that gives back to the community.

For some companies, a summer internship is an extended interview, particularly in the business sector. You'll find your summer to be a delicate balancing act between using the time to test out a few career options and laying the necessary groundwork for whatever that career will be. It's worth investigating by speaking with your major advisor as well as folks in that industry. The career center may be particularly helpful in connecting you with alums in that field.

If you can afford to work for free during the summer, you have even more options available to you (and many of them admittedly cooler than the paying jobs). A time-honored path for college students is working as interns in DC for any one of countless think tanks. While this sort of job typically isn't paid and may not necessarily lead to a career on the Hill, it adds sparkle to your narrative and creates a small professional network to draw from later.

Should you decide to go a more traditional employment route, summer is not so much a testing ground for a specific company as it is for an industry in general, as well as an opportunity to socialize and meet people in your potential field. It is rare to find a quality internship as a freshman, though it's been known to happen. Don't stress too much about the wow factor of the job you take the summer after your freshman year. If possible, develop a financial plan that will allow for an impressive (aka unpaid) internship the summer before your senior year.

If you can't afford to work for free *ever*, there are still some incredible paying summer jobs out there, but they're few in number so apply NOW. Even if it's a year or two away, you'll rarely apply too early. If you find you've already missed the deadline for applying to work at Disneyland two summers from now, there is no shame in taking any job that pays. Waiting tables of needy patrons can be a wonderful training ground for learning how to deal with demanding clients.

Clocking in at an average sort of job has its own perks as you develop the reputation of a trustworthy and responsible employee and learn how "the rest of America" works. Sue—yes, the dean who wrote this book—was a waitress for two summers. To this day, she tidies up her own table at restaurants because she knows how hard the job can be. There's a lot to be said for the value of empathy derived from the everyday experience, and it can make for a compelling interview when you recount how you spent your summer.

Study abroad and summer school are alternatives. We tend not to recommend the latter unless you're in an academic or financial pinch, since you need some time to decompress from campus life (and many of your top professors will be on vacation), but it is the right choice for some. Study abroad is a much more tempting possibility—after all, how often can you earn credit for traveling the world? It's like being paid to eat dessert. More on that topic in chapter 10.

Developing Your Own Year-by-Year Plan

Okay, so we've sold you on the benefits of planning. How about a list of what to do when? If you're coming into this chapter after your freshman year, it would be worth your time to read through all the headings in case there is something earlier on that you missed. However, if you're reading this as a newly minted freshman, we recommend that you read your section below as well as the other three while you're at it. Then, at the end of each school year, review the upcoming section once more and revisit it during the year as necessary.

FRESHMEN

The biggest advantage freshmen have is more lead time for engaging in academic experiments and for considering future careers.

Develop a working strategy. Jot the plan down, but not in permanent marker. A fair amount of maturation occurs in college, and what excites you socially or academically as a freshman may not get your wheels spinning as a senior. Included in this strategy is revisiting the boundaries and goals you established for yourself in chapter 5 (charting an academic sketch of what you'd like to accomplish and identifying people you'd like to know better). Figure out a way that all these goals can flow seamlessly together.

Explore with some distant goal in mind. For now, your job is to keep in mind the notion that you will graduate someday soon, and to take steps toward that end without letting it consume you. Take a rich romp through a variety of courses, disciplines, and jobs; be leisurely about it if you like. But have some end in mind to provide your exploration with structure so that you have a sturdy narrative when you are through instead of your resume shouting, "I had no clue and was purposeless in my decisions at all times."

Begin scouting professors. You may want to reread chapter 6 on professors and take some notes on how to start grooming some relationships that can generate strong letters of recommendation. Look for either a deep appreciation for how a prof handles the subject matter or some sort of personal chemistry as you begin your search for professors you'd like to know better.

Research sophomore perks. Some colleges offer unique seminars or programs available only to sophomores that you need to register for as a freshman. Since this is largely dependent on your college, we must remain vague. Stop by your advisor's office or career center to see if there's anything more you should be taking advantage of this year.

SOPHOMORES

You know you're a sophomore when you begin to recognize a whole new set of acronyms.

Study for the GMAT, MCAT, LSAT, or GRE. These tests tend to be taken later on, but it is not too early to squirrel away some time now and begin your test prep. The standard procedure for preparing for these exams is to take workshops specific to your test to help you prepare not only for the knowledge base but for the unique test structure you will encounter with your sweaty #2 pencil (or mouse) in hand. It's not abnormal to attend a session two to three times a week in the evening, even as early as your sophomore year, especially if you plan to take a course or social overload or study abroad your junior year. By planning ahead, you will have more chances to retake the test should your initial scores not be as high as you hoped.

Explore MFA, MBA, or MDiv programs. If you are interested in pursuing a graduate degree, make an appointment with a professor in that field whom you already know. With his help, sketch out what you need to know and what your future may require of you should you pursue further education in this field. You might consider getting to know a few grad students in this field as well, since they will have recently finished one or more of those whopping entrance tests and will know the process of getting accepted to grad school. You'll also want to check in with your career center at this point to see what exactly will be required of you as an undergrad (in terms of courses, tests, and internships) to apply to this field for future study.

End with a BS or BA? What if you aren't considering grad school as a postgraduation option—should you be? Not necessarily. Grad school isn't for everyone, especially if you don't think your future career will be able to shovel you out of school debt very quickly (such as if you become a public high school teacher). If you are fairly certain that grad school is not for you, breathe a huge sigh of relief.

Apply for SI. No, not *Sports Illustrated*—student internship. Use your summers to discern what careers might be of interest to you by interning in similar areas. Perhaps you already know what you want to do—even better. Intern for a summer in that line of work; next year, intern in something *completely* different to be sure the first career is what you had in mind. Remember Frances and her med school mistake we mentioned earlier? Had she spent a summer volunteering in a hospital as an undergrad, she might have discovered her true preferences earlier on. The career center will be able to give you some suggestions as well as make other connections you may have missed (such as seminars, workshops, or upcoming guest lectures) in teasing out potential careers.

Tabulate GR1, GR2, GR3, GR4, and GR5. Graduation requirements tend to vary in name from college to college, but the shudder feels about the same. Now would be a good time to take a gander at what you have left to cover in your general and departmental graduation requirements so you aren't caught off guard. Don't feel obligated to complete them all by Christmas, but do begin to look for ways to knock a couple out in the next year.

See the world. No acronyms needed for that one. If you haven't done study abroad yet and still want to, fall of your junior year is your best remaining option (which most often means you have to apply as a sophomore). Many majors offer programs to study abroad, but even if they don't, there are often national programs available that offer accredited courses which are transferable. We offer a veritable feast of information on the subject in chapter 10, in the event the topic sounds delicious.

JUNIORS

Some say this is the hardest academic year (assuming you don't continue on to grad school) that you'll ever face, but if you've been following along with us since day one as a freshman and have your ducks in a row, it may turn out just, well, ducky.

Wrap it up. Junior year is a great time to finish up any standardized test preparation and take your GMAT, GRE, LSAT, or MCAT. Once you feel well prepared, take the test as soon as you can. Not only will your mind be sharper, but you will also have a larger window of time to retake the test in the event your scores aren't beefy.

Revisit those reqs. It is well past time to review those graduation and major requirements so you are on track for completing them. It's not necessary that you know exactly which term you will take what, but by the beginning of your junior year, you'd better have more than a general idea of how much is ahead of you (and whether or not you can get a two-fer by overlapping some requirements).

Research your future. If you haven't been to the career center yet, shame, shame. Take some time and invest in your future. Trust us. At worst, you'll waste forty-five minutes on a rainy afternoon; at best, you'll save yourself from some catastrophic career move that otherwise would have cost you significant time, money, or both!

Challenge your course load. If at all possible, schedule an intensive seminar or tutorial with a professor early in your junior year. Not only is it a memorable learning experience, it is also good timing for requesting a letter of recommendation that reflects your ability to maintain a focused engagement with a faculty member. This is especially important if you are planning to apply to graduate school. Since grad school applications are due in late fall of your senior year, most of the material in the letters of recommendation will be based on work you did in your junior year or before.

Start planning for next summer now. The summer between your junior and senior years will be the most critical for your next career move. If you can manage to secure a solid internship or job, or some other notable experience, it will give you plenty of rich material for your job interviews. We can almost guarantee they'll ask what you did last summer. Many of the desirable or impressive internships have big lead times in their application process, so you'll want to start yours in September or October—almost a full year in advance.

Effectively this long "to do" list turns the first few weeks of your junior year into a serious brainstorming session. Should you decide to study abroad during the fall of your junior year, you'll need to back your strategizing up even further, to be completed at the end of your sophomore year, since life won't wait for you to get back and unpack.

SENIORS

If you've played your cards right, there shouldn't be an unmanageable load left for your senior year. Don't be surprised if you see comrades scurrying to finish their test prep and quickly take the GRE, or folks just realizing they have more major requirements to fulfill than time. These things happen. But you are on the ball, so you have the whole year to look forward to.

What do you want to be when you grow up? It is not uncommon for seniors to quickly come to hate the question "What will you do after you graduate?" It will become increasingly annoying by winter of your senior year. Most of the time the question is being asked by people who don't know what else to talk about but who would like to strike up a conversation with you; as a result, the question can easily be redirected into talking about a course you enjoyed and will pursue in your free time, a new hobby you'd like to develop, or travel plans. However, what many seniors hear in the question is either "What do you want to be when you grow up?" or worse, "What do you expect to do with the next forty-five years of your life?", which leaves them in a tailspin. And who wouldn't be flummoxed? It's an unreasonable question, and most folks aren't even asking it. If they are, buy them a drink and aim them toward a different corner of the party.

Expect the future to intrude on the present and adjust accordingly. Senior year is a tough balance because you want to enjoy it to the hilt, but you also need to attend to some academic requirements that require an intense amount of focus. It may even feel reminiscent of your senior year in high school, only the intellectual opportunities are richer and the cost of checking out early is significantly greater.

At this point in your career, interviewing for jobs is itself almost a full-time job. It's easily as much work as an additional whopper of a class, what with all the research, applications, interviews, and maybe even distant interviews on location. Many classes that are frequented by seniors have attendance requirements because professors know how hard it is for seniors to keep up with their course work when their futures are calling—so shop for courses carefully if you think your interviews will have you traveling off campus frequently. Choose courses that meet the fundamental priorities for your education but that will also have attendance requirements that are realistic, given your schedule. This issue typically affects the fall semester the most, since that is when the competition for top-notch jobs is most intense.

The goal is to arrange a course schedule that will allow you to both interview at companies and pursue your classes. Hopefully there will be some flexibility with the potential employer so that you can request to interview on Friday instead of Tuesday. Be willing to investigate whether or not there is some leeway, and don't assume that by asking for a different date you are ruining your chances of getting the job. We talked with Colin (an executive of a well-respected international consulting firm that has particularly stringent recruiting habits—at times the firm requires seven interviews from a single candidate before offering a position!) and queried him on this very topic.

Colin said, "Were a student unable to arrive for an interview due to a course schedule, the best action to take would be one of honest professionalism. Explain to the recruiter why you cannot miss the course, whether it be limited absences allowed or a test that cannot be moved, and ask if it is possible to come at a different time. And—this part is critical—be accommodating. Offer a few times that work for you, but show you are also willing to go out of your way to take red-eye flights or drive at odd hours to make it work for the company. Most firms recognize you have a life beyond the application process, and how you handle the situation could reflect positively on your application."

It should go without saying—but we will say it anyway—make sure you keep your professors apprised of your interview travel and any other distractions from your studies. Professors will be more accommodating if you've been courteous by informing them in advance that you will be absent. However, that doesn't necessarily mean they will be indulgent. Actually, the advice offered above from the executive could just as easily come from the professor in terms of making absences work, as much as possible, for everyone involved.

Understand that you are not making "forever" decisions. As you search for the perfect job, try not to stress out too much about signing your life away: "What if my first job is a disaster? What if I don't like it? Will it look bad if I change jobs too quickly?" The bottom line is that you can always change, and if you're like the average American, you will—many, many times. PJ is a recent graduate who—though he was a promising student—could only find a job selling Internet satellites when it came time to graduate. It wasn't his dream job. Three years and two job changes later he is working in higher-level management in a prestigious bank and loves it. How, you ask? Short of Providence, the best reasoning PJ gives is that each job change highlighted a set of talents or strengths he wanted to develop in himself—as opposed to staying in a field simply because the job training was similar. So even though the industries varied, the leadership skills he was honing at each company improved from one move to the next.

Take workshops that will prepare you for life after college. One last thing to look for are workshops geared toward seniors and life after college. Many colleges offer brief forums on topics such as medical insurance, how to buy a house, how to handle credit cards responsibly, and how to plan for retirement. Most often these sorts of practical life courses are offered in . . . where else? The career center. (It's too bad you don't get a dollar every time we mention that place. Your college loans could be paid off by now.)

Early in my senior year, I had an assignment to contact fifteen industry professionals in my chosen career path and ask to interview them about their experiences. In my case, these were complete strangers, and not only that but intimidating strangers. Many of these folks had the power to move my career forward or halt it, and I had to introduce myself to them by asking for a favor! I had dreaded it since the day I saw it printed on the syllabus, but when I finally started making the calls, I found that nobody minded helping out a college kid who had a great deal to learn about the industry. Their advice has saved me from many common pitfalls and rookie mistakes that I would have paid for dearly.

Rebecca—recent grad, Point Loma Nazarene U

SURPRISE!
How Not to Be Caught Off Guard by the Big Stuff

Until now, we have focused on positive things you can do to position yourself for success after college. You also need to play some defense, avoiding mistakes we have seen too many recent graduates make.

THE CAR

As much as it may pain you to hear this, don't rush out and buy yourself a "happy graduation" car. Even as a gift, a car involves major ongoing expenses. We've seen it before. The happy graduate heads to the dealership and signs up for a car he can barely afford, which in turn limits his options because he can only take jobs that ensure that he can meet those payments. Many exotic jobs involve low pay in the beginning and often open tremendous doors later on.

LIFESTYLE

An all-too-common trap for recent graduates is trying to live by their parents' standard of living. This may seem reasonable because they grew up with it, but this standard is in fact not reasonable at all—at least, not for a recent college graduate.

The twenties is a great time to be relatively poor. (It's certainly a lot easier than attempting it later, should you be married with kids.) We've been encouraging you from the beginning to experiment, and this is another place to take a calculated risk. Try out something you've always wanted to do that may involve low pay now but that has a long-term payoff. The job that provides great professional networks or learning experiences or public exposure can be risky but rewarding—more so than the job with a higher starting salary and dead-end prospects. As you head into your job search, draw up a budget of what you think you need to earn, given your spending habits (and what you'd like to save). If jobs aren't available with that sort of pay scale, adjust the budget as needed—or consider different jobs.

ALUMNI CLUBS

Fancy Bumper Sticker or Future Investment?

If you attend a large university, your alumni website will most likely have information to connect you with alumni and alumni clubs across the world, and if you are moving to a new city, it could be a helpful resource in building some new networks. Even if you attend a small college or an elite university, your alumni office will probably keep files on alums and their careers, which could be useful in the event you need a few introductions.

The alumni office is a great resource. In addition to helping you connect with other alums wherever you live, it may also offer discounts on extras like travel or car insurance. Since the network you develop in college is almost as valuable as the college itself, keep your contact information current in their files.

Don't worry about giving them your phone number either. Most colleges know better than to beleaguer recent grads with requests for money.

There are numerous books and seminars on the topic of financial planning, so we won't go into all that here. We will, however, draw your attention to two important facts that seem to underscore their point:

- The miracle of compound interest means that saving in your twenties is turbocharged when compared to saving in your thirties, forties, and fifties.

- Good financial management is 90 percent discipline and habit and 10 percent wisdom and luck. You can't control luck, but if you are wise enough to set up properly disciplined habits, then your investments (and dividends) will most likely reflect that.

INSURANCE

Health insurance can be another doozy, and with all of the changes in US policy, our best advice is to research this further. Happily, as a college graduate, you know how to do this.

Health insurance can be one of the toughest things to nail down since you don't know what insurance plan your prospective company will have, if any, and you won't have access to that information until you receive an offer. Figure that if you're going into a traditional career, it's likely you'll have some sort of coverage. If you are in the fortunate position to have multiple offers, take a close look at their benefits when evaluating compensation.

Regardless of what your insurance plan turns out to be, we *strongly* advise against having a lapse in coverage. We repeat: *there should be absolutely no window of time when you are not covered by some policy*, first and foremost because of the major risk to your health (though some hospitals *will* treat you even without coverage), and second because of the crippling financial burden it would become should you become seriously injured or ill. Your life can change for the worse in an instant if you have no insurance to provide for those unforeseeable situations. The good news is that you are exactly the kind of person insurance companies are looking for: young and thus more likely to be healthy (which makes for a great policyholder from their point of view). At your age, it makes sense to have major medical coverage. Unless you have a chronic condition (and if you don't know whether you do, get yourself checked out while still at college and covered by good medical insurance), you probably won't need a gold-plated policy.

SAVING

Another surprise to meet head-on is saving for retirement. It may seem like eons away but before you know it, you'll be of age to retire. When you turn to look for that nest egg, will it be shiny? Cracked? Egg, what egg? That depends. It's *never* too early to start investing. Once you earn an income, be sure you pay your future self immediately. What that means practically is that each time you earn a paycheck you contribute as much as you can either to a retirement plan or a savings account that you *don't* touch. It's not that we expect you'll be making a lot of money early on. Heck, you may only be able to put in $5 a month. The value of that $5 goes beyond the principal to the principle: you are cultivating an important lifetime habit that will have positive returns for years to come.

DILIGENCE AND INTEGRITY

Just as we've said that it's not so much where you attend school as what you accomplish while you're there, we reassert that it's not so much what your first job is as how you perform in that job. Good recommendations (and bad) will follow you wherever you go.

We knew of one businesswoman—let's call her Matilda—who directed an online start-up company, which we will call LousyBusinessPlan.com. Despite her initial goodwill, she turned out to be a snake and sold the company downriver, making off with the profits and leaving the employees out in the cold. It was infuriating and the rest of the management team was helpless. A year or so later, Matilda applied for a prestigious role in another company—the sort of position she'd been working her whole career to reach. In looking over Matilda's impressive profile, one of the board members of that company happened to recognize the name LousyBusinessPlan.com (his son's best friend was the former COO). Wouldn't you know, that board member got an earful when he gave the former COO a quick call, and Matilda lost out on a major career move. Your performance has a way of keeping track of you. Make that a good thing.

One Last Thought before Sending You Off into Success

As hard as you have worked to put yourself through school these past twenty years, and as hard as your parents have worked to support you in your ventures, don't kid yourself: that you are standing here today on your way to receiving a college diploma is still Providence. You have just won the genetic lottery. No, it's not irrelevant that you were up all night preparing for your anthropology midterm or merely luck that you passed your biochemistry class.

What we mean to say is that none of us chose to be born into this state of privilege. None of us selected our family or our upbringing. None of us even selected the era in which we would live. But somehow we were born here and now, and there you stand ready to begin your bright future, having already been given more than most individuals in this richly populated world will receive in a lifetime. You have been given vaccinations, taught to read, trained in a healthy lifestyle, given clean air to breathe. And you are now blessed with a life's education. It really is awesome when you think about it.

Find a way to financially or personally give back to the world a portion of what you have taken thus far—it will never be easier to give back than it is now. You have a lifetime to cash in on the prestige that comes from being in the upper echelon of educated people in the world. For now, use your innate talents and your college-honed skills to right someone's wrong, to confront a global challenge, to create a new opportunity, or to meet a local need. Who knows, this sort of giving back may become a wonderful addiction. And someday, when you are feeling nostalgic and looking back on your journey, you'll be glad you were not just another well-fed person on the sidelines pointing out problems; you were part of the solution.

INDEX

Grades
  bad, 52, 164
  impact of, 64
  questions about, 127
  standards for, 182–83
Grad requirements, 60–61, 269, 270
Graduate schools, 64, 246–47,
    264–65, 268–69
GRE, 268, 270
Greek system, 82–85
Guests, overnight, 11, 15

H

Health insurance, 276–77
Health issues, 87, 120, 202, 206,
    209–10, 225
Help
  need for, 197, 198, 203, 209–12
  sources of, 197–98, 203–8
  timeliness of, 198, 199–200
High school
  college vs., 150–54
  friends from, 38
Holidays, 189
Home
  changes at, 32–33, 35–36
  leaving, 27–28, 29–32
  -sickness, 37–39, 42, 171–72,
    175, 212
  trips back to, 33, 37, 39
Homosexuality, 24–25, 113
Housekeeping, 18, 21–22
Housing, 7–9. See also Move-in day;
    Roommates

I

IDs, fake, 99
Immaturity, 215, 217
Independent study, 122–25
Insurance, 276–77
Integrity, importance of, 277–78
International centers, 177–78

International students
  academic honesty and, 186–87
  alcohol and, 188
  communication difficulties for,
    181, 183, 190
  community service by, 189, 192
  cross-cultural experience of,
    179–80, 191–95
  culture shock and, 187–90
  diversity brought by, 169–71
  financial costs for, 175
  grading standards and, 182–83
  holidays and, 189
  homesickness and, 171–72, 175
  motivations of, 179
  networking by, 190–91
  parents' expectations of, 178–79
  professors and, 181–87
  religion and, 193
  as roommates, 14–15
  school choice and, 173–74
  in seminars, 184–85
  support systems for, 173, 175–78
Internet, postings on, 99–101
Internships, 80–82, 228, 265–66,
    269, 271

J

Jobs. See Careers; Employment
Juniors, advice for, 270–71

L

Law schools, 64
Learning disabilities, 202
Learning styles, 56–57, 62
Leave of absence, 224–28, 235
Legal issues, 97–99, 101, 110–11, 234
Lesbianism, 24–25, 113
Liberal arts education, value of,
    240–41
LSAT, 268, 270

ABOUT THE AUTHORS

Peter D. Feaver (PhD, Harvard, 1990) is a professor of political science and public policy at Duke University. He has over twenty years of teaching experience—as a teaching fellow at Harvard and as a professor at Duke. He won the Harvard Certificate of Distinction in Teaching (1985–86 and 1986–87), the Trinity College (Duke) Distinguished Teaching Award (1994–95), and the Duke Alumni Distinguished Undergraduate Teaching Award (2001). He has published numerous scholarly books and articles on national security issues, and he has served on the National Security Council at the White House, first as director for defense policy and arms control under President Bill Clinton and most recently as special advisor for strategic planning and institutional reform under President George W. Bush. As long as his knees will let him, he can be found waddling up and down the basketball court—or more often these days, cheering his daughter and two sons from the sidelines.

Sue Wasiolek (affectionately known as Dean Sue among the students) is assistant vice president for student affairs and dean of students at Duke University. She was premed at Duke (she never got into medical school), completed a master's of health administration at Duke (only worked in health care for eighteen months), completed her JD at North Carolina Central University and her LLM at Duke (only practiced law for nine months), and has been working at Duke for the past thirty years. Sue loves the classroom, both as a teacher (she teaches education law) and as a student (she completed her EdD at Penn in 2008). Sue encourages students to study what they love and base their careers around what they love, even if those two things are totally different. Her time with students is not a job but a way of life. In her free time,

Sue can be found jogging around Durham or working out at the gym with students.

Anne Crossman studied at both Stanford and Duke Universities, earning a BA in English and a Certificate in Education. She began a career in education by teaching in public high schools, in military barracks, and around kitchen tables to students ranging from academic underdogs to honor society prodigies. In 2011 she published *Study Smart, Study Less*, a compact guide that makes learning fast, fun, and memorable by mingling current research on memory and the brain with creativity and a sense of humor to help students identify and work to their study strengths. She has also recently published her first book of poems, *Trying to Remember*, a memoir about Alzheimer's disease. For more information about Anne or her work, visit www.AnneCrossman.com.

ABOUT THE STUDENT CONTRIBUTORS

Andrea is a freshman in the directing program at Carnegie Mellon University (Pittsburgh, PA). She went to a performing arts high school for acting and took a gap year before college to gain experience in her field. She plans to graduate college with a minor in music theory and go on to direct musicals and operas.

Billy is a sophomore at High Point University (High Point, NC), majoring in communications. When he isn't in class, he's out playing intramural sports, driving the free ice cream truck on campus, and enjoying the company of great friends. "This book really gave me the heads-up on what to expect and prepared me very well. I feel lucky to have landed at HPU and made such great friends here." Billy is from Durham, NC.

Brian is a freshman at the University of Oregon (Eugene). He was given this book as a graduation present and read it with his father a month before his first term at U of O. "I thought that there was a lot of helpful information in here and recommend that all college students, especially freshmen, read this book. It will make their transition into college a whole lot smoother."

David is a recent graduate of Stanford University (Stanford, CA), where he received a BS in computer science. (His three and a half academic years at Stanford were spread across seven chronological years, with a brief hiatus in the middle.) David admits he is a technology entrepreneur at heart, having started numerous companies, including Redfin and MyTwoFrontTeeth (now Family Giving Tree). David has worked at Amazon.com and Overstock.com and is currently the founder and CEO of RichRelevance. David lives in the San Francisco Bay Area with his daughter, Abigail; his wife, Cynthia; his two godsons, Miko and Kimo; and their dogs, Coconut and Valentino.

Hans recently graduated summa cum laude (and Phi Beta Kappa) from Duke University (Durham, NC) and may be the only student to have earned a seminar semester grade of A+ from Peter Feaver. While at Duke, Hans served as student co-director of the Duke Community Service Center and earned national recognition for his efforts helping victims of Hurricane Katrina. He is currently teaching middle school science in New Orleans as a member of Teach for America. His graduate school aspirations include dual business/public policy degrees to further his desire to fight social injustice. Hans is a native of Martha's Vineyard, Massachusetts.

Helen is a sophomore at the University of Chicago (IL). She has loved animals ever since she was little and is a vegetarian. This has inspired her to become a biology major, perhaps with a concentration in genetics and a minor in Spanish. In her spare time, she loves hanging out with friends, listening to music, and dancing. At the University of Chicago, Helen participates in ballet, belly dance, and Irish dance, and tutors local elementary school students. In the future, she hopes to go to medical school or maybe get her PhD and go into biological genetic research.

Joshua, who is from Zimbabwe, is a sophomore at Duke University (Durham, NC) and plans to major in biology with a prehealth track. He is an external policy analyst of the International Association and likes to work closely with other international students. This summer he will do HIV vaccine research at the Duke Human Vaccine Institute and hopes to contribute in the search for a cure for AIDS. He likes playing soccer and, as a staunch Liverpool fan, has a natural dislike for Manchester United. "By the standards of my country, Zimbabwe," he says, "I am from a small family." He has an older brother and two young sisters.

Lauren is a sophomore at Northeastern University (Boston, MA), where she is pursuing a major in international business with a concentration in marketing and a minor in Spanish. She is scheduled to graduate on time after completing all of her credits as well as two co-ops, one domestically and one internationally. She loves traveling, snowboarding, and photography.

Nick recently graduated from Point Loma Nazarene University (San Diego, CA) with a BA in business administration. He spent his free time at PLNU leading a worship band, leading Bible studies, and surfing. Nick currently resides in the utopian metropolis we know as San Diego, along with his sweet wife, Autumn; their palm tree, Baby Judy; and succulent, Little Buddy. He works as an office broker with CB Richard Ellis and spends his free time volunteering and playing the guitar.

Onome is a junior at Stanford University (Stanford, CA) studying electrical engineering with a concentration in computer software. She enjoys working with technology, and her goal is to someday be in a position to use technology as a tool for social change and economic advancement in Nigeria. She grew up in Lagos, a coastal and metropolitan city in the western part of Nigeria, and came to the US for the first time to matriculate as a freshman at Stanford. "I definitely miss being at home with my family, childhood friends, and all things familiar," she says, "but Stanford has been instrumental in my development as an individual by providing me with opportunities, resources, and people to help me learn, both in and outside of the classroom."

Philip is a freshman at Virginia Commonwealth University (Richmond, VA) hoping to major in communication arts (illustration). In high school, he was active in both the visual arts and music performance, and at VCU he has been active with InterVarsity and the Society of Communication Arts. If all goes as planned, he will someday have a career in storyboarding or freelance illustration.

Rebecca recently graduated from Point Loma Nazarene University (San Diego, CA) and proudly holds a BA in theater and a minor in music. Much to the chagrin of those who doubted her answer to the big "what do you want to do with your life?" question, she is thankful to be currently working (and actually making money) as a professional actress and pole vault coach in Phoenix, Arizona.

MORE COLLEGE GUIDANCE
from Ten Speed Press

10 Things Employers Want You to Learn in College, Revised
The Skills You Need to Succeed
Bill Coplin
$14.99 (Canada: $17.99)
ISBN: 978-1-60774-145-9
eBook ISBN: 978-0-307-76849-0

Lecture Notes
A Professor's Inside Guide to College Success
Philip Mitchell Freeman
$14.99 (Canada: $18.99)
ISBN: 978-1-58008-754-4
eBook ISBN: 978-1-58008-429-1

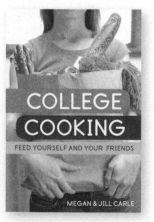

College Cooking
Feed Yourself and Your Friends
Megan Carle and Jill Carle
$19.99 (Canada: $24.99)
ISBN: 978-1-58008-826-8
eBook ISBN: 978-1-60774-121-3